ESSENTIAL GUIDE TO WINTER RECREATION

LEARN THE SKILLS YOU NEED— HIKING, SNOWSHOEING, FIRST AID, AND MORE—FOR A SAFE AND ADVENTUROUS SEASON OUTDOORS

BY ANDREW VIETZE

AMC SKILLS SERIES

Appalachian Mountain Club Books
Boston, Massachusetts

AMC is a nonprofit organization, and sales of AMC Books fund our mission of protecting the Northeast outdoors. If you appreciate our efforts and would like to become a member or make a donation to AMC, visit outdoors.org, call 800-372-1758, or contact us at Appalachian Mountain Club, 10 City Square, Boston, MA 02129.

outdoors.org/books-maps

Distributed by National Book Network.

Front cover photo of the New England National Scenic Trail, near Erving, Massachusetts, and back cover photo of Third Roach Pond at AMC's Medawisla Lodge & Cabins in the Maine Woods © Paula Champagne/AMC
Cover design by Katie Metz
Interior design by Abigail Coyle
Illustrations by Deb Eccleston

Library of Congress Cataloging-in-Publication Data
  Names: Vietze, Andrew, author.
  Title: Essential guide to winter recreation : learn the skills you need-hiking, snowshoeing, first aid, and more-for a safe and adventurous season outdoors / by Andrew Vietze.
  Description: Boston, Massachusetts : Appalachian Mountain Club Books, 2019. | Series: AMC skills series | Includes index. | Summary: "This comprehensive guide to winter recreation features practical advice that emphasizes preparation, safety, outdoor stewardship, and fun. For hikers, snowshoers, skiers, backpackers, and anyone else looking for a winter adventure"–Provided by publisher.
  Identifiers: LCCN 2019028731 (print) | LCCN 2019028732 (ebook) | ISBN 9781628420517 (paperback) | ISBN 9781628420524 (epub) | ISBN 9781628420531 (mobi)
  Subjects: LCSH: Winter sports–Safety measures. | Outdoor recreation–Safety measures.
  Classification: LCC GV841 .V54 2019 (print) | LCC GV841 (ebook) | DDC 796.9028/9–dc23
  LC record available at https://lccn.loc.gov/2019028731
  LC ebook record available at https://lccn.loc.gov/2019028732

The paper used in this publication meets the minimum requirements of the American National Standard for Information Sciences-Permanence of Paper for Printed Library Materials, ANSI Z39.48-1984. ∞

Outdoor recreation activities by their very nature are potentially hazardous. This book is not a substitute for good personal judgment and training in outdoor skills. Due to changes in conditions, use of the information in this book is at the sole risk of the user. The authors and the Appalachian Mountain Club assume no liability for accidents happening to, or injuries sustained by, readers who engage in the activities described in this book.

Interior pages and cover are printed on responsibly harvest paper stock certified by the Forest Stewardship Council®, an independent auditor of responsible forestry practices. Printed in the United States of America, using vegetable-based inks.

22 21 20 19   1 2 3 4

FSC
www.fsc.org
MIX
Paper from responsible sources
FSC® C005010

This book goes out to my fellow rangers at Baxter State Park.

CONTENTS

Acknowledgments   ix
Introduction   xi

⑦ 1: BEFORE YOU GO   1

Prior Experience   2
Trip Planning   4
Essential Trip Planning Resources   12

❄ 2: UNDERSTANDING THE WEATHER   15

Meteorological Winter   16
Why Winter   17
Fronts   19
Observation and Evaluation   22

🜨 3: DRESSING FOR WINTER   29

The WISE System   30
Thermodynamics   32
Fabric and Insulation Choices   33
Outerwear   34
Protecting Your Extremities   36
Not Breaking the Bank   44

🥾 4: BACKPACKING GEAR   47

Backpacks   47
Shelters   51
Sleep Systems   54
Camp Kitchen Gear   59
Gear Care   63

⚠ 5: SAFETY

First-Aid Preparedness   67
Environmental Challenges   76
The Human Element   86
Mental Challenges   87
When Things Go Wrong   88
Avalanche and Rescue Gear   95
Animal Danger   98

✪ 6: NAVIGATION

Maps   104
Compasses   108
Route Finding   112
GPS   115
Smartphones   119
Celestial   120
Additional Navigation Tools   121
Setting Your Pace in Winter   123
Tracking Animals in Winter   124

✚ 7: HEALTH AND HYGIENE

Your Body in Winter   126
Water Sources   129
Water Filtration Methods   130
How to Keep Water Liquid   133
Nutrition   134
Hygiene   137
The Restroom   139

⛺ 8: CAMPSITES

Siting Your Camp   141
Fire Building   142
Permanent Structures   150
Backcountry Camping   152

9: ACTIVITY GEAR AND SKILLS   162

Winter Hiking   162
Snowshoeing   165
Skiing   170
Splitboarding   176
Ice Climbing   177
Pulks   179
Fat Bikes   182

10: A DISAPPEARING SEASON   185

Impact on Future Recreation   186
What AMC Is Doing   187
Get Involved   188

Appendix A: Personal Gear Checklist   189
Appendix B: Participant Information Form   193
Appendix C: Expedition Preparation Checklist   195
Appendix D: Drinking-Water Treatment Methods   197
Appendix E: List of Charts, Tables, and Figures   200
Index   203
About the Author   208
About AMC   209

ACKNOWLEDGMENTS

Many thanks to everyone involved in bringing this book to shelves, especially the Appalachian Mountain Club's editorial director, Jennifer Wehunt, for her patience and support, and books editor, Tim Mudie, for his expert guidance and tireless bird-dogging. I'd also like to thank all of the outdoor professionals who read and provided wise counsel. These include Colby Meehan, Kristi Hobson Edmonston, Aaron Gorban, Jonathan Niehof, Dexter Robinson, Mark Warren, Karen Barsanti, Paul Glazebrook, Leo Kelly, David Mong, Bill Brooke, John Rogers, Richard Breusch, and Wanda Rice. For her work turning a manuscript into an actual book, thank you to AMC's books production manager, Abigail Coyle. To Deb Eccleston for creating the illustrations, Erin McGarvey for copyediting, and to Ryan Smith and Matt Mills for providing additional material.

INTRODUCTION

"I have never seen a grander or more beautiful sight than the northern woods in winter," wrote Theodore Roosevelt, waxing lyrical about the snow-draped forests of Maine after exploring them one March during a break from his studies at Harvard. Traveling through Aroostook County changed the future president's life, setting him on course to become the nation's most famous outdoorsperson.

The winter woods can have that effect on people. Under the soft cover of snow, the outdoors becomes a new place, taking on an entirely different aspect. With the advent of cold and snow, the world outside instantly becomes wilder. Mountains look taller, more majestic. Views open up into panoramas, with no leaves to hide them. Trees stand out all the more in contrast to the white that surrounds. Stars seem to multiply overhead, sparkling in the firmament more brightly than ever, because the cold air has banished the haze.

With the pristine white snow painting everything to perfection, it's an inviting place, as anyone who's ever strapped on a pair of snowshoes knows. The tourists leave with the foliage, and the woods take on a deep, intense quietude, as if wearing a great crystalline muffler. They're more peaceful and restorative than they are at any other time of year. On most days, you have them all to yourself. There are few sounds and no bugs to harry you as you head out to explore. And nothing can compete with the satisfaction of returning from a day romping in the snow like sitting near the fire and warming up with a mug of cocoa.

But for all its beauty, winter is equally unforgiving. Winter is the great magnifier, demanding much more of those who venture outside, carrying more risk than any other time of year. Trips take more time, more planning, more gear, and more outdoor ability. They require better decision making and more common sense.

The consequences of winter are writ large, too. Winter is a season of amplification; errors in judgment that would hardly be noticed in summer can carry massive ramifications. Mistakes made at -10 degrees Fahrenheit can be catastrophic in a way that similar problems during the other three seasons are not.

Getting lost, for example. If a hiker gets stuck for a night on the shoulders of Katahdin in July, it might be uncomfortable and less fun than the original plan, but it shouldn't pose a threat to one's life. Find a mossy patch, sit down for a snack and some water, wait for the sun to come up, and be off. In February, when it's 4 degrees Fahrenheit and the winds are blowing at 20 MPH, the story changes altogether. With windchill, the air suddenly feels like -32 Fahrenheit, and at that temperature, a body consumes its recommended daily allowance of 2,000 calories just trying to warm itself, leaving little for physical energy. Frostbite, hypothermia, and death due to exposure all become very real possibilities.

In winter, the days are shorter, and snow and ice generally make travel slower. Without proper gear (a whole lot of high-calorie food, a sleeping bag, many layers of dry clothing, a shelter), your life can be in jeopardy. Little mistakes quickly compound themselves. Forget the map in a new area in summer? Depending where you're going, it might not be a big deal. Forget the map in a new area in winter? That could spell doom. Forget the matches in summer? Again, probably not a major issue. Forget the matches in winter? Potentially life threatening. Neglect to tell someone where you're going in June? Not smart, but not necessarily the worst thing you could do. Neglect to tell someone where you're going in January? It could be the worst call you've ever made.

The season requires a certain set of skills and expertise. And you must give the cold woods their due respect. But if you do so, you can have the time of your life out there. While many sit inside, cranky and complaining about yet another winter storm, those in the know venture out into it, reveling in a winter wonderland, enjoying the spectacular beauty of the season. For many skiers, snowshoers, and winter campers, it really is the most wonderful time of the year.

→ HOW TO USE THIS BOOK

Getting outside at any time of year has been scientifically proven to lift our spirits. Hiking and camping and exploring nurture the soul, insulating us from the problems and worries of the modern world. And there's no need to avoid the outdoors simply because snow has fallen and the thermometer's mercury has dropped a few inches. In fact, outdoor adventure is more vital this time of year than ever, the antidote to cabin fever and seasonal affective disorder.

You just have to be smart and prepared. This book is designed to help you become so. If you're a newbie who never has woken up to find fresh snow coating your camp or wrestled with an icy snowshoe buckle, you'll find all the information you need to get started in the winter woods. If you're a more experienced outdoor lover, you'll discover new tips and techniques to enhance your appreciation and refine your skills. From trip planning to navigation to rescue, this book explores all aspects of winter traveling and camping, with safety always paramount.

People of all abilities can find their own way into the *Essential Guide to Winter Recreation* and use this resource in different ways. You can read from cover to cover, absorbing all that's inside, or use it as a reference work, searching for specific pieces of information. We recommend beginners start at the beginning and make their way through, chapter by chapter. To that end, we've laid out the information in a logical fashion, opening with the most elemental skills: planning, reading the weather, dressing for winter, and gearing up. By the end, we move into more advanced techniques, such as shelter building, rescue, winter water treatment, and DIY sled construction.

If you have some experience outdoors, you still may find it helpful to read from cover to cover. You'll happen upon neat tricks you may not have considered before, learn safety techniques, and deepen your knowledge in a variety of areas. Perhaps you're a snowboarder but have never considered backcountry splitboarding. Inside, you'll learn about skins and freeheel skiing. Or maybe you've been hiking and camping for years but never knew how to properly use a map and compass. (Your numbers are legion.) It's in here. More advanced readers may want to pick and choose their way through the text, looking for those areas in which they could brush up.

Wise campers know that no matter how much we learn, we can always learn more.

➔ LEAVE NO TRACE

The Appalachian Mountain Club (AMC) has a lengthy history with Leave No Trace (LNT) and champions its principles in this book. With the sheer number of people in the outdoors these days and encroaching pressures on open space everywhere, we all must make an effort to minimize our impact on the land. AMC offers LNT master educator classes in partnership with the Leave No Trace Center for Outdoor Ethics to train those who will help train others.

The LNT program in the United States was created in the 1980s as a cooperative effort between the U.S. Forest Service, the National Park Service, and the Bureau of Land Management. Its purpose was to develop hiking and camping principles that promoted a new wilderness land ethic. In the early '90s, the U.S. Forest Service partnered with the National Outdoor Leadership School to develop a science-based curriculum for training public land managers, outdoor professionals, and outdoor recreationists. Today, the seven LNT principles are widely accepted as the seven commandments of any serious and educated hiker or backpacker. They are easy to understand and, with some guidance, quite simple to put into practice.

It is important to note that in many locations, public land agencies have used some of the seven LNT principles to establish rules and regulations for outdoor users. This means that not practicing some of these principles results in infractions with concrete consequences, such as a fine or expulsion from a public land area. There are some pristine natural areas in the United States that users cannot enter without demonstrating they have received basic LNT training.

LNT training is available to all recreationists and/or professionals in the United States and Canada. The training structure includes three levels: (1) LNT master educator certification, a five-day course designed for professionals in the outdoor industry who intend to instruct LNT trainer or awareness workshops; (2) LNT trainer certification, a two-day course designed for educators, guides, agency employees, and other outdoor professionals that enables LNT trainers to provide LNT awareness workshops to the general public and outdoor recreationists; and

(3) LNT awareness workshop certification, a short training that can last from 30 minutes to a few hours, intended to bring awareness to various groups, such as educators, children, college students, outdoor camp counselors, Girl Scouts, Boy Scouts, trail crews, hiking club members, and others interested in LNT skills and ethics. AMC provides LNT training courses throughout the year, and it might be wise to take one of these formal training workshops if you are an avid hiker or backpacker, or if you intend to lead others into the backcountry. Find a course near you at outdoors.org/activities.

LNT principles also must be included in a common-sense approach to risk management. During a critical incident, any actions taken to mitigate the situation should prioritize the following elements, in this order:

- Safety of the individual (that is, yourself and others)

- Safety of the equipment

- Safety of the environment

If you keep this in mind, you will be able to respond to an emergency without feeling bad about the impact your action might have on the environment. For instance, in a situation in which someone in your party has broken through ice and is soaked, it would be appropriate to set up camp near the site of the incident, even if it is near a water source, and to build a large fire to dry the wet clothing while actively warming the person. You might be breaking a few LNT principles, but this situation calls for you to prioritize the unfortunate companion.

THE SEVEN LNT PRINCIPLES

 Below you will find the seven LNT principles adopted by the Leave No Trace Center for Outdoor Ethics, which manages and promotes LNT in North America.

1. Plan Ahead and Prepare

- Know the regulations and special concerns for the area you'll visit.

- Prepare for extreme weather, hazards, and emergencies.

- Schedule your trip to avoid times of high use.

- Visit in small groups when possible. Consider splitting larger groups into smaller groups.

- Repackage food to minimize waste.

- Use a map and compass to eliminate the use of marking paint, rock cairns, or flagging.

2. Travel and Camp on Durable Surfaces

- Durable surfaces include established trails and campsites, rock, gravel, dry grasses, or snow.

- Protect riparian areas by camping at least 200 feet from lakes and streams.

- Good campsites are found, not made. Altering a site is not necessary.

- In popular areas, concentrate use on existing trails and campsites; walk single file in the middle of the trail, even when wet or muddy; and keep campsites small. Focus activity in areas where vegetation is absent.

- In pristine areas, disperse use to prevent the creation of campsites and trails and avoid places where impacts are just beginning.

3. Dispose of Waste Properly

- Pack it in, pack it out. Inspect your campsite and rest areas for trash or spilled foods.

- Pack out all trash, leftover food, and litter.

- Deposit solid human waste in cat holes dug 6 to 8 inches deep, at least 200 feet from water, camp, and trails. Cover and disguise the cat hole when finished.

- Pack out toilet paper and hygiene products.

- To wash yourself or your dishes, carry water 200 feet away from streams or lakes and use small amounts of biodegradable soap. Scatter strained dishwater.

4. Leave What You Find

- Preserve the past: Examine but do not touch cultural or historic structures and artifacts.

- Leave rocks, plants, and other natural objects as you found them.

- Avoid introducing or transporting non-native species.

- Do not build structures or furniture and do not dig trenches.

5. Minimize Campfire Impacts

- Campfires can leave a lasting impact on the backcountry. Use a lightweight stove for cooking and enjoy a candle lantern for light.

- Where fires are permitted, use established fire rings, fire pans, or mound fires.

- Keep fires small. Use only sticks from the ground that can be broken by hand.

- Burn all wood and coals to ash, put out the campfire completely, and then scatter the cooled ashes.

6. Respect Wildlife

- Observe wildlife from a distance. Do not follow or approach animals.

- Never feed animals. Feeding wildlife damages their health, alters natural behaviors, and exposes them to predators and other dangers.

- Protect wildlife and your food by storing rations and trash securely.

- Learn the area's regulations for pets and obey those rules. If you cannot control your dog, leave it at home.

- Avoid wildlife during sensitive times, such as when animals are mating, nesting, raising young, or during winter.

7. Be Considerate of Other Visitors

- Respect other visitors and protect the quality of their experience.

- Be courteous. Yield to other users on the trail.

- Step to the downhill side of the trail when encountering horses and other pack stock.

- Take breaks and camp away from trails and other visitors.

- Let nature's sounds prevail. Avoid loud voices and noises.

ADAPTING LNT PRACTICES TO THE ECOSYSTEM

Although this book focuses on hiking and backpacking skills related to forest and mountain regions, the LNT practices presented here are relevant for other ecosystems as well. The LNT principles were created with wide application in mind and can be adapted to various environments.

For instance, the third LNT principle, "Dispose of Waste Properly," instructs you to dig a cat hole away from water sources, campsites, and official trails to properly dispose of human waste when traveling in forest or mountain regions. Along certain seashores, however, it would be more appropriate to use a portable latrine that would allow you to carry out your waste. Be aware of any regulations that might apply to the areas you visit.

Another example of ecosystem adaptation, this time associated with the second LNT principle, "Travel and Camp on Durable Surfaces," states that in forest regions, it is appropriate to disperse a group of hikers when traveling off-trail to minimize the chance of creating a new trail. That practice would not be appropriate for the desert regions of the American Southwest, however. When traveling in very fragile terrain, such as cryptogamic or cryptobiotic soil (a biological soil crust that hosts a rich and delicate community of living organisms), it might be better to walk single file, matching the leader's steps. There are many other LNT adaptations for various ecosystems and outdoor activities.

Although this book is not the proper forum to identify and explain all of these variations, you can review the *Outdoor Skills & Ethics* booklets published by the Leave No Trace Center for Outdoor Ethics for more in-depth information. These focus on LNT principles and techniques for specific areas or activities. The collection includes the titles *Alaska Wildlands, Northeast Mountains, Pacific Northwest, Rocky Mountains, Sierra Nevada*, and more. These booklets also cover various outdoor activities: fishing, mountain biking, rock climbing, and more. All of these can be purchased at lnt.org.

LEARN FROM THE EXPERTS

AMC's Outdoor Learning and Leadership team vetted each chapter of the *Essential Guide to Winter Recreation*, so you can rest safe in the knowledge that the content of this book checks out among even the most seasoned pros. Everything herein coincides with AMC's best practices.

As for me, I've been actively exploring the woods of the Northeast in all seasons for more than 40 years and writing about it for an array of publications for the past 25. I've been a Registered Maine Guide since the late 1990s and have spent the past 17 years working as a ranger in Maine's "forever wild" Baxter State Park, the northern terminus of the Appalachian Trail. As a ranger, I've gone through intensive outdoor training, earning Wilderness First Responder certification, and taking innumerable classes in search and rescue and outdoor safety. I've put what I've learned to use in countless rescues, hauling hikers down the mountain in burrito wraps and searching for people who didn't bother to bring a map and found themselves lost. And I've built many a campfire for freezing campers who didn't know how. I've peppered the book with pro tips picked up along the way.

I hope you have as much fun reading this book as I did during the many years I unknowingly spent researching it.

CHAPTER 1
BEFORE
YOU GO

➜ **Prior Experience**   2
➜ **Trip Planning**   4
➜ **Essential Trip Planning Resources**   12

Every year in New England, we hear stories about people getting into trouble on their outdoor adventures in places like the White Mountains, and the root cause is almost always the same. The scenario goes something like this: A couple of friends decide to go for a hike in the majestic, snow-draped mountains, grab a few snacks and their winter coats, and head out. The day begins beautifully, and they cover a few miles on trails that are almost bare. As the pair climbs, the air begins to chill, and they find the going gets more difficult as the snow deepens. They know they're nearing the top, though, and they don't want to turn back without bagging the summit.

Soon they're post-holing, their legs plunging into thigh-deep drifts, and tiring rapidly. Their food and water are long gone, and their jeans are soaking up the wet snow. The sun falls behind the mountains earlier than it does elsewhere, and the shadows lengthen as the short winter day begins to wink out. With the deepening snow and darkness setting in, they lose sight of the cairns and trail markers they were using to navigate. Then, with warning signs that were hard to see through the canopy of snow-draped trees, black clouds move in, and the sky lets loose in a snow squall, blowing a gale and limiting visibility to less than 10 yards.

Now the intrepid pair is in trouble.

The two didn't think to pack a map or a compass. They figured they'd just use their phones' GPS, but they've been on the trail longer than they expected, and the batteries died hours ago—if they even had reception in the remote mountains to begin with. The pants and coats they put on for this midwinter romp in the snow are now drenched and providing little warmth. Preparing for only a day hike, they neglected to bring matches or headlamps or a set of dry clothes. In fact, all they have left in their packs are empty water bottles and energy bar wrappers.

Now they're in serious life-or-death trouble.

This sort of thing happens all winter long in the White Mountains, according to a 2017 story in the *Boston Globe*. Colonel Kevin Jordan of the New Hampshire Fish and Game Department, the agency tasked with rescuing hapless hikers, says the

1

numbers are growing. He estimated his organization responded to more than 200 missions in 2017, up from 173 the prior fiscal year. Now, winter in New Hampshire can feel interminable, but we can estimate it's at least three months, or 90 days, long. Do the math, and the state's wardens are carrying out more than two rescues a day. "We're getting a ton of them," Colonel Jordan told the Globe, "because people aren't prepared for the winter conditions we're finding."[1]

Hiking in winter demands more. More preparedness and more planning. More outdoor experience and ability, and—perhaps most easily overlooked—more time. The cold months require better decision making and a more cautious mindset. The same trail you hiked in summer six months ago is a different world now. Just as windchill intensifies cold, winter has a way of magnifying mistakes.

Knowing what you're getting into, checking the weather, making a friend aware of your plans, wearing and carrying the appropriate gear for the time of year and terrain: These are the basics of hiking *any* time of year. But they're never more important than in winter.

➜ PRIOR EXPERIENCE

Not long ago at Maine's "forever wild" Baxter State Park, rangers at Chimney Pond Campground sat down with everyone planning a winter ascent up Katahdin. These campers typically stayed overnight at the beautiful bowl midway up Maine's largest mountain, and they'd stop by the ranger station to discuss gear, plan, route, size of group, and experience levels. Those who appeared to be novices with inappropriate gear were given suggestions for alternate routes at lower elevations. Baxter would allow only groups of four or more into the park in the winter, with at least one experienced winter climber in the lead.

These practices have changed in favor of an "at-your-own-risk" policy, but the idea behind them remains a good one: Everyone who ventures into wild terrain at any time of year—but especially in cold, snowy, and unpredictable conditions—should have appropriate gear and some practice under their web-tech belts.

How much experience one needs to tackle winter hiking is debatable. But just as you wouldn't expect to take on Everest without months of training, you probably shouldn't consider Katahdin, the Presidential Mountains in New Hampshire, or anything over 3,000 feet in winter until you've put in a lot of time at lower elevations. In Maine, Acadia National Park is a perfect place for literally getting your feet wet with winter camping and climbing. The park's Blackwoods Campground is open year-round, and it feels quiet and secluded, protected from noise by the long approach road. Anyone can pitch a tent, fire up the camp stove, and spend a weekend enjoying the "jewel of the National Park System" all to themselves. But it's close enough to Route 3 that if you get scared or have any issues, you can retreat

[1] Bryan MacQuarrie, "Harsh Winter Leads to More Rescue Missions in N.H., Taxing Rescuers," *Boston Globe*, May 15, 2017. Accessed online.

to the safety of Bar Harbor in no time. The park is filled with picturesque peaks that are easy to summit, ideal slopes on which to get comfortable using snowshoes and traction devices (such as Microspikes and crampons, which we will discuss in Chapter 9, Recreation Gear and Skills, page 162) and to practice the all-important climbing skill of self-arrest.

What is the minimum level of experience to venture into the winter woods? That's a debatable question and entirely dependent on the itinerary, but certainly there are some absolute necessities. Everything in winter is relative to the distance from help. Winter both helps and hinders backcountry rescue. Many remote areas become more difficult to reach when roads are closed. Some, however, are easier to get to, thanks to snowmobiles, which can venture farther and faster than anyone on foot.

How much experience you need depends on your fitness level, your comfort level, common sense, and the route you intend to attempt.

PRESEASON TRAINING

Simply walking on a snowy trail is more difficult than the same hike on bare ground. Snow slows each step. And, just as you tire faster running on sand than you do running on grass, travel on snow requires more effort. This is simple physics. You're no doubt wearing heavier footwear and bulkier layers of clothing; add to that the surface beneath you giving way when you step, requiring more effort to go the same distance. When the snow is deep and you're breaking trail, it's even harder.

All of which means you need to physically prepare before your winter outing. Many outdoor experts recommend a fitness regimen for outdoor activity that in-cludes a mixture of cardiovascular and strength training. Weights, too, are a good idea; for example, squats with kettlebells. A backpack loaded with a few weights on your daily walk does a good job emulating what it's like on the trail. Many of the commercial outdoor magazines and outfitters have fitness ideas on their websites.

No one would think to attempt a marathon without building up stamina on many successive shorter runs. The same thinking applies to hiking or any other outdoor activity. The best way to get fit and comfortable for climbing a 4,000-footer is to scale a few easier peaks. Skip the elevator and run the stairs at home or work. If you work out at a gym, hit the StairMaster or crank the inclinometer on the treadmill.

Other preseason ideas: If you intend to snowshoe, make sure you're comfort-able on snowshoes. Romp around the backyard in them. Try climbing small hills. Chase the dog. Soon they'll simply feel like extensions of your boots. If you plan to climb any serious inclines in winter, it's crucial you're familiar with using an ice ax and you understand self-arrest. Many outdoor organizations, including the Ap-palachian Mountain Club and even adult-education programs at your local high school, host courses designed to boost your wilderness skills. You can also sign up with a skill-specific program at outdoor outfitters.

1

➜ TRIP PLANNING

So now you're physically fit and have a basic idea of how to use your gear. Time to head out, right? Not quite. Preparedness comes in many forms and includes having an idea where you're going, how to get there, how long this adventure should take, what you need to bring for the conditions, and what to do if the unexpected happens. (In the woods, the unexpected almost always happens. That's the hallmark of adventure—and why it's fun.)

> ➜ **PRO TIP** Pick up a Hike Safe Card when you see one on your travels. These plastic cards, which are only available in New Hampshire, display all the above information in a handy checklist, and their sales help fund search and rescue operations. As an added bonus, people who carry the cards are not held liable to pay for their rescue, should they need one, unless they make some egregious choices. Find out more at wildlife.state.nh.us/safe.

Baxter State Park rangers often are amazed when they're called out to rescue southbound Appalachian Trail thru-hikers only to find them wearing jeans and cotton shirts and carrying 150-pound packs that contain canned foods, frying pans, and giant bowie knives but no headlamps or maps. In other words, these hikers have traveled half the country, all the way to the Northeast's wildest corner, to embark on a 2,100-mile odyssey with no idea what they need and no clue what they're getting into.

In winter, this lack of preparation very easily could result in death.

A sound plan is vitally important to outdoor adventure at all times of year but never more so than when it's deeply cold and snowy.

The White Mountain National Forest and the New Hampshire Fish and Game Department came up with a checklist of sorts that gives a good idea of the very basics of what's needed when venturing into the woods. Called hikeSafe, the program makes it clear that it's every adventurer's responsibility to return home at night and lists the bare essentials.

You are responsible for yourself, so be prepared:

1. **With knowledge and gear.** Become self-reliant by learning about the terrain, conditions, local weather, and your equipment before you start.

2. **To leave your plans.** Tell someone where you are going, the trails you are hiking, when you will return, and your emergency plans.

3. **To stay together.** When you start as a group, hike as a group and end as a group. In winter, the team should set a slow enough pace that no one breaks a sweat and everyone keeps their clothing dry.

4. **To turn back.** Weather changes quickly in the mountains. Fatigue and unexpected conditions can also affect your hike. Know your limitations and when to postpone your hike. The mountains will be there another day.

5. **For emergencies.** Even if you are headed out for just an hour, an injury, severe weather, or a wrong turn could become life threatening. Don't assume you will be rescued; know how to rescue yourself.

6. **To share the hiker code with others.**

Common sense, right? You can find out more at hikesafe.com.

Author Alex Kosseff addressed these ideas in the original *AMC Guide to Outdoor Leadership* but with different prompts. He suggests that trip planners address a series of questions while laying out their itineraries, and it's the kind of list any journalist would recognize. These questions are why, who, where, when, how, and what if?

1

WHY?

This is a question so many of us overlook when heading out for some outdoor fun. Why are we going? It's important that people recognize their goals and, perhaps more importantly, the aims and objectives of the rest of the members of their traveling party. Does everyone want the same thing?

One of the most common problems rangers encounter in backcountry rescue happens when groups separate, leading to lost members and people getting injured without help or any chance of self-rescue. Oftentimes, groups split because some members want to go faster and conquer a peak, while others are interested in a casual snowshoe in the winter woods, some fresh air, and time with friends. These differing ideas not only lead to potentially dangerous situations, they also cause discord within a group. Even if nothing bad happens, having several people with different goals for a trip inevitably creates conflict and makes for less fun.

Luckily, the fix couldn't be any simpler: Sit down and talk beforehand, discussing the plan with all members of the party. Allow everyone input and consider an alternate route if someone is uncomfortable with the plan. Perhaps split into two groups—one for a rigorous hike and the other a lowland jaunt—that will join back up for a delicious campfire dinner at the end of the day. Maybe someone simply would rather not come this time. Laying out the plan beforehand gives people options—and prevents arguments and safety issues later.

Don't forget to consider the why question, even if you're traveling alone. Consider your personal motivations for where you're going and be sure you understand your own objectives and how they jibe with your physical limits and abilities.

WHO?

The composition of a group determines a lot about a plan. Your buddies may have extensive mountaineering experience. But did you invite your workmate who's recovering from a heart attack? Is your friend bringing his small kids or his elderly

1

father? Does one member have asthma or perhaps a peanut allergy? Does one traveler really dislike another? Is this someone's first time on skis or snowshoes?

Knowing who is coming—their interests, abilities, experience levels, and even medical issues—is vital to trip planning. Nothing is worse than being on the side of a mountain only to find out that one of your hiking companions put nuts in the trail mix and another forgot to bring her EpiPen. Or that your workmate is not physically able to complete the hike, is complaining about the cold, and wants to turn around.

Knowing how many people are in a traveling party is critical to planning. There are the obvious considerations regarding the amount of food and supplies to bring and who is sleeping where and with whom. But there are other less obvious issues: some hiking areas—like Baxter Park, the White Mountains, and the Adirondacks, for example—limit group size to preserve the wilderness experience. The Appalachian Trail doesn't allow more than ten people to camp or 25 people to hike together. It's vital to know numbers for things like permits and land use and Leave No Trace ethics, too. (The leader of a trip to the High Peaks Wilderness Area in the Adirondacks was issued a ticket in 2016 for bringing a bus tour of 67 to climb Algonquin Mountain!)

Big parties often bring their own problems, and some people prefer to travel in small groups, although we do not recommend winter adventuring in groups smaller than four people. Hiking and camping trips, especially in winter or during adverse conditions, are great opportunities to get to know others. The forced togetherness, the shared experience, often creates enduring friendships, and this can be diminished in larger gatherings. Smaller groups can break camp faster, clean up easier, travel farther, and see more, especially when it comes to wildlife. There's nothing like a long, loud train of people to scare off moose and birds and that elusive winter lynx. Many people consider four a great group size for outdoor adventure, especially in cold weather. If anyone does get hurt, this allows you to send two for help while one person remains with the patient.

Some might want to bring kids on their outdoor adventures, and there are many benefits to introducing children to the outdoors. Many campers wonder what the appropriate age is to bring kids on an outdoor adventure. The answer is . . . it depends. If you're going to climb Katahdin in

> **→ PRO TIP** Start slowly with kids. Consider trying a few day hikes to gauge their abilities in winter. Bring along a lot of their favorite snacks. When you go for your first winter camping trip, hike a distance they feel comfortable with and set up a base camp, using that to explore an area. The kids should be familiar with day hikes already, and this allows you more time in camp for play, making snow shelters, and getting comfortable. It also requires you to tote less gear on a daily basis when you're out for the day. Bring a few toys and games and make it fun. Make cocoa upon your return to camp. Read stories at night.

winter, leave the children at home. Kids under six are not allowed above treeline. If you're winter camping in Acadia, enjoying the small peaks and dramatic sea views of the country's most easterly national park, bundle them up and bring them along. If it's a backcountry ski with some buddies from work, moving quick and climbing high, probably best not.

Whether or not to include your kids on a winter camping trip is largely a common-sense question to which there are no hard-and-fast rules. Your number one role as a parent is to keep your children safe. If you feel you can do so and show them a good time in the winter woods, great. By most measures these days, kids spend too much time indoors. They can benefit from wind in their hair, sun on their faces, overcoming challenges, and romping in the snow just as much as you can. Getting kids outdoors—in the right way—can instill a love that will last their lifetime. You can create bonds, teach them important skills and life lessons, and build self-confidence. Keep in mind, though, that kids need to be more bundled up than adults and will travel more slowly.

Which brings us to our furry friends. Many dogs are natural outdoor companions and can add a lot to a winter camping party. Going for a walk is among the many ways pooches bond with their humans, so a hiking excursion makes a lot of sense. Scads of Appalachian Trail thru-hikers, for example, bring their dogs along with them. Dogs can even lighten the load, pulling sleds or wearing their own packs. They can keep you warm, improve your mood, warn you of danger, and even save your life.

Whether or not to take yours depends in large part upon the animal. Do you walk together several times a week at home? Then the woods should be fine. If not, consider putting in some miles before embarking on a winter camping expedition. Does your dog listen well? Does it like to chase? You must have full control of your pet at all times whenever you're in a park or wilderness setting. Before heading out, check with the land manager at your destination. A lot of parks and preserves do not allow canine companions. Many national parks do.

Once it's clear who's coming on this outdoor adventure, there are other things to consider. Politics, for example. In any group there's always politics. Who is the leader? If a dangerous situation does arise in a remote location, who makes the hard call? This role usually defaults to the person with the most outdoor experience or the coolest head, and that's probably right, but leadership should be discussed ahead of time. Everyone should be comfortable with who's in charge.

WHERE?

This one typically takes care of itself. Where to go is usually the first topic of discussion when it comes to outdoor adventure. And the answer generally leaps to mind without a whole lot of thought, automatically setting the parameters for the whole trip.

It shouldn't.

1

The matter of *where* should be given considerable deliberation, and it shouldn't be thought of as independent from the other considerations of why and who. They are all inextricably tied together. Imagine, for example, that you and your friend decide to attempt a difficult but nontechnical route in the White Mountains over a weekend. You're both very experienced winter warriors but don't have a lot of time, due to family commitments. Another friend overhears and invites himself along. He is older and slower and doesn't have a lot of experience in off-season camping or climbing. You hesitate but agree, sticking to your original plan. Best-case scenario, this situation leads to a happy weekend expedition and some new skills and memories for your friend. More likely outcomes, however, are less pleasant. The two hardcore buddies leave their friend far behind, it gets dark, and the friend gets lost. Or the friend tries to push himself to keep up and gets injured. Or everyone argues all weekend. Better to stick to the plan and tell the third party to come along next time, or find a new, less strenuous course that is inclusive of everyone's ability levels.

The destination has a way of defining the whole trip and putting everything into perspective. Once the *where* is decided, you know roughly what gear you need and how long it will take to get to the trailhead. But it also raises many questions of its own. A visitor to your average Northeastern park can choose between lowland walks, strenuous ascents, and easy day hikes to enjoy views. Other considerations naturally arise:

- Where will you stay? Tent camping or a cabin? Lean-to or hut? Will there be parking at the trailhead? Is it plowed?

- What kind of permits/reservations do you need?

- What will you do when you get there? Do you want to snowshoe or ski? Do you need crampons or Microspikes? Are you backpacking or pulling a sled?

- What route will you take? Is one car sufficient, or will you make a loop? Some great weekend treks require spotting a second vehicle.

- What's the climate like where you're going? Is the weather affected by elevation, for example, or by the ocean?

- Are there hazards? Do you have to cross ice or worry about an avalanche on your selected route?

- Is the park staffed in winter? How will you get help? How far is your route from the road? Are there bail-out options if you get into trouble?

You must answer all of these questions for a safe, exciting adventure. Guidebooks, blogs, friends, maps, and park websites and hotlines are all good resources to turn to when researching a trip. It's always necessary to set up contingency plans, in case weather, gear, or closed parking lots render your planned itinerary unsafe. Always remember: The hiker's primary responsibility is to get home in one piece.

WHEN?

Another question that seems fairly obvious. The when of any trip is whenever you can get time off from work and a few days away from the family, right? Well, that's a good start, but like all of these other prompts, *when* raises a number of other questions: How does winter weather affect your area of interest? Is the lake you have to cross frozen over? Rivers? Are the roads plowed to get there?

1

Is the peak you're hoping to visit even open in winter? Many are not.

Is the route that interests your group available year-round? Some parks close trails when there's snow cover.

How does less daylight factor in? Is there enough light during a single day to complete your chosen route? Should you budget in an overnight to give yourself more time? Certainly, you should make sure to get an early start when the days are shorter.

What are the accommodations like that time of year? What sorts of permits are needed? At many parks and preserves, winter rules differ from those in summer. Are there any special seasonal restrictions?

How busy is it this time of year? Some of the most popular outdoor recreational areas can be bustling with winter adventurers looking to climb or ski the backcountry. Finding bunkhouse space at Baxter Park's Chimney Pond, for example, is difficult even in February and March, and Tuckerman Ravine in the White Mountains is often thronged in the off-season, especially as winter edges toward spring.

WHAT?

What to bring? As you can imagine, supplies and provisions vary with the itinerary. Spending time at Katahdin Lake Wilderness Camps, where shelter and meals are provided, requires packing less on the sled than a winter camping trip deep in the bush of the Adirondacks. We'll cover gear for specific activities in later chapters, but every pack should always contain a handful of items—often referred to as the Ten Essentials—no matter the destination or time of year:

1. **Map.**

2. **Compass.**

3. **Extra clothing.** Winter demands more than summer, obviously, but you should always be able to put on something dry, toes to toque.

4. **Extra food and water.** Again, winter requires more because your body burns so many calories simply trying to keep itself warm. Water, unbeknownst to many, actually helps stave off hypothermia.

5. **Flashlight or headlamp.** The sun goes down earlier this time of year and that flashlight app on your cell phone doesn't count. Extra batteries are a good idea as well.

6. **Matches or fire starter.**

1

7. **First-aid kit and repair kit.** You'll be amazed by the many backcountry uses for duct tape. And you're always awfully glad to have that moleskin.

8. **Whistle.** Three short blasts is the universal signal for distress and it cuts right through the quiet of the winter woods.

9. **Pocketknife.**

10. **Weatherproof upper and lower layers.**

    Extra winter essentials might include:

11. **Baby wipes.** When it's too cold to bathe, these things are magic.

12. **Avalanche rescue gear.** Depending upon where you're going.

13. **Tarp.** Whether you use it as an emergency shelter, a hypothermia burrito wrap, a kindling sled, or to retain heat across the face of your lean-to, a tarp is endlessly helpful.

14. **Sunscreen and sunglasses.** Snow glare does a number on your peepers.

15. **Lightweight nylon rope (paracord).** This always comes in handy.

WHAT IF?

Ah, contingencies. One of the most critical parts of any plan and the one most often overlooked. *What if?* What will you do when something goes awry? Does your group have the skills and tools necessary to extricate itself from a bad situation? Do you know where the emergency exits are on your route? Every good plan A should have a plan B for when things inevitably go wrong. Remember the new mantra in the woods: Hikers are responsible for their own rescue.

When you're planning your fun winter getaway, you must consider the what ifs. What if someone breaks a leg? Where are the bail-out points along your route? Are there any? Where are the nearest roads? What are the closest sources of help? Identify these on the map—and make sure everyone in the group knows them. It does no good if the leader has all of the contingency plans in her head and tumbles down the trail slamming said head on the ice, rendering her incapacitated. Make sure everyone in the party knows the intended route, exits, and overall plan, and the name of the specific trails. It's amazing how many times people call 911 unable to describe their location with any precision.

Imagine a worst-case scenario. What will you do if you can't leave? Do you have the supplies to shelter in place? Do you know whom to call if you need help? It's a good idea to keep a sheet of paper in a zippered plastic bag that lists all the numbers of the local agencies on it. Calling 911 usually does the trick, but it's smart to have backups. You can even text 911 now in some states, so check if that is a possibility before you go adventuring.

And don't forget to think of ways to help potential rescuers. Leave the particulars of your plan with a friend or loved one who's back home and available by phone. This should include a very detailed itinerary: where you're going, trails you intend to hike, where you plan to stay, and when you intend to return. It should also mention everyone in the group by name, with ages and medical information if necessary. Appendix B: Participant Information Form (see page 193) provides a helpful resource for this aspect of trip planning.

1

HOW?

Now we're getting to the nitty-gritty. Once you've decided why you want to undertake this adventure, who's coming, when and where you're going, and what your break-glass options are, you need to consider travel plans. How are you getting there? Who's driving? Do you need multiple vehicles for the size of your group? If you're starting and ending at different locations, do you need a second car (often referred to as "spotting" a car)? Are the selected vehicles up to the task? Many backcountry areas, especially in winter, pose challenges for low-clearance cars, for example. The Golden Road, which allows access to many recreational areas in Maine's North Woods, including Baxter Park and several sporting camps, is plowed all winter long, but it's unforgiving on small cars without four-wheel-drive capabilities. It's important to make sure your vehicle is as winter ready as you are. Snow tires, kitty litter for weight and traction, a shovel, jumper cables, and blankets all make sense this time of year.

Some winter camps offer snowmobile shuttles and/or bush plane transport, which can add extra days of skiing and snowshoeing to your itinerary.

HOW MUCH?

Outdoor adventure can be one of the least expensive hobbies going. Just a pair of boots and some Goodwill clothes, right? That may be true in summer, but in winter, you have to add in costs for things like skis, snowshoes, Microspikes, appropriate extra layers, double boots, and crampons and ice axes if you need them. Make sure to familiarize yourself with the various expenses of your destination ahead of time. Discuss options with your group, so there are no surprises when you arrive and it's twice the cash outlay people were expecting. See if you can borrow gear from friends or rent it from an outfitter. There are more specific suggestions on gear throughout the book. Also look into membership with organizations, such as the Appalachian Mountain Club, that offer discounts on lodging and camping. Find out more at outdoors.org/membership.

Of course, *how much* also refers to the amount of gear to carry. Winter expeditions require more gear, more food, and more time. Your pack necessarily grows in winter, and many trekkers add a sled to handle all of that additional gear. Expect to carry almost twice

1

as much food and for your pack to weigh 30 to 40 percent more than it does during other seasons (see Chapter 4, Backpacking Gear, specifically Figure 11 on page 49).

THEN WHAT?

You haven't even gone yet and you're planning for the end-of-trip cleanup? You certainly should. You'll have far more energy before you leave than you will after a weekend of breaking trail, climbing peaks, and post-holing in the deep snow. When you reach the warm confines of home after an epic winter odyssey, there's still a lot to do, especially in winter when everything, even on the sunniest days, gets wet to some degree.

1. Make sure you let everyone know you're safe. Simple, but easily forgotten. Your contact person, especially, should be alerted that you're out of any danger. A call or text when you get back to your car is a great idea, which hopefully will preclude any worrying.

2. Dry out your gear. Your future self will thank you. Sleeping bags, tents, and anything else made of nylon will grow mildew, shortening its life and making it a mess the next time you pull it out for use. Hanging your stuff over chairs or the shower rod for a day should be fine. Just don't dry anything too close to a heat source.

3. Some of your down belongings—sleeping bags, packable pillows, etcetera— can go into the dryer. Throw in a tennis ball or an old shoe to keep them fluffy.

4. Wash your clothes.

5. Put your utensils and tableware in the dishwasher and clean your pots and pans.

6. Take out the garbage. Hopefully, you packed out all of your scraps. Now's the time to get rid of them, unless you did so in a trash can on the road home.

7. Return any rented items. Be sure they're clean and dry.

8. Stuff some old newspaper into your boots to absorb moisture and lay them by the fire (but not too close). Or try removing the inner soles, stuffing the boots with towels, and placing them near a fan.

9. Pack away your gear for next time. Store your stove fuel in an appropriate location. Take batteries out of headlamps and GPS units to avoid corrosion.

➜ ESSENTIAL TRIP PLANNING RESOURCES

So, you've done all of your big-picture planning and now need to fill in the details. Thanks to the internet, outdoor blogs, outfitter sites, park sites, guidebooks, and map archives, there's no shortage of places to turn for trip planning information. A half hour on the laptop is about all it takes. (This is why rangers are astonished when people show up without an inkling of what they're getting into.) You can even find printable checklists of everything you need to bring. We've included some of our own in Appendix C, Expedition Preparation Checklist (see page 195).

MAPS

Many of us have gotten so used to the GPS in our cars and phones that we couldn't imagine going anywhere without them; however, these devices often don't work in wilderness areas. Some remote places simply have no cell service, and many digital cartographers don't go into much detail in the backcountry. Phones also seem to have a habit of running out of juice when you most need them.

1

Which brings us to maps, the GPS of yore. An up-to-date map, even the illustrated ones you can find in trailhead boxes, can be a literal lifesaver in the woods. Maps come in all shapes, sizes, and scales. Many parks have maps that can be printed right from their websites and larger Tyvek ones that can be purchased at their visitor centers. Guidebooks often contain them these days. And there are those old outdoor standbys, those topographical treasures, the U.S. Geological Survey (USGS) maps we've been carrying since seemingly forever. The USGS's most well-known series is the 7.5-minute, 1:24,000 scale quadrangle topographic maps, which are accessible for free to the public. You can download a PDF of any USGS topographic quadrangle map from store.usgs.gov/map-locator or purchase a print. For those with a solid understanding of navigation fundamentals, CalTopo.com is an excellent source of printable maps. AMC produces a selection of maps rendered and verified by its staff cartographer, including coverage of Maine's 100-Mile Wilderness and Acadia National Park, as well as a new winter recreation-specific map of the White Mountains. Learn more at outdoors.org/books-maps.

GUIDEBOOKS

Guidebooks and trail guides are a great place to start when trip planning. But it should be noted that guidebooks are just that: guides. The amount of time that passes between writing, printing, binding, shipping, and hitting the retail shelves can mean that vital information provided in guidebooks changes, due to natural forces, such as a hurricane, or less destructive but inconvenient occurrences, such as a trailhead closing or a phone number changing. Always call ahead or research online before setting out to explore an area recommended in a guidebook. You are responsible for yourself, so make sure you're aware of current conditions. Guidebooks remain a good resource, however, because they tend to offer local details on a very fine level, they're easy to transport (or to take pictures of relevant pages with your cell phone), they're eminently shareable, and they make for good reading in a tent or cabin. Guidebooks cover most major parks, vacation areas, states, and regions. It's always a good idea to use the most recent edition of any travel or trail guide, but even a vintage copy can contain relevant information; just be sure to call the land manager or agency and confirm the details before setting out. Find a list of current AMC guidebooks, as well as updates to existing and past editions, at outdoors.org/books-maps.

INTERNET RESOURCES

The internet is the information supertrail when it comes to the outdoors: an immensely powerful tool. On the web, you can find maps, guides, blog posts, gear reviews, how-tos, rental prices, satellite photos, permit and fee information, magazine articles, discussion boards, weather forecasts, and even friends to hike with. Just be sure to use the net wisely. Sources should always be corroborated and be careful to whom you give your information.

CONDITION REPORTS

Many clubs, parks, and outdoor organizations provide trail and snow condition reports via telephone hotlines or the web. These are typically updated daily or weekly, giving you boots-on-the-ground information. AMC, for example, posts up-to-date backcountry weather and trail conditions for all its huts and lodges at outdoors.org/conditions. The rangers at Baxter State Park post current conditions at Chimney Pond on Facebook every day in winter. New York State's Department of Environmental Conservation offers an email subscription with the latest on trail conditions and news. And websites such as newenglandtrailconditions.com provide reports from hikers and weather observers scattered across New England.

CHAPTER 2
UNDERSTANDING THE WEATHER

→ **Meteorological Winter**   16
→ **Why Winter**   17
→ **Fronts**   19
→ **Observation and Evaluation**   22

The weather is perhaps the single greatest factor affecting outdoor plans. It's what makes winter *winter*. Or, at least, it's what makes us notice that the seasons have changed. Weather can determine our itineraries, alter our routes, or cancel days out altogether. Weather has no mercy and no malice; it just is. Weather, or our preparedness for it, can be the difference between a fun trip and a miserable slog. It has the power to determine whether we live or die.

But what is it, exactly?

In February 2015, a congressional climate change skeptic brought a snowball into the United States Senate to disprove this whole global warming idea. If the world was heating up, Senator James Inhofe (R-Okla.) argued, why was it snowing outside? Like so many people, the esteemed congressman confused weather with climate. Climate, of course, is an overall set of meteorological conditions governing the weather patterns of a place. It's a consequence of both a region's location on Earth and Earth's location in the solar system, and it is a long-term measurement, factoring in averages across years and decades. Weather, on the other hand, is the set of atmospheric conditions occurring in a specific location at any given moment. Weather is often determined by a region's climate, but it is a brief temporal phenomenon. Weather changes by the hour, sometimes even by the minute, but climate changes across eons. Over at NASA, they like to describe the difference this way: Climate is what you expect; weather is what you get. In other words, we expect hot days in late July and cold days in January because that has been the norm for our lifetimes. We get unexpected rain and afternoon thunderstorms in July and snow squalls in January.

Weather in North America occurs largely due to two powerful, opposing forces: warm air from the equator and cold air from the Arctic. These two constantly compete for control of the continent, like warring nations, or like Heat Miser and Snow Miser from the old holiday TV special, "The Year Without a Santa Claus." Many other factors play a role, including the moisture of the oceans, the tilt of the planet, the temperature of the atmosphere, and the rotation of the Earth. But everything in the United States, Canada, and Mexico begins as a binary battle between what scientists call continental tropical and continental polar air masses.

In very basic terms, while the planet spins, the sun heats the air, which rises into the atmosphere, leaving space behind for cool air to move into. This motion causes wind. The wind moves weather systems, called fronts, across the continent. The warmed-up air tends to be lighter and drier than its polar counterpart and is thus able to absorb moisture as it rises into the atmosphere. Colder air is generally heavier and denser, with molecules packed closer together, and pushes down toward the ground.

The area where the two air types contact one another is called a front, and fronts become either a cold front or a warm front depending upon the prevailing weather system. In warm fronts, a heated mass of air rolls over a cooler one. When cold air slides under a warmer air mass, it's called a cold front. Both frontal systems can occur any time of year.

Understanding these relatively simple thermodynamics makes it easy to predict what the weather will be in the near future—although predictions aren't always correct.

➜ METEOROLOGICAL WINTER

Listen to a TV meteorologist, and winter lasts from December 1 until the end of February. But the winter solstice, the actual astronomical start of winter, doesn't occur until December 21, and the spring equinox, the astronomical *end* of winter, isn't until March 21. There's a three-week discrepancy at either end of winter. What gives? How can meteorologists be so out of whack with the planet?

This temporal misalignment is the difference between meteorological winter and astronomical winter. Essentially, meteorologists and government scientists created meteorological winter based on temperature norms. Winter is the coldest season, so winter should be the coldest three months. Makes sense. They did this to simplify and standardize the calendar, making it easier to create reports and climatological statistics, the kind of data upon which farmers and fishermen—and meteorologists—rely.

Astronomical winter, meanwhile, follows the rotation of the planet on its journey around the sun. The universe didn't set Earth on its flight plan for human convenience, and its schedule is as precise as an overbooked airline flight. The planet takes 365.24 days to complete its orbit. Those .24 days add up to a whole day every four years, what we call a leap year, and those days cause the solstice and equinox calendar to vary from year to year. Earth's rotation on its axis also causes seasonal forecasting headaches. The astronomical seasons in some areas may differ by as many as four days in a year, thanks to the planet's elliptical orbit.

And so, meteorological winter was invented to keep things straightforward, which is why meteorological winter in North America lasts from December through February.

➔ WHY WINTER

There's a popular misconception about the reason behind the seasons. Many people believe Earth is closer to the sun in summer and farther away in winter: When the planet spins close to the big solar furnace, it's warmer, and when it's the farthest distance away, it's colder. While that makes a certain amount of sense, it doesn't exactly explain the appeal of the Caribbean to New Yorkers in February or the snowbird phenomenon, which sees Mainers jetting to Arizona for the period between December and March. Or why it's summer in the southern hemisphere when it's wintertime in North America.

In actuality, winter occurs due to the tilt of the rotational axis of Earth relative to its orbit. Although it's counterintuitive, the planet is closer to the sun in January than it is in July, but the sun in the northern hemisphere is lower in the sky as seen from Earth, so the same amount of energy is spread over a larger patch of ground, and the days are shorter. The northern hemisphere thus becomes colder. In July, it's the opposite. The big belt along the equator, where those tropical getaways all line up, doesn't cant (or tilt) as much one way or the other and thus gets an even, steady amount of sun, which makes it appealing in winter to people looking to escape colder climes.

KOPPEN CLASSIFICATION SYSTEM

As a young botanist studying at the University of St. Petersburg, Wladimir Koppen noticed the difference that temperature and topography made to the flora he saw as he traveled from his university on the plains to his home in coastal Crimea. The relationship between plant life and temperature fascinated the Russian-born scholar, and he wrote his doctoral dissertation on the subject in the late 1860s. After graduating, Koppen moved to Germany to take a job as a meteorologist, but his interest in plants and temperature never cooled. In 1884, he introduced a world map divided into temperature zones, which were determined by the number of months a region would be higher or lower than certain temperatures. In 1900, Koppen made meteorological history by developing this map even further, factoring in not just temperature but aridity. Koppen assigned numerical values to the five major climate types to produce a groundbreaking global climate classification system. Gardeners have been rejoicing ever since.

The Koppen classification system benefited many people beyond those with green thumbs, of course. Meteorologists had their jobs simplified. Koppen also made it easier to explain to desert dwellers why their washes and culverts so rarely saw any action.

Most importantly for our purposes, Koppen's system makes it easier for outdoor lovers to understand what to expect and plan what to pack for their adventures. Those of us who love winters filled with bountiful snow prefer Koppen's continental and cold climate zones: subarctic and polar regions. In the former, precipitation is not as high as it is in the tropics and humid middle latitudes, and temperatures tend to fluctuate wildly with the seasons. In designated cold climate areas, ice and tundra remain year-round, and temperatures climb above freezing only a few months out of the year.

When traveling in continental climate zones, it makes sense to have more layers and to prepare for precipitation that might fall as rain or snow. You'll want to make sure you can regulate your temperature dramatically, peeling off fleeces and shells as the day grows warmer and piling on puffers and hats as the night brings the mercury back down. In cold climate areas, you need your most heavy-duty winter gear almost all of the time.

2 REGIONAL WEATHER

North America is one big weather meet and greet, where arctic air masses dropping down from Canada meet sticky tropical air from the Southeast and the cool ocean breezes of the Atlantic; where storms sweeping in from the Midwest slam into nor'easters off the coast of New England; and el Niño-born warm fronts bring winter rains. The continent combines so many climatic regions—arctic, subarctic, tropics, high peaks, rain forests, and deserts—that it's always creating a rich froth of weather for somebody somewhere.

The trick—or the skill, rather—is to learn the trends for your location.

Maritime

Drive toward the sea from inland areas, and you'll often notice that the weather changes about 6 or 8 miles from the water. The ocean is where much of our weather in North America gets its start. Moisture from the seawater gets sucked up into the atmosphere, pushed around by winds, and dumped back down on the ground in the form of rain. The ocean retains heat in winter, making nearby areas warmer than regions just a few miles inland, and it is generally colder than the air in summer, bringing cooling breezes.

In places like Maine and New Hampshire, where the summits meet the sea, the coast often gets hit with ice and sleet, while the inland peaks receive giant mounds of snow. The difference of a few miles, particularly at elevation, can be stark. Keep this in mind when traveling in the Northeast. Expect dramatically different conditions, for example, between Acadia and Baxter parks. The greatest effect for winter adventurers could be traction, route planning, and sudden changes in weather patterns. You may be planning a weekend snowshoe in Acadia only to find bare ground when you get there.

That's maritime or oceanic climate, in practical terms. Technically speaking, this is not the Koppen-defined maritime climate. That applies to the southern Appalachians, parts of seaside Massachusetts, and northwestern California, Washington, and Oregon. Koppen described the oceanic climate as a place where the sea mitigates temperatures, keeping them from the extremes. The monthly mean temperature is typically below 72 degrees Fahrenheit during the warmest months and above 32 degrees during the coldest. And precipitation remains steady throughout the year, precluding dry seasons or wet seasons. Keep in mind that Koppen made his observations before scientists recognized the effects of human-driven climate change, which has made weather more volatile and unpredictable.

Continental

Hot summers, cold winters, and relatively dry conditions characterize continental climate. The temperature swings in these inland regions are often very dramatic. The mean temperature in continental zones stays below 26.6 degrees Fahrenheit in winter and above 50 degrees for four months or more during the hottest season. According to Koppen, most of Canada falls into this category and much of the U.S. Midwest. Even coastal cities like Portland, Maine; Boston; and Juneau fit this bill, somehow, despite the mitigating ocean.

Traveling through the continental climate during winter means being prepared for a lot of snow—and cold that doesn't go away. When the white stuff falls in this region, it sticks around, often for months. You want your warmest winter gear.

➜ FRONTS
WARM FRONTS

Just as front lines are where opposing forces meet in battle, weather fronts occur at the point where two air masses come into contact. In a warm front, temperate air meets a body of cold air and slides up and over it while pushing it back. Heat rises, of course, which is why the warmer air lofts up over the cooler air, almost as if it is riding an escalator to the atmosphere. Warm fronts in North America typically start in the West, picking up moisture as they travel northeast. They initially appear with high, wispy cirrus clouds, which steadily give way to thicker cloud cover. The clouds gather, and the ceiling falls, often all the way to the ground in the form of fog. Winds shift to the south-southeast, and temperatures tend to rise noticeably. Rain follows, generally light drizzle, though sometimes steadier. Winds become variable, as the warm front engulfs a region.

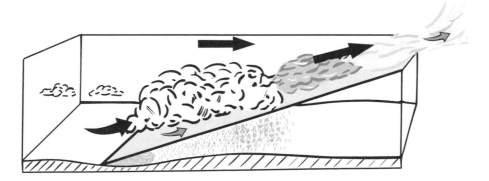

FIGURE 1. Warm, less dense air moves up and away from Earth, rising over cold air.

As the warm air of a warm front rises, it interacts with other air masses, eventually creating less air pressure on the ground, causing barometers everywhere to fall. Because the warm air is lighter and less dense than the cold air, warm fronts often move slowly, having a difficult time displacing the weightier cold air. The process can take days.

What does this mean for outdoor enthusiasts? You generally can predict a warm front by watching the sky. The arrival of cirrus clouds is a great indicator. As more air rises and collects, cirrostratus, then altostratus, and finally nimbostratus clouds form. The direction that the upper atmosphere moves is another sign. If the highest clouds move left to right, relative to the wind at your back, a warm front is on the way. If they move right to left, cold is advancing.

Another sign to look for overhead is the contrail of a plane. Jets tend to leave more noticeable contrails in warm, moist air, because their exhaust vapor has no place to go in wet air. Dry air absorbs this excess moisture, and it isn't as noticeable from Earth.

Think of another old saw when you're looking at the clouds: "Long foretold, long last; short noticed, soon passed." In other words, warm fronts with their many predictors tend to stick around a while, as they endeavor to displace the cold air. More muscular cold fronts power through, passing quicker.

COLD FRONTS

Cold fronts tend to generate bigger storms than warm fronts. They also move much faster. In a cold front, a mass of cool air displaces a mass of more heated air. The density of the cool air forces the warmer air to rise into the atmosphere, bulldozing it off Earth's surface. When the warm air rises, its temperature falls. This shift often creates unstable weather, bringing snow, rain, and heavy winds. In summer it touches off thunderstorms, although these are rare in winter. Cold air does not hang on to moisture as well as warmer air, and thus water gets dumped back down onto the ground.

In North America, cold fronts most often move from the northwest to the southeast, bringing arctic air from Canada down into the United States. The "cold" in a cold front can be quite dramatic, dropping temperatures 15 or 20 degrees in a matter of hours. When a cold front approaches, the winds pick up in strong gusts, usually from the south-southwest. Barometric pressure rises. Precipitation steadily intensifies, becoming heavy at times.

The cloud pattern can warn of an impending cold front. Because of the speed of these fronts—sometimes moving as fast as 40 to 50 MPH—clouds stack up quickly into big, dense towers of moisture. Cold fronts usually begin with cirrus clouds, followed by cirrostratus, and then the ominous cumulonimbus clouds as they grow and grow. From the side of a mountain, you can watch these giant lines of clouds develop.

Unlike warm fronts, which can hover over regions for several days at a time, cold fronts usually move through quickly. Precipitation tends to hit concentrated areas and last less than six hours. Stable air masses with bright skies, but cooler temperatures, typically follow.

FIGURE 2. A cold front occurs when a cold air mass pushes against a warm air mass. This can produce dramatic changes in weather, such as high wind, heavy rain, hail, and thunderstorms.

OCCLUDED AND STATIONARY FRONTS

To occlude something, you obstruct it. Thus, an occluded front forms when one air mass catches up to or gets in the way of another air mass. An occluded front generally forms as a result of two cold fronts colliding with a warm front in between them. The colder of the two air masses moves toward the less cool air, forcing the warm air upward. Cold occlusions behave similarly to cold fronts, causing unstable weather. Warm occlusions likewise often take on the characteristics of warm fronts.

In a stationary front, a warm front and a cold front meet on the field of battle, and neither is strong enough to move the other. So they simply sit there in a stalemate, sometimes for days. Stationary fronts can bring several days of snow, rain, or fog. These fronts can ruin the vacations of fair-weather outdoor adventurers. Of course, they can also provide a week of clear skies.

OROGRAPHIC LIFTING

Ever hear your favorite mountain referred to as a cloud factory? This is due to a meteorological phenomenon known as orographic lifting. When topographical features, such as mountains, cause air masses to move up and over them, the upward air in that mass cools. This can lead to precipitation and wind on the windward side of a peak. Hikers in the Northeast often see snow or other forms of precipitation on the exposed or unprotected side of a peak, particularly near the crests of mountains. On the leeward side, air slides back down the mountain, warming and drying out as it does so, creating a much drier clime. This is typical in the northern Appalachians, where the mountains orient north-south and prevailing winds blow in from the west.

2

Several types of clouds are commonly associated with orographic lifting, including lenticular clouds, the flat, UFO-shaped clouds that ring peaks; banner clouds, or large masses that sit near the summit, as if on a flagpole; and wave clouds, such as the arch cloud, which rolls up and over the tops of mountains like a cresting breaker. These patterns provide clues for what to expect as you climb, and they are particularly useful for selecting routes and places to seek shelter and establish camp.

TEMPERATURE INVERSIONS

Meteorologists describe inversions as the opposite of normal atmospheric behavior, and they are almost always related to temperature. In a temperature inversion, warm air remains warm even as it drifts up into higher altitudes. This warm air sits in place over colder air below, holding it in place. The result is a low ceiling that prevents air from moving, trapping smoke and soot and other particulates. Good examples of this are places like Los Angeles and Beijing, where smog gets caught by inversion and blankets the ground. Temperature inversions often mean the weather will be sticking around a while.

→ OBSERVATION AND EVALUATION

We've all heard the old sayings about red skies at night and farmer's britches and rings around the sun or moon. These old proverbs became household sayings because they contain a fair bit of wisdom. Learning to read the weather and understand its signs is a skill that benefits anyone who spends time outdoors. This is especially true in winter, when a sudden storm can potentially place you and your group in real peril.

LOCATION

Before you head into any woods, it's prudent to know a bit about what sort of weather to expect in them. As we've learned, regions have their own weather patterns, which change due to factors including topography and elevation. The weather in one corner of Baxter State Park, for example, might be far different than in another part of the same 200,000-acre park. Sometimes all it takes is a mile or two to enter a different microclimate. It is common to start a hike on an uncovered path at sea level and find yourself deep in the white stuff at 1,500 feet, or to start off down a trail in a snowy forest only to discover bare ground when you reach the coast.

In your planning, make sure to explore the seasonal weather conditions typical for the region where you're headed. Things change weekly in many places, so factor in the time of the month. You may prepare for a region's winter conditions only to find out the hard way that the ice is soft in March, thanks to warming temperatures. Some routes that are easily traversable in January are barely passable in late winter and early spring. Check local forecasts and explore online for whatever additional information you can find. This might include condition updates at parks, warden service warnings about ice, or even discussions on hunting and fishing blogs.

PRECIPITATION

As anyone who's ever visited New England knows, winter weather takes all shapes and forms, often during the same storm. Snow, sleet, freezing rain, and rain all tumble from the sky during the cold-weather months, presenting outdoor lovers with an array of conditions. The shape that precipitation takes, of course, depends on the temperature—and not just at the ground.

Snow forms as ice crystals high in clouds, when water molecules coalesce around a speck of dust or pollen at below-freezing temperatures. When they become heavy enough, these crystals begin to fall, attracting more moisture as they pass through clouds. Droplets freeze onto the crystals, creating snowflakes. When they become too heavy for clouds to hold, they drop from the sky as snow. If they fall through moist air, they clump together and become bigger, fluffy flakes. This slightly wet snow makes for perfect snowballs but is less fun to ski. When the air is cold and dry, snow comes down in a finer, powdery form, the sort of lofty fluff that downhill skiers and snowboarders love. When the ground temperatures remain cold, it sticks around.

The science may be simple, but the presentation is complex. Those ice crystals can turn into sleet if they pass through warm air on the way down but refreeze in colder air before they hit. They can turn into rain if they hit warm air that remains warm all the way to the ground or become freezing rain if water droplets encounter cold temperatures near Earth's surface. Snowflakes can be huge or tiny. Under perfect conditions, you can see snowflakes "bigger than Frisbees" or "larger than milk pans," as a rancher in Montana pointed out in January 1887. During one particular storm that month, Montanans measured a snowflake that was 15 inches across. It still holds the world record.

The rate at which snow falls varies with the type of storm, the temperature, and the humidity in the air. Some of the heaviest snowfalls have been recorded in lake-effect areas near the Great Lakes. Meteorologists consider snow rates of 2 inches per hour heavy snowfall, but it is not unusual to see snow accumulate more rapidly. In 2015, winter storm Nemo deposited snow in Connecticut at 6 inches per hour.

All the same factors that affect snow in the air—temperature, wind, humidity, etcetera—affect how it sits on the ground. When ambient temperatures are warm, accumulated precipitation begins to melt. If it's windy when snowflakes are falling, they split into more packable piles and can layer more densely on the ground. Winds also move powder around on the ground.

Snow can prove totally unpredictable. Some of the snowiest places in the world receive snow very infrequently. Parts of Antarctica, for example, are technically deserts, but they're covered in snow and ice. Some of the interior regions of the continent receive less annual precipitation than Arizona, but the 2 inches of snow they get each year hangs on because it's too cold to melt. As a matter of fact, snow falls more readily when it's warmer than when it's colder. Often, when temperatures get deeply cold, the air dries out, making snowfall unlikely. Snow prefers temperatures between 15 and 32 degrees Fahrenheit best of all.

2

SKY

We can learn a lot about weather by watching the firmament. Seems simple enough, right? The sky is where the weather comes from. But there's more to it than that. If you can understand what clouds and auras and sunsets are telling you, you can anticipate a lot of the weather coming your way. This gives you time to adapt on the ground, making changes to your routes, plans, and gear. Is the sky about to get unwelcoming? Is a rare winter thunderstorm approaching? Time to vacate the summit. Is a cold front about to radically change the conditions? It may be time to think about turning back. Is freezing rain about to make an already difficult trail nearly impossible? These are the kinds of things you can tell just by spending a few moments looking up.

The color of the sky is itself a big clue. Blue is good, gray is bad; everyone knows that. And it's true. Fair-weather skies are a rich cerulean. Any white or gray indicates that dust or soot is being driven by winds in the air, which often indicates a storm is approaching.

Clouds, too, are great communicators. When they are thick and gray and ominous, we know precipitation is likely. That's kindergarten-level sky reading. But did you know cirrus clouds often portend a weather change? Or that a halo around the sun or moon usually means snow or rain will fall within 24 hours? Clouds often indicate the weather will be different tomorrow than it is today or even that it will alter within a few hours. But first we must learn to differentiate the types of clouds and what they portend.

Cirrostratus clouds are long, thin, almost translucent clouds that sit high in the sky. Sometimes described as veil-like or sheetlike, they cover the sky like stretched gauze. Made of ice crystals, they often herald the arrival of moisture, typically in the form of a warm front. Watch their movement across the sky, and you can generally tell from which direction the front will approach. Cirrostratus clouds form the halos around the sun or moon, which signal the weather will likely get wetter within 24 hours.

Cirrocumulus clouds are the small, wispy cousins of the "cirro" family, and they fill the high sky with bunches of little cloudlets, often huddled together in long rows. These are the mackerel skies of folklore, and they are useful predictors when seen with other clouds. If by themselves, cirrocumulus usually mean a continuation of fair skies. When paired with cirrostratus or cirrus clouds, they forecast a shift in the weather within eight hours.

Clouds in the middle layer of sky—those in the "alto" family—are often gray or blue, might appear slightly thicker, and typically precede an impending storm. Tall altocumulus clouds in the morning, for example, generally mean a cold front will hit by afternoon, because they indicate that warm air is climbing up, cooling, and stacking into more dangerous cumulonimbus clouds. In the summer they herald thunderstorms.

Stratus clouds, which sit lower and stretch from horizon to horizon, creating a cotton ball quilt, indicate that weather is sticking around. Sometimes associated with temperature inversions, they're usually the result of a lingering warm front.

Rainbows and sundogs tell of good things to come. Formed by moisture or ice crystals in the atmosphere, both indicate that weather is changing for the better.

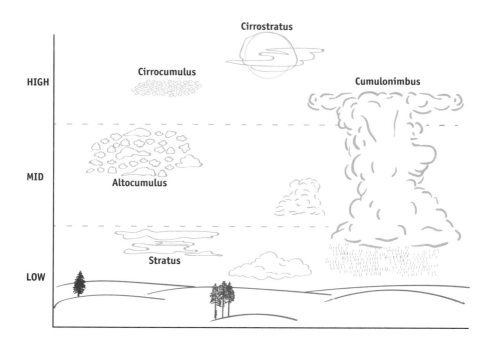

FIGURE 3. You can tell a lot about the weather by watching the clouds. High in the atmosphere, cirrostratus clouds herald the arrival of wetter air and precipitation, while cirrocumulus clouds predict a continuation of fair weather. Altocumulus clouds in the middle layer of the sky often stack into cumulonimbus clouds, and so the appearance of either portends a storm. Low-lying stratus clouds, meanwhile, indicate a lingering warm front and non-moving weather systems.

Rainbows usually follow rainstorms, appearing in the sky as the clouds give way to the sun. Sundogs are similar though rarer. These stripes in the clouds look like dull rainbow segments; farmers used to say that a sundog meant conditions would improve the following day. They were usually right. When sundogs sit near the sun in the early morning or evening, it tends to mean cold weather is coming.

TEMPERATURE

Temperature, it turns out, is a relative thing. Everyone has his or her own comfort level. What feels cold to someone from Florida may seem balmy to someone from Maine: 40 degrees Fahrenheit is shorts weather Down East. The human body is highly adaptable to temperatures, and what makes us feel cold changes with the seasons. When temperatures hit the 60s in early fall, for example, we turn on the house's heat. But when it's the same temperature on a humid, late July evening and we're trying to sleep, it feels sticky and uncomfortably hot.

Personal temperature preferences reveal themselves on the trail. When deep, below-zero cold hits, you'll often find yourself the only one out and about in the winter woods. When thermometers crawl up above freezing, the forests and sum-mits suddenly come alive. As you plan for your trips, keep in mind the temperature patterns for the region you're exploring. The coldest part of any day is typically right before the sun comes up in the morning. The warmest is usually when the sun is the highest. Not only does light fall when the sun sets; so does the temperature.

Remember, too, that in winter, the closer you get to the ocean, the warmer you'll find the air. Like a big household radiator, the North Atlantic is very effective at holding on to heat, taking a long time to cool. Yet when you're in seaside or open areas, you're generally exposed to the wind, which can have a dramatic effect on how cold you feel. The woods also have an impact on the ambient temperature, blocking out the sun. Hiking in certain areas, you can feel the temperature difference from sun-drenched plateau to woodland trail, sometimes swinging by 10 degrees or more.

WIND

Every hiker knows how wind affects an outdoor adventure. We've all huddled be-hind a boulder on a summit, trying to find a few feet of relief from the chilling breeze. We've also welcomed warm zephyrs that feel refreshing on a sweaty neck.

Atmospheric pressure causes the wind. Simply put, air travels from areas of high pressure to areas of low pressure. The rotation of Earth and the dramatic difference in temperature between the poles and the equator contribute to many atmospheric depressions where the pressure is low, which the wind fills in. The intensity of the wind depends on the degree of difference between pressure zones, heat, humidity, and other factors.

The prevailing winds in North America blow from the Southwest to the Northeast. This accounts for smog in Acadia, which blows in from the factories of the Midwest. And it accounts for the fact that the upper Maine coast is called the Down East region, since ships sailed downwind, heading east. Obviously, that's just the general trend, and not every wind swirling through North America is from the southwest. In the Northeast, weather does tend to sail in from the west, unless it's one of New England's famous nor'easters, which spin in from the ocean and slam the coast from the right side of the compass rose. Knowing that weather typically moves from a specific direction can help you forecast, plan, and select campsites on the ground.

Besides its ability to chill us and shove weather around, wind plays many other roles in our outdoor adventures. When wind transports snow, it can present a real problem in the woods. Heavy snow pushed by 35-MPH winds is considered a blizzard, and visibility quickly reduces to zero feet, causing whiteout conditions. Whiteouts bring true peril, especially when on mountain trails, anywhere where you could fall, or in places with which you're unfamiliar. Blowing snow quickly covers signage, making route finding hard. It covers tracks, making it difficult to backtrack. Wind also knocks down or steals protective tarps, leaving us exposed. It dumps snow on our tents and puts unwelcome drifts in the wrong places. We discuss what to do in these situations in Chapter 5.

Make sure you understand these possibilities before you hit the trail, checking weather conditions, basic topography, alternate routes, and avenues of escape should you need one.

SNOWPACK

Snow provides us with the base for many of our winter adventures. It comes in a variety of shapes and sizes, as anyone who's spent a winter on it knows. It's a good idea to have a general idea of the snowpack before you set out on a hike or arrive at a spot to set up camp. Has the snow fallen recently? Has it been on the ground for days or even weeks? Roughly how deep is it? What have the temperatures and the weather conditions been like? Has there been a lot of blowing and drifting? These are the kinds of factors to consider.

Knowing what to expect is not just for convenience; it's a gear and safety issue. You don't want to spend your whole trip post-holing because you didn't think you'd need snowshoes. You also don't want to dull your crampons on bare ground and rock or forget the ski wax when you're up against drippy, wet snow. Setting up camp in melting puddles requires different thinking than building a bivy in deep, fluffy powder. Will you be able to see signage? There are myriad considerations when it comes to snowpack.

Most important of all is avalanche danger. It lurks in many of the high places where we like to play in winter, and according to National Geographic, avalanches kill more than 150 people worldwide each year. But with proper planning, you can mitigate avalanche danger, as we explore on pages 76–79 in Chapter 5.

The National Weather Service makes it easy to check snow conditions. Government forecasters track snow depth across the country on a weekly basis at www.nohrsc.noaa.gov/nsa. Their handy map breaks the nation into more than a dozen regions, so you can focus on the area where you're headed with a fair amount of precision. Other ways to get local details on snowpack include calling or checking the websites of nearby ski areas, park sites, and outdoor clubs.

BAROMETRIC PRESSURE

Many outdoorspeople, especially sailors, carry barometers on their adventures. Not long ago, this meant lugging around a tall piece of wood and glass with three dials. Nowadays, for $20 you can buy a pocket barometer that helps you monitor barometric pressure. Traditionally, barometers detected how much air pressure was pushing down on a pool of mercury. Most modern barometers use sensors in place of that dangerous element.

Generally speaking, when the barometer shows air pressure falling, a low-pressure system is moving in, and we can guess the weather soon will be wetter and likely warmer. When pressure rises, the weather typically will turn cooler and drier. These barometric measurements warn us about 12 or 24 hours before a storm arrives. Elevation throws a wrinkle into the workings of barometers, but they are handy tools in the field nonetheless, and you can buy small, relatively cheap ones that easily fit in a backpack pocket and include thermometers, altimeters, and compasses. Some even boast wind gauges. (You can also get an idea of air pressure by watching your campfire. Note the smoke rising as you sit around a blaze at the end of the day. If it flows straight up, you can expect good weather. If it stays low, hugging the ground as it dissipates, it could mean a storm is approaching.)

DEW/FROST POINT

Morning dew—or during winter, frost—is another easy-to-read weather indicator. The dew point represents conditions in which the air cools until it's saturated with water vapor. In summer, because cool air sinks, dew usually clings to the cold ground. The frost point is similar to the dew point, but it reflects the temperature at which water molecules in the air can cling to a surface without passing through the liquid phase. In winter, we notice frost on grass and other vegetation or on cold, flat surfaces, such as windshields.

Meteorologists use dew point to measure the relative humidity of the air. (As the old saying goes, "it's not the heat, it's the dew point. . . .") The higher the dew point, the more water content in the atmosphere. In the winter, high frost points lead to hazardous conditions underfoot, such as hoarfrost and ice.

CHAPTER 3
DRESSING FOR WINTER

➜ **The WISE System**   30
➜ **Thermodynamics**   32
➜ **Fabric and Insulation Choices**   33
➜ **Outerwear**   34
➜ **Protecting Your Extremities**   36
➜ **Not Breaking the Bank**   44

Dr. Gordon Giesbrecht likes to quote a Norwegian proverb: "There is no such thing as bad weather . . . only bad clothing." A physiologist at the University of Manitoba in Winnipeg, Giesbrecht earned the nickname "Professor Popsicle" from *Outside* magazine for his cold-water immersion studies. He knows a thing or two about bodies and the cold. To explore how long humans can survive in frigid water, the brave Canadian routinely cleared holes in the ice and climbed in. After years of study, he concluded that we humans are "tropical animals and poorly designed to withstand a cold environment," as he explained to an audience at a wilderness medicine conference in Jackson Hole in 2003. Due to this simple, immutable fact, clothing choices become all important when venturing outside in winter.

For Professor Giesbrecht and many other outdoor professionals, the single most important consideration when selecting clothes for winter adventures is minimizing the amount of moisture that accumulates next to the body. The idea is that water next to skin provides rapid cooling. That's why we sweat when we exert ourselves. In summer, moist skin cooled by motion or breezes helps to regulate temperatures and avoid overheating. In winter, it can lead to hypothermia and even prove deadly.

The winter outdoors provides many different ways for us to get wet. Rain, snow, and sleet fall onto us from the sky; we post-hole in the snow; we stumble into puddles. And that's just for starters. Our clothes not only have to protect us from these external sources, acting as winter body armor; they also must keep us safe from the sweat of our own exertions. Even when it's 15 degrees Fahrenheit out, walking up a hill makes us perspire.

In the past, the secret to keeping warm when wet was wool. Then fleece came along, a synthetic alternative to wool that serves the same purpose, maintaining its insulating properties when damp, with the added advantages of weighing less and

drying more quickly than natural fibers. These days technology has bounded even farther down the trail, exponentially expanding our outdoor clothing options. Just as modern musicians with computers have far more recording power at their disposal than did the Beatles, today's hikers and climbers can select from an array of modern fabrics that make the mountaineers of the '60s look like relics of a bygone age. Some of the most remarkable developments in winter textiles have come in the form of breathing and wicking, preventing dangerous moisture from accumulating both by releasing heat so we don't perspire as much while pulling what we do perspire away from the skin.

→ THE WISE SYSTEM

Despite these advances, the basic premise of dressing for the winter woods hasn't changed all that much. The key, as you've surely heard, is layering. You want to wear multiple thin layers rather than one bulky layer, the idea being that, as you get warm, you can remove pieces. Instead of sweating in a heavy parka that provides all your insulation (and leaves you completely exposed when you take it off), it's better to wear a couple of thin insulating layers and a shell on the outside so that you can more easily regulate your temperature. You want to avoid sweat buildup at all costs. The ideal winter clothing scheme consists of a wicking layer next to the skin; a couple of insulating, heat-retaining layers; an outer covering that provides sheltering from the weather; and perhaps a few extra items, if things get wet or the temperature drops. The Wilderness Education Association invented an acronym for this system: WISE, for wicking, insulation, sheltering, and extra.

WICKING

As Professor Popsicle suggested, the base layer needs to move moisture away from the skin. In cold temperatures, you never want to wear cotton, which retains moisture. A good wicking layer made from silk, wool, polypropylene, or another synthetic draws sweat away from the skin, moving the moisture through the fabric and releasing it into the air. Because of this, your innermost layer should fit snugly, in close contact with your body. This serves the purpose of protecting skin from extreme cold when you're traveling through the winter woods, and it also helps with another, less life-threatening concern: chafing. Wet rubbing parts can lead to severe discomfort as skin becomes raw. When traveling in winter, it makes sense to have multiple base layers so you always have a dry spare to put on. And don't forget your feet: Thin wicking socks can be the difference between blisters and comfort.

INSULATING

Insulating layers vary widely. Their role is to trap warmth against the body, creating a comfortable airspace between the wicking layer and the exterior shell. The more air space, or loft, the warmer you are, just like with the down comforter on your bed. Insulators might include microfleece tops, wool overshirts, raglan sweaters, or quilted puffer jackets. And they're not limited to just one. Winter hikers often combine them, pulling a down vest over a midweight fleece atop a sweater that sits on the base layer. This way, when you feel yourself getting too hot, you can easily remove a layer without losing too much heat. The same rules apply with insulating layers: They must stay dry in order to be effective. That is, unless they're wool or fleece, which retain the ability to warm even when wet.

SHELTERING

Just as it sounds, this layer protects you from the elements, providing shelter against wind and water. The sheltering layer for a winter adventure should be impervious to weather and cover the entire body. This almost always means two pieces: a hooded jacket for the upper half and some form of pants for the lower body. Most of the better "shells" available also remain breathable, allowing moisture to escape but not to enter. Some have vents that allow moisture to escape and air to circulate, while others are made of waterproof, breathable fabrics, such as Gore-Tex. Many people elect to buy a jacket one or two sizes larger than they would wear on the street to allow for layering underneath.

3

FIGURE 4. The WISE system calls for layering clothes in the following order, working from nearest to skin outward: wicking, insulating, shell, extra.

EXTREMITIES AND EXTRA LAYERS

We can't, of course, forget feet, hands, and head. Anyone who has endured wet boots on a hike knows how closely our comfort level corresponds to the condition of our feet. Many hikers today, especially in winter, wear a pair of silk or polypro liners under their usual winter socks to wick away moisture and prevent blisters. Over these go waterproof boots, preferably with a layer of insulation and a rugged tread. When it comes to the hands, many outdoor enthusiasts have strong preferences. Mittens are objectively warmer, but many prefer the improved dexterity that gloves provide. Some winter adventurers like all-in-one gloves that feature thick insulation and can be slipped off easily. Others want two layers of mittens: a waterproof outer layer over a heavy underlayer. Hats provide another layer of warmth under the hood of your shell, while neck gaiters and balaclavas help protect your face from the cold and elements. You really want to keep as much skin as possible covered in the cold for reasons we touch on later.

The "E" in the acronym WISE stands for extra, because it's always wise to bring along a change of everything, from socks to gloves to hats, and additional layers you can add if you find yourself cold. The temperature swing during an average winter day can be dramatic—usually starting cold, warming with the sun, then becoming cold again when darkness descends—so it's a good idea to be able to add and subtract layers as necessary.

➔ THERMODYNAMICS

Dressing for winter comes down to basic physics. Specifically, thermodynamics, the branch of physics that involves heat, temperature, and energy. Understanding how these forces work can make it easier to dress for outdoor adventures and provides a better idea of what to expect when you're out in the elements. When you recognize that wind pulls heat off your body and that evaporation leads to windchill, you'll know to wear a windproof jacket and shelter behind boulders to avoid wind, and its cooling effects. Learn the following basic principles, and you'll be ready to take on the winter outdoors.

CONDUCTION

You know the chill you get when you sit in a snowbank, and you can feel the snow sucking away your heat? That's conduction. Technically speaking, conduction is the transference of heat between two objects in contact. Conduction happens when you put your sleeping bag directly on packed snow for the night. The snow draws warmth out of your body, chilling you as you sleep. This is why you want as many layers of insulation between yourself and the solid bodies (that is, the ground) with which you come into contact (see "Sleeping Pads" in Chapter 4, Backpacking Gear, page 57).

CONVECTION

Convection occurs when wind blows past you on a summit, taking your heat with it. It's the scientific principle of heat transference through currents, whether they be air or water. When you're snowboarding and creating wind, that wind is robbing your heat as you move down the mountain. On a windy day, you can lose much of your body warmth through convection.

RADIATION

When you sit atop a summit and feel the sun's warmth on your face, you're enjoying a bit of radiation, the transfer of heat across empty space. You also lose heat, however, by radiating it away. When the ambient temperature hits 68 degrees Fahrenheit or less, you begin to lose your body warmth, like a woodstove letting off heat. On cold days, your body pumps out 65 percent of your heat into the air through radiation.

3

EVAPORATION

When you sweat, you lose heat through evaporation. In summer, when the breeze blows over you and removes the perspiration from your skin, it cools you off, which feels great. In cold weather, when the wind does the same thing, it's called wind-chill, and it can be dangerous. If you're wearing the wrong clothing (say, a cotton T-shirt), you'll lose additional heat by having wet gear, as evaporation conspires with conduction. Water removes heat from the body 25 times faster than dry air.

With these basic principles in mind, it becomes easy to build body armor against winter weather. Basically, we want to keep the skin dry and to retain as much body heat as necessary to keep our core temperature where it needs to be. It's OK to lose body heat, even in winter. When we engage in vigorous outdoor activity, we're going to sweat. The trick is not to lose too much body heat and to keep what we need for safety and comfort.

Our clothing should create pockets of warmth and be able to breathe to allow excess warmth to escape. It should prevent our skin from getting wet and hold on to needed body warmth against all of the forces—conduction, convection, radiation, and evaporation—that are conspiring to steal it.

→ FABRIC AND INSULATION CHOICES

Today's outdoorsperson has a host of options when it comes to under- and outerwear, and the first basic consideration is natural versus synthetic. Most modern gear manufacturers use synthetics in the construction of their clothing. Base layers might be made of polypropylene, nylon, spandex, rayon, or any number of other human-made materials. Synthetics tend to be lighter and cheaper than wool. They stretch better and wick about as well, and some people find synthetics less itchy than woolens. Be sure the synthetics you select don't feature any cotton, which some manufacturers add to certain items. Also be aware that synthetics are more flammable and can melt if you get too close to the campfire.

Some outdoor adventurers prefer natural fibers over synthetics. These include silk or even a soft wool like merino, which is enjoying a comeback. Midlayers often include some form of fleece, but may also feature merinos, thicker woolens, or knit sweaters. Many outfitters are now combining natural and synthetic fibers for the best of both worlds. New "shackets," for example, feature the fashionable look of wool with a soft inner lining of polypropylene. Thanks to modern technology, the same stretchy midlayer can keep you cozy at 40 degrees Fahrenheit and still keep you snug at 0 degrees. Outerwear might be Gore-Tex or another proprietary waterproof/breathable fabric, a combination of the synthetic and the natural in a down jacket, or an even heavier wool. The secret is to find what's comfortable, affordable, and works for you.

Most of today's exterior shells feature some form of waterproof/breathable fabric on the exterior. Underneath that layer, many have a layer of insulation. This typically includes some form of synthetic fiber that lofts in the interior, providing an air cavity and thus warmth. Sometimes these fibers are knitted together; sometimes they float about in quilted sacks, mimicking down. The advantage of polyester and other synthetics is that they retain heat when wet, unlike goose feathers. But the latest down jackets include down that has been treated to be water repellent and often feature vents to dump heat when you're really moving. Most stay soft, even in extreme cold and wet conditions.

→ OUTERWEAR

Mountaineers from the past, such as Sir Edmund Hillary and Tenzing Norgay, would hardly recognize today's shells and jackets. The level of sophistication built into modern outerwear dwarfs the dingy old anoraks the legendary pair wore to summit Everest: down coats combined with synthetics so that feathers stay dry in their own waterproof compartments; jackets that can compress into a tiny sack and remain warm to below zero; coats with electric heat distribution; "media-compatible" puffer hoodies with built-in pockets for phones and holes for earbud cables. Companies now design whole outerwear *systems*, including waterproof, breathable shells with as many as two liners, doing all of the layering and planning for you. The number of choices can overwhelm, but if you stick to the basic principles, you can equip yourself in short order better than Hillary ever could.

SNOW JACKETS/PANTS

Snow jackets and snow pants come in all shapes and sizes and for all weather conditions. You can buy a single jacket that purports to do it all, with a shell that fits over the included interior layers, or a single shell designed to be pulled over separate underlayers. They even make puffers, or quilted jackets, that are "emergency-bivy" capable (meaning you could take refuge in them for hours in the event of a storm) and that weigh little more than a pound.

As with any clothing purchase, comfort is key. Make sure that whatever you buy fits you well and allows for the kind of mobility you need for whatever it is you plan to do. You might be able to get away with a big stuffed coat if you're sitting around a hole, ice fishing all day, but you wouldn't want to wear one on a backcountry hiking trek. Layers almost always make more sense than big, single-piece outerwear items, giving you the flexibility to adapt. You could wear a breathable, waterproof shell atop a puffer over a sweater on that ice-fishing excursion and use it for a lung-pumping uphill traverse on another day. For most outdoor adventures, a good shell is adaptable to most of your needs. You can even wear the same one in summer and winter if you buy well and choose one that is unlined or has a removable liner.

The same holds true for pants. A bulky, farmer john–style pair of snow pants would be ideal for a snowmobiling trip to the North Woods but clumsy and awkward for hiking. A shell of waterproof, breathable pants over silk or fleece long johns and a pair of fleece pants makes for much more comfortable hiking. That sort of system allows plenty of flexibility and motion for walking, and if you get too warm, you can always remove a layer. The latest snow pants have built-in flex, ventilation, big pockets, and removable suspenders. If you can find them, try snow pants that you can remove without taking your boots off—a nice and quick feature that keeps you and others in your group from standing around getting cold.

RAIN JACKETS/PANTS

Anyone who's spent any time outdoors in rain gear knows the phenomenon: You pause for a moment in a shelter and discover you're wet under your raincoat, and you don't know if it's because rain seeped in from the outside or perspiration condensed on the inside. Outfitters have been battling this problem since the invention of the rubber coat. The advent of Gore-Tex and other waterproof and breathable fabrics and ventilation zippers in the pits and pants certainly helped, but interior moisture persists, and it perfectly illustrates the dual challenges of modern rainwear.

The primary role of a rain jacket is, of course, to keep out the elements. These days, that's accomplished in a variety of ways. Rain gear might be laminated, coated, or treated with durable water repellent (DWR). Lamination consists of gluing a thin water barrier to the interior of the jacket's exterior, which prevents water from penetrating the fabric. This is how Gore-Tex and eVent, for example, are applied. Coatings are liquid treatments applied to the inside of the jacket that prevent water from penetrating. DWR is the traditional, spray-on film that dries on the surface of a raincoat, causing water to form drops that simply slide down the jacket, like rain on a windshield, rather than soaking in. These jackets tend to be on the expensive side and require reapplication of the DWR coating or a wax substitute. (DWR and similar treatments have recently come under fire for their reliance on PFCs, chemicals that can have a deleterious effect on the environment. For greener alternatives, look for labels that read, "PFC-free.")

Of course, the same barrier that keeps rain out does a fine job of keeping perspiration in, necessitating some way of dispersing heat and moisture. Solving this conundrum was the goal of every designer of outdoor clothing for years, but it wasn't until 1969 that scientists William and Bob Gore developed a fabric made of polytetrafluoroethylene (PTFE), the chemical that gave us Teflon, kicking off an outerwear revolution. The father and son team discovered that PTFE, when stretched out, blocked liquid from passing through but allowed water vapor to permeate. In other words, it was impervious to precipitation but not perspiration. The Gores patented their invention and gave it the name Gore-Tex, and by the late 1970s it began to appear in clothing. When the original patent expired in the late 1990s, a host of companies began to introduce their own versions of waterproof and breathable fabric.

Most of the same principles apply to snow pants and jackets. Many outdoorspeople wear the same shell for spring rain that they do for winter snow. They just put more layers on underneath.

➔ PROTECTING YOUR EXTREMITIES
HATS/BALACLAVAS

In the 1950s, the U.S. Army released a study showing that the body releases the majority of its heat through the head. Since disproven—the skin all over the body releases warmth at roughly the same rate—this myth persists. Regardless, it's always a good idea to have a cozy hat. Just as we're exponentially more comfortable when our feet are dry and warm, we are that much more content when our heads are protected from frosty winds.

Winter hats come in all types: bulky, tight, wool, synthetic, above the ears, over the ears. Every outdoor adventurer has a personal preference. Many serious outdoor athletes like to wear beanies made of polyester with a fleece liner, which insulates the head but at the same time wicks away sweat. These can be worn under the hood of a shell and fit easily into a pocket when the day grows warm. Other adventurers swear by wool. Some prefer simple ear bands, strips of felt or fleece that cover only the ears, which they wear under baseball caps, whereas others prefer felted or fleece baseball caps with ear flaps. There are no rules, just the same common-sense principles that apply to the rest of the body: Layering is good, wicking is ideal, comfort is key.

On days when the cold is serious and determined, consider a balaclava. Not to be confused with the Greek pastries, balaclavas are head-and-face covers reminiscent of ninja masks. Typically made from varying thicknesses of synthetics or fleece, though sometimes you can find wool versions at army-navy stores, these hoods protect everything except the eyes from the elements. They fit well under helmets and parka hoods, often with bibs to tuck into jackets, and pair nicely with goggles. Some are formless pullovers with just an oval space for the eyes; others have structure, beaking out at the nose. The more expensive balaclavas even provide ventilation at the nostrils and mouth. Hoodies under your jacket can perform the same function. Some people like the "snood," or neck gaiter, which is a heavy-duty scarf of sorts that encircles the neck. As ever, comfort is the most important factor.

SUNGLASSES AND GOGGLES

Don't forget your eyes. On a brilliant winter day when the sky is a rich cerulean and the sun is making the snow impossibly, almost painfully, sparkly, forgetting your sunglasses in your car might mean the end of your adventure. "Snow blind" is more than a classic rock song. It's a genuine condition that afflicts climbers in winter, especially those in exposed snowfields above treeline. The intensity of the sun reflecting off all of those frozen crystals can expose your eyes to harsh levels of ultraviolet radiation. This can lead to sunburn of the eyes, a painful condition known as photokeratitis. *Photo*, of course, means light, and *keratitis* is inflammation of the cornea. In bad cases, it can lead to temporary blindness.

A quality pair of sunglasses prevents this and should always be in your winter pack. Pick a largish pair that allows in the least amount of light. Some outdoorspeople prefer glacier glasses with side flaps that prevent any light from penetrating. Make sure, too, that your sunglasses offer real UV protection. These days many feature yellow lenses to contrast all of the blue light associated with winter snow and ice. A strap that keeps hold of your glasses when you take a terrible tumble is also a good idea. See page 75 in Chapter 5 to learn more about snow blindness and how to prevent it.

Sometimes even the best sunglasses are not enough. If the wind is driving, if the snow is pelting, or if you're venturing high above treeline, goggles may be in order. Just as downhill skiers sport goggles to shield their eyes, climbers and other winter adventurers often find that the added protection of goggles, with foam gaskets to prevent wind or snow from getting in and held securely by a strap, are perfect for high altitudes. Many have high-contrast optics to protect against snow glare and dual lenses to add insulation, like a Thermopane window. Some feature changeable lenses, allowing you to pop in a new color or shade. The latest, highest-tech models make switching lenses even simpler using electrochromatics powered by USB. Don't need as much protection when clouds move in? Just push a button to change to another lens.

GLOVES/MITTENS

Many outdoorspeople still swear by choppers, those bulky leather mittens that slide over a fleece or wool mitten or glove. They're hard to beat even with modern technology. The treated leather shell provides a waterproof outer layer that's impervious to snow or ice. Pull them off temporarily, and the inner glove allows you to use your hands for tying bootlaces, buckling snowshoes, or adjusting backpack straps. If it warms up during the course of the day or you find yourself getting warm from activity, you always have the option of removing the outer layer. When it gets cold, plunge your hands back into the warm, weatherproof comfort. Today's manufacturers have built similar hand "systems," combining a waterproof synthetic shell with removable

➜ **PRO TIP** For those who tend to have cold hands or hands that perspire, one strategy is to wear surgical gloves under liner gloves. The surgical gloves serve as a vapor barrier, keeping the liner gloves dry.

interior layers, and they work just as well. Once again, it's about keeping the skin dry and comfortable, and layering is the most effective way to accomplish that.

Modern gloves and mittens follow the same basic design principles as the rest of outerwear. Most employ some form of layering, with a lighter layer next to the skin, insulation, and a shell that protects from the elements on the outside. In some cases, this is obvious, with linings that can be removed and a protective outer layer, but other gloves might have these pieces sewn together. The most sophisticated models use wicking for the innermost layer and waterproof/breathable technology for the outermost.

Thanks to childhood, we all know that mittens are warmer than gloves because they keep all digits together in a single space, where they generate heat together and raise the temperature. Gloves isolate each extremity, which prevents this mutual warming. The benefit of gloves, however, is that they allow maximum dexterity, making it possible to use each individual digit and simplifying complex tasks like rebuckling a snowshoe or tying a boot. Lobster-style mittens, which provide access to the thumb and index finger, are one method of improving hand coordination while keeping most fingers as warm as possible.

Glove and mitten manufacturers use many different materials in their products, just like other forms of outerwear. Proprietary wicking and waterproof/breathable fabrics, down, wool, and various synthetics all go into the construction of gloves and mittens, and they have the same pros and cons as for any other article of clothing. When selecting your gloves and mittens, keep in mind the activity that you're planning to pursue. Many gloves and mittens are designed for particular sports or pastimes. The best gloves for heavy aerobic activities, like nordic skiing and snowshoeing, for instance, typically are lighter than other types and include wicking inners and waterproof/breathable exteriors, so that sweat can be whisked from the skin and dispersed. For sports that are less active, such as snowmobiling and ice fishing, gauntletlike mittens, large and bulky with thick insulation and water-resistant shells, ward off serious cold. Somewhere in between are mittens for downhill skiing, snowboarding, and mountaineering, which tend to run large and retain heat well.

SOCKS

Though many people simply pull on socks and boots for a winter excursion, the same layering principles apply to feet as to elsewhere on the body. In-the-know hikers slide into a base layer before putting on their heavy socks. Thin liners made of silk or synthetics, such

➜ **PRO TIP** A comfortable pair of boots is among the most important outdoor gear purchases, and it's always smart to try before you buy. Extended hikes in footwear that doesn't fit right is not only uncomfortable it can be dangerous. Ill-fitting boots often result in blisters, which can easily become infected on multiday excursions, due to those momentary lapses in hygiene that can occur in the woods. Make sure yours are a good fit. Make sure to lace them all the way up, walk around the store, march up and down stairs, and jump up and down in them. It's best to wear socks similar to the ones you will wear hiking.

as polypropylene, go directly against the skin for the same purpose as every other base layer: to prevent moisture from collecting on the skin. Perspiring feet lead to worse consequences than, say, sweaty hands: blisters. A wicking fabric protects against this and helps prevent socks from bunching up inside boots. A warmer pair of insulating socks, often wool or some sort of synthetic pile, pulls over the liners and does a better job of keeping the feet warm because it adds loft.

Some hikers and snowshoers like to wear plastic bread bags or single-use oven baking bags between their liners and their insulating layers, forming a vapor barrier. This is a version of the trick you perform when you forget your waterproof boots at home on a rainy day and simply make a pair using a plastic bag. This is a good idea because your feet sweat more than any other place on your body except your armpits, and when you're active, that makes for wet socks. When socks get damp and the temperature falls, you have a problem. Vapor barriers for the feet prevent this phenomenon by forming a wall between your wet feet and your dry socks.

The key to happy feet is dryness, and the key to dryness is an extra pair or two of socks. This way, one pair can dry while you're wearing the other. Hang them by the fire at camp or by the woodstove in the cabin when you return from exploring and you'll always have a ready pair.

BOOTS

As with every other decision you make when dressing for winter, choice of boot is usually situation dependent. In other words, pick a pair that's right for the adventure on which you're embarking. No matter what you're doing, though, you always want a winter boot to meet certain criteria. It should: (a) keep your feet dry; (b) accommodate warm socks; and (c) have appropriate tread. Usually this means a lug sole—that is, one with a thick tread. But the level of insulation you want depends on your activity.

Be sure to try on your boots before venturing off into the backcountry and give them as much break-in time as you can. Comfort is crucial, and you don't want to find yourself two days into the woods with infected blisters. Climb stairs when you try boots on at the store to make sure there's no slippage inside the boot. Make sure the heel fits snugly. Check the ankle support. Spend a few minutes walking around the showroom.

Hiking Boots

Many outfitters now sell hiking boots specifically for winter treks and snowshoeing. They often look like a slightly bulkier version of a traditional hiking boot, but some have the duck-boot bottoms made popular by L.L. Bean's Maine Hunting Shoe. These boots generally have a waterproof outer layer, a layer of insulation, and lug soles, and they're ideal for a variety of outdoor pursuits, assuming you are moving around and it's not deeply cold. Just as with jackets, boot insulation takes a variety of forms, almost all of them synthetic. Manufacturers have their own proprietary varieties, most consisting of

FIGURE 5. Winter hiking boots are similar to three-season hiking boots but generally have a waterproof outer layer, a layer of insulation, and more deeply treaded lug soles.

human-made fibers that create tiny pockets of air. The amount of insulation is typically referred to in grams per square meter. A 200-gram pair of boots would be comfortable in slightly cold temperatures. A 2,000-gram boot would keep your toes toasty in temperatures below zero. Most winter hiking boots, assuming they're for people on the go and generating their own heat, fall into the 400 to 1,200 range.

Made for walking, winter hiking boots usually have enough stiffness to accommodate a pair of snowshoes. Some even boast D-rings on the toes to attach gaiters (see page 43 for more on gaiters). Many manufacturers publish the temperature range for their boots, and it's wise to take note, although, if you plan to go somewhere on a bitter day or to be sedentary, they might not be your best option. Some hikers are loathe to part with cash for a pair of winter hiking boots when they already have a pair of waterproof three-season hiking boots, and on trails with little snow, you may be able to get away with the same boots you wear the rest of the year, assuming you can get a warm sock in there. But when the snow begins to fall and the mercury plummets, you'll be glad you invested in an insulated pair intended specifically for winter hiking.

Pac Boots

The traditional winter footwear owned by nearly everyone in cold-weather regions, these big, boxy boots almost always feature a waterproof outer layer, an insulating layer, and a synthetic bottom of lug rubber. Many also feature liners that can be taken out to dry. They come in umpteen styles, from neoprene uppers like chore boots, to those nylon-upper, rubber-lower L-shaped boots with felt liners you had as a kid. (Those liners make for great camp slippers in the evening.) Pac boots

FIGURE 6. This classic style of boot consists of a waterproof outer layer, an insulating inner later, and a deeply treaded bottom. Some outdoor adventurers complain that pac boots are too warm for extended activity and that the footwear isn't comfortable over long hikes. For short outdoor excursions, however, pac boots provide an option that many cold-climate dwellers may already have in their closets.

FIGURE 7. Often made from the same durable plastic shells as downhill ski boots, double boots are designed to accommodate crampons and feature a removable insulating layer.

are typically very warm, easy to thaw out, and do a great job of keeping the feet comfortable at 0 degrees and below. They do have their detractors when it comes to backcountry use, however. Many people find them tiring to walk long distances in, and others think they're too warm, making for sweaty feet. For this reason, some manufacturers have created special liners that you can buy separately to replace overly hot ones. Pac boots are usually fine for short jaunts, and some pair well with snowshoes but don't do as well with crampons. But if you're serious about getting out and into the backcountry, you might prefer another type of footwear.

Double Boots

Also known as mountaineering boots, these clunky plastic clompers were designed to accommodate crampons, and they're often made from the same sort of durable shell materials as downhill ski boots. Stiff and waterproof, double boots almost always have a removable insulating bootie (hence the name), making it easy to dry them out après hike. Made for serious ascents in deeply cold climes, they can keep your feet comfortably warm at very low temperatures and are ideal for attaching crampons and other traction devices, such as Microspikes. Their heavy-lug, Vibram rubber soles grip well on rock or snow. But they're not as comfortable for long walks on snowless trails and can be heavy and inflexible. Some come with their own built-in, heavy-duty Cordura gaiters; others have internal

3

3

vapor barriers. Double boots tend to be weighty, adding 2 or 3 pounds to each foot, and very expensive. If you climb infrequently, it might make sense to rent rather than purchase a pair, as you might with ski boots (see "Not Breaking the Bank" on page 44 of this chapter).

Mouse Boots

Named for their likeness to Mickey's big, bulbous black feet, "mouse" boots became widely used during the Korean War, when they were issued to GIs to insulate their feet from the coldest of temperatures. Constructed from layers of rubber, with wool and felt sandwiched between, they are oversized and utilitarian, making no concessions to fashion. Some outdoor lovers swear they are the warmest winter boots available. Designed for temperatures as low as -20 degrees Fahrenheit, mouse boots are great for any cold-weather pastime where you sit as much as you move (think snowmobiling or ice fishing). They're definitely homely, but there's no denying that they do their job—unless you feel like taking them on a long jaunt, in which case you'll find them hot and heavy. In fact, they can keep your feet so warm a vapor barrier might be in order. They also tend to be inexpensive, found in surplus stores and online. Those valves on the side were for relieving pressure when flying. The white variety are often referred to as bunny boots.

Nordic Ski Boots

Designed for cross-country skiing, these boots come in a variety of styles and shapes. Most feature firm ankle support and some form of insulation, though not much, because nordic ski-

FIGURE 8. Mouse boots are extremely warm, but they are also heavy, which makes them less than ideal for activities where you will be moving around a lot, such as hiking.

FIGURE 9. Nordic ski boots come in a variety of styles, but they typically feature firm ankle support and are designed to slip into ski bindings.

ing is famously taxing. Many have relatively treadless bottoms and are constructed to slip into coordinated bindings for a session of kick and glide. Others look more like hiking boots and have full lug soles, intended for a combination of backcountry trekking and skiing. Uppers might be leather in older styles or brightly colored synthetic in the latest cross-country styles.

GAITERS/OVERBOOTS

Gaiters look like the spats that army soldiers wore during World War I or the leg warmers sported by '80s dancers. Built to keep mud and snow out of your boots, these wraparound coverings are usually made from a waterproof material, like Gore-Tex. Most use a Velcro closure and feature a stirrup strap that goes underneath the sole of the boot and a cinchable top. Made from a heavy-duty material, they typically boast scuff-guard or ripstop qualities. Some hikers swear by them; others figure rain or snow pants essentially serve the same purpose. Most cover the span from the top of your boot to just below the knee, although in recent years, shorter versions constructed with clingy spandex have become popular (mostly among trail runners). If you do want a gaiter for winter, go for a taller, 17- or 18-inch model.

Overboots take the gaiter concept and extend it over your whole boot, including the sole. These are essentially heavy-duty boots in themselves, which are built to be worn over another shoe or light boot, such as full-size galoshes. With high-traction bottoms and waterproof uppers, they keep your actual footwear warm and dry, and give you the grip you need to navigate slippery paths. They come in a wide variety of styles, from zip-up rubbers with cleats on the bottom to Gore-Tex nylon with Vibram soles. Some cover everything but the sole of the shoe. Most are not comfortable enough for extended stretches on the trail, feeling clumpy and awkward. The exceptions are those made by several nordic ski manufacturers that are designed specifically to fit over ski boots.

FIGURE 10. Gaiters are an easy addition to your outdoor wardrobe and indispensable when you're looking to keep snow and mud out of your boots.

CAMP BOOTIES

The wise winter warrior brings booties. One of life's great pleasures is pulling off a stiff, heavy, insulated boot at the end of a day and trading it for a light, warm, soft slipper. A comfortable pair of booties can offer powerful relief to tired dogs. Today there is a wide range of options from which to choose. These include goose down, over-the-ankle booties, comfortable enough to wear in your sleeping bag; woolen slippers with rubber outsoles, which can handle a late-night trip to the car or the outhouse; and even slip-ons that combine the cushy fit of slippers with the rugged, outdoor-ready lug soles of trail shoes.

BOOT DRYER

Rangers, mountaineers, ice fishers, guides: They're all wise to the benefits of a boot dryer. Essentially narrow warm heaters that slide into boots, these do a fantastic job of removing moisture from shoe interiors. If you're the kind of person who needs to use your boots in cold, wet terrain multiple days in a row, boot dryers are for you. They can be purchased relatively inexpensively at big-box stores.

3 → **NOT BREAKING THE BANK**
BARGAIN BIN OR INVESTMENT PIECE?

Now that we know what we need, how do we afford it all? Pricing gear can be daunting. Buying a nice shell alone can set you back as much as $300 or more, and then you have to purchase everything that goes underneath it. Shopping at the higher end means shelling out hundreds, even thousands of dollars for a routine trip into the winter woods. But it doesn't have to be that way.

For decades, many outdoor enthusiasts have combed the aisles at Goodwill, Salvation Army, and even the local army-navy store. In Maine, many people know the state's most famous outfitter donates regularly to the local Goodwill stores, and you can pick up slightly used items at serious discounts. Thrift stores are great places to look for outerwear, fleece, and layering pieces made of wool or silk. (Maybe not so much for long underwear.) Often, these individual items cost the most when purchased retail, so careful searching can result in real savings.

Army-navy stores, when you can find them, are also great places to hunt for gear. You can occasionally find government-issued fleece and outerwear for extreme conditions, down booties, wool/silk long johns, and wool hats and socks. You may also happen upon things for the pack, such as compass whistles, compact first-aid kits, and waterproof match containers. And, of course, surplus stores are the home of mouse boots. Oh, and tarps. You can always find a great deal on tarps at surplus stores.

Many winter wanderers have success on the internet, where slightly used goods or seconds can be had for a fraction of the cost of new items. Because shopping online means you don't have the opportunity to try before you buy, some folks will order a new parka, and if it doesn't fit the way they want or match the color of their eyes, they'll turn around and sell it cheap on the web. Their loss equals your new jacket. Several discount retailers, such as Campmor and Sierra Trading Post, offer close-outs, seconds, and last year's gear from major outfitters at exceptional savings and are worth perusing. You can buy outerwear, underwear, socks, layers—virtually anything you need—online. But it's best not to buy your boots without trying them on first.

Other options for buying gear without breaking the bank include the classifieds, Craigslist, discount stores, and even big-box retailers. Be careful shopping for outdoor gear at Walmart and Target, though. Some items will serve you just fine, but make sure to check each one over and look up reviews of individual pieces before laying out the cash. Quality, especially for big-ticket items, is often not what it needs to be. But you can often find smaller items like cookware, synthetic base layers, filtration, stuff sacks, tent stakes, fleece base layers, and other items that are perfectly serviceable. You just have to do your homework and know what you're looking for.

Recently, a spate of used gear repair programs have risen, often partnering with big-name outdoor brands. These programs take in high-quality used gear, repair any damage, and resell it at a discount. Find out more about these programs, and where you can find them, at outdoors.org/used-gear-repair.

Boots and shells are where you want to spend the bulk of your budget. Always make sure these items fit and purchase the highest quality you can afford. Both will last a long time and serve you well, but the wrong pair of boots can turn an extended trip into a nightmare. They can even veer toward dangerous if they give you blisters that get infected, if they slow you down so you get stuck in darkness or storms, or if they cause you to walk funny and lose your balance.

BUYING USED

Thrift stores and the Salvation Army are great places to look for many items for your next outdoor adventure. You might find wool and fleece, tents, bags, sweaters, down jackets, vests, hiking pants, hats, mittens, and even nordic skis or snowshoes if you visit frequently and root around in the corners. When buying used, it pays to spend some time inspecting your finds before taking them to the counter. Look over the entire item thoroughly. Consider its age. Rain gear, for example, loses its effectiveness over time, and any piece of clothing wears out eventually. Are the elbows and knees worn? Look for holes and stains. Carefully inspect the stitching, zip the zipper, and test the drawstrings. Turn it inside out. For goodness' sake, try things on. Try to resist impulse buys and carefully consider bargain finds, and you can often save yourself a bundle.

MAINTAINING YOUR CLOTHING

You wash your clothes too much—if you're the average cleanliness-obsessed American, that is. Be mindful of this when you pull your winter gear out of your pack after a long trip. Most outerwear, especially waterproof/breathable fabrics and down, needs to be washed infrequently, and too many reps at the laundromat eventually will break down the material.

The degree to which your outdoor gear needs washing corresponds to its proximity to your skin. In other words, your innermost layers, which soak up sweat, need to be laundered more often than your outermost layers, which are several strata away from your smelly body. Your base layers need to be washed after every adventure, whereas your shell or down jacket or puffer most likely won't.

The best advice is to read the label and follow the instructions. Polypropylene and other synthetics will shrink, so be careful drying them. Woolens may or may not be machine washable; many need to be dry cleaned. Fleece usually can hold up to many sessions in the washer, but be sure to read the label to avoid pilling or unraveling. Many of today's fabrics, including fleece and wool, last longer and retain their size and shape better when dried on the line rather than in a dryer.

3

CHAPTER 4
BACKPACKING GEAR

➜ Backpacks 47
➜ Shelters 51
➜ Sleep Systems 54
➜ Camp Kitchen Gear 59
➜ Gear Care 63

➜ BACKPACKS

Like outerwear, backpacks have bounded far ahead on the technological trail since the days of those ubiquitous, poky, metal-frame external packs that shifted wildly on your back, cut into your shoulders, and snagged on branches. These days, 40-liter overnight backpacks look almost like colorful rucksacks: streamlined, rounded, and form-fitting. Built of Cordura, a thick, rugged form of high-thread-count nylon, packs now keep the gear dry and the load light, with some models weighing in at less than 2 pounds. They're designed to allow a wide range of motion without riding up or affecting your balance. Many include exterior straps for carrying winter essentials, such as ice axes, helmets, and crampons. Internal frames have overtaken exterior frames in popularity, with most featuring aluminum stays or foam panels for structure. Some even use inflatable systems, requiring air canisters or battery-powered fans to retain their shape. Backpacks today are a world away from their primitive cousins and ideal for carrying the larger loads that winter requires.

As always, when shopping for a pack, keep in mind what you will use it for. Are you planning a single-day outing or a weekend-long backpacking trek? Will you be carrying extra gear for someone else or for the group? Will you be pulling a tote sled? Do you need a lot of creature comforts on the trail or do you tend toward the ultralight? Winter makes certain demands simply due to safety concerns, so you'll never be able to travel as lightly as you can in summer. But the size of the pack doesn't necessarily have to be huge, especially if you're planning a short jaunt or you have a pull-behind sled heaped with gear.

Pack sizes are measured by liters, as in how many liters of stuff you can smoosh into them. Small packs for winter use will be in the 30- to 50-liter range, good for a few hours out in the wild. Midsize rucks for a winter overnight will be 50 to 80 liters. Big, full-size packs for extended excursions can accommodate 70 or more liters of gear.

DAY PACKS

The same day pack you use in summer is likely too small for a winter trip. In cold weather, it's necessary to have a load of warm layers, and it's always wise to carry a sleeping bag for emergency use. A winter day pack will be along the lines of the 30- to 50-liter jobs that outfitters call "weekend" packs. In the snowy season, they fill quickly with a sleeping bag, puffer jacket, exterior shell, hats, gloves, emergency shelter, first-aid kit, map, GPS, avalanche beacon, and the extra food needed for winter safety.

Many of the considerations for these packs are the same as when selecting any sort of backpack. Packs are measured by the length from shoulder to waist, as opposed to overall height. Look for a pack that feels comfortable across your shoulders and snugs nicely to your hips. Some packs are adjustable for torso length, so be sure to make the proper adjustments when trying them on. And do try them on. Make sure you stuff a pack full of gear and march around the showroom, too. Once you have it filled, adjust the straps at the shoulders and waist until it feels right for you. Adjust the load lifters as well, if your pack has them. Make sure the hip belt falls across the top of your hips, not your abdomen, and that it cinches fully. When a pack is fitted correctly, the majority of the weight—more than three-quarters—should ride on your hips, so it's crucial there's no play in the hip belt. Some manufacturers make swappable hip belts in different sizes, and they also design packs (and other gear) specifically for women, optimized for women's frames.

No matter which pack you choose, it should feel form-fitting, comfortable around the waist, snug to the back, and bear most of the load at the hips. If it doesn't feel right for you, it's not right for you, no matter how much you like the color or the look or the price tag. Like boots, backpacks are one of the gear choices where you want to be certain you've chosen properly.

EXTERNAL FRAME PACKS

You can still buy external frame packs, but they've been largely left behind by internal models. External frames look much the same as they did during the big backpacking boom of the 1970s, with the square fabric bag hanging off the large, rectangular aluminum tubes. The packs themselves have been updated with compression buckles, more pockets, and other modern features. And the overall load is more comfortable, with extra padding and better weight distribution than before. But most people still prefer internals because they hug the body, slide around less, and enable you to be more agile. They fit down narrower trails and through smaller gaps. Anyone moving around a lot; climbing; skiing; or traveling on twisty, rooty, rocky trails usually prefers an internal frame pack on their back.

External frame packs have their uses, however. They are better for strapping things to, which is why they're used by rangers, trail workers, and others who carry tools and extra gear. They also breathe better than internal packs, because they sit farther from the back, allowing air to circulate. Some people find it easier to access gear in an external frame because these packs generally have more compartments, more spread out. On a wide, flat, prescribed trek, you can haul more stuff. You can also use external packs in a rescue, lashing them together to create a makeshift litter. And they're generally much cheaper. There will always be that guy or girl who prefers them.

INTERNAL FRAME PACKS

Internal frame packs are the norm these days, far outselling their exoskeletal counterparts. Many outfitters don't even carry external frame packs because consumer demand is too low. So why did outdoorspeople switch loyalty over the past twenty years and largely send the external frame packing? There are many reasons, but primary among them is probably that shrinking the aluminum stays and sewing them into the back of the pack creates a much more compact, form-fitting ruck. Internal frames follow the contours of the body for greater comfort and mobility. A correctly sized, properly adjusted internal frame pack lets a backpacker be far more agile, allowing a range of motion that their square, external cousins can't come close

4

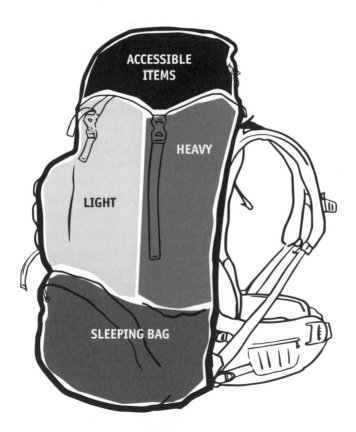

FIGURE 11. When packing a backpack, distributing weight as illustrated above reduces the risk of hip and back injury, transferring much of the work to the legs.

to offering. Unlike the old days, today's packs don't sway wildly when you move around, which is especially important during winter, when cold-weather activities—skiing, snowshoeing, swinging an ice ax—involve regular shifting of body weight. And the shoulder straps and hip belts tend to be more adjustable than those on the external frame packs of yore, allowing you to fine-tune the pack for your body. They also make better carry-on luggage, because they are far easier to jam into an overhead bin than an external frame.

➔ **PRO TIP** Hydration bladders are a popular backpack addition, and some are specially designed for winter, with insulated linings and neoprene sleeves to keep the water tubes from freezing. Some include a warmer that slides over the mouthpiece to prevent it from icing. When using hydration bladders in winter, blow into the mouthpiece after each drink to discourage ice buildup. Tubes still might freeze, but we'll cover how to keep water thawed on page 133 in Chapter 7.

Most internal frame packs feature one large compartment that runs the length of the pack, around which are a handful of smaller pockets. Access to the large compartment either can be from the top or through a zippered opening in the front. More care must be exercised when packing a top-loading pack. You will want frequently used or quickly needed gear at the top, for easy access. Compression straps keep interior spaces compact. Many have springy mesh pockets on the outside for water bottles or other frequently needed items. Some feature sleeping bag compartments at the very bottom, where you can stuff your sack, as well as external loops for attaching your sleeping pad, hiking poles, and the like. Fancy models might even include a removable day pack as part of the top lid. Interior hydration bladder pockets have become quite common, although they are not as useful for winter excursions of more than a few hours because the valves tend to freeze.

Internal frame packs are often made of Cordura or denier nylon, a synthetic fabric with high fiber counts. The higher the rating, the more fibers and the tougher the fabric. Many boast ripstop fabric, which can save the life of the pack if it accidentally gets poked by a sharp branch—or, worse, a hiking pole or crampons. Most are water resistant; some are waterproof or have waterproof bottoms. Thanks to the ultralight craze, some models have foam panels rather than aluminum rods for structure, and the panels can be removed at night and used as a sleeping pad.

Just like external frame packs, however, internals aren't perfect. With one large inside compartment, they can make it difficult to access gear buried at the pack's bottom. Because interior frame packs conform to the shape of your body and don't allow much airspace between gear and back, they can get sweaty on long hikes. Some manufacturers have created mesh back panels and ventilation chimneys to allow for better airflow. Unlike external frames, they don't force you to walk upright as if you're wearing a back splint; in fact, they encourage you to lean forward, which can lead to a sore back at the end of the day. They're also pricey.

SPECIALIZED PACKS

You can now find packs specifically designed for winter use. These packs are among the most form-fitting available, with flexible suspension and a super-compact shape to keep them steady during skiing, snowboarding, climbing, and other weight-shifting activities. They sport an array of features that makes them handy for cold-weather adventuring, including extra-rugged nylon construction to resist pokes and tears from sharp winter tools; buckles and straps designed for gloved hands; loops for skis; holsters for ice tools; insulated hydration pockets; and quick-open compartments for avalanche beacons and satellite communicator devices.

AVALANCHE AIRBAG PACKS

Similar in features to other winter-use packs, "av" airbags are inflatable, filling with air in the event of an avalanche. The premise behind them is similar to when you eat popcorn out of a bowl: Larger items move to the surface when you shake an aggregate of items. As soon as you feel the tremors of an avalanche, inflate your pack, and it will make you that much bigger and give you the best chance of survival. (Turn to pages 76–79 in Chapter 5 for more on avalanche survival.)

4

DRY BAGS

Dry bags are a welcome pack accessory on winter wanders. Originally designed for canoe trips and other waterborne adventures, these durable sacks are made of waterproof material, and the tops roll down to lock out moisture, which makes them ideal for traveling through snow country. Put your sleeping bag inside, and you know it will be dry when you pull it out. Dry bags pack well into a pull-behind sled, and backpack straps on many models make them easy to shoulder, should the need arise.

CONVERSION PACKS

Not necessarily designed for winter use, these packs allow you to transform them from backpack to duffle and back again using straps and buckles. They make for easier travel on the way to your next mountaineering adventure, fitting into overhead compartments and luggage carriers.

➔ SHELTERS
TENTS

Depending on the model, you may be able to use your favorite three-season shelter on a February camping trip, especially if you plan to set up below treeline or if the weather looks relatively fair. Most three-season tents can handle some snow, but if you're headed anywhere extreme—up a mountain to high-wind zones and cold temperatures or into a blizzard—you're going to want a tent specifically constructed to withstand the cold, wetness, gales, and heavy loads of winter.

Winter tents come in a range of models and styles. They don't look all that different from three-season tents at a distance. But up close, you'll notice almost all feature snow flies (an extra layer that serves as a snow shield) covering the entire tent, rather than the skimpy rain flies many three-season tents sport for summer. Poles are usually made of aluminum rather than fiberglass, and they are attached via sleeves in the tent body rather than via clips. You'll also see the material tends to be heavier nylon, 1,800 weight, for example, and that winter tents have few or no windows and less mesh for ventilation. The more serious mountaineering tents boast double walls for added protection against the blustery winds and heavy snows of high places. Most feature at least one vestibule and often two, which are perfect for storing gear outside and allow you to remove your boots before you track snow into the tent. The great drawback of these stouter tents, of course, is they're considerably heavier than their three-season cousins. Many people distribute the weight of the tent among those who are going to be using it, giving someone the fly and poles, and someone else the tent body, for example.

Some winter lovers favor the heavy, canvas-wall tents of the old Maine Guides over today's modern nylon wonders. The beauty of these old-school, cabinlike shelters is that they often accommodate chimneys, allowing you to set up a lightweight box stove inside. Many are made of canvas treated to be resistant to cotton fabric's old nemeses—water, mildew, and fire—and they feature reinforced pockets for ridgepoles. Some have floors; others do not. They are great for longer outings, and you can wait out the most vicious of storms in them, but you pay for their comfort in weight—not to mention they make your bivy look like a Revolutionary War camp.

MIDS

Not as useful in winter as they can be in fairer climes (and not recommended for novice winter campers), mids are essentially the roof of a tent without the floor or walls. Some outdoorspeople buy commercially made varieties, which come with their own suspension systems and resemble pyramids (hence the name); others simply use tarps. If you're planning to camp below treeline and build a shelter using snow for walls and a mid as a roof, these can work exceedingly well in winter. Just make sure there's enough pliable snow available. Otherwise, they don't provide enough protection. Mids can also pair well with bivy bags, which provide extra comfort.

BIVOUAC SACK (BIVY)

Created as a way to provide an overnight sleeping option to rock climbers on multi-day ascents, bivy (or bivouac) sacks were originally lightweight sleeping bag covers. They became very popular among ultralight backpackers, eventually growing and morphing into tiny tents just large enough to accommodate a single person in a sleeping bag. They share a similar construction with their bigger, three-season tent

4

FIGURE 12. A bivouac sack, or bivy, works best in winter when paired with another form of shelter, locating it inside a quinzee or a tarp-covered dugout.

cousins in that they usually have a waterproof, breathable upper section and a more durable, weatherproof lower section. These days, they even find their way into the winter woods. Bivy sacks function best in cold weather when used in conjunction with another shelter. They can add more protection underneath a mid or be deployed inside a snow shelter, such as a snow cave, igloo, or quinzee. You could set one up under a tarp or even spend a night in one far below treeline if you find a glen protected from the wind. Used on their own, though, bivys are not enough to keep you safe in a heavy storm. Some users find them claustrophobic, and winter can exacerbate that sensation, because you'll want to close the roof while you sleep to keep from waking up covered in snow. Others complain about the inability of bivy sacks to handle internal moisture—they sit not far from your face—which can pose a safety concern in cold weather.

TARPS

These days, many ultralight hikers carry nothing but a basic tarp to keep out the elements at night. Some survivalists swear by a winter shelter constructed only from a tarp hung lean-to style, with a reflective (safety) blanket underneath it and a fire out front, cowboy-style. If you go this way, be sure to orient your tarp so that it won't catch the wind and blow away. It's also wise to know what weather you're expecting and to have a good supply of wood on hand. Other winter adventurers use tarps as the roofs of snow shelters, stretched above a trench or snow walls. Unless you plan to build an igloo or quinzee, tarps are about as light as it gets for transport.

They're also extraordinarily handy for winter camping, and you should always have one in your pack. You can hang a tarp across the front of a shelter or Appalachian Trail lean-to; you can use them to drag wood or snow across the snowpack; you can cover your sled against the falling flakes; you can burrito wrap someone with hypothermia . . . the uses are endless.

FIGURE 13. When the weather isn't too rough, you can construct an easy winter shelter by stringing up a tarp and hanging a reflective blanket underneath. When you build a fire out front, the heat will reflect onto you from the blanket. Make sure to put a sleeping pad or two under your bag to insulate yourself from the cold ground.

HYBRID SHELTERS

Hybrids look like the result of a big tent, hammock, and bivy sack mashup. They perhaps most closely resemble bivy sacks but are much stouter and more tentlike. Plus, they can hang hammock-style, lifting you off the ground. Most feature a taller space for the head than the average bivy and a covering for the bottom half of the body, and they tend to flare out at either end. Some of the cleverer designers created hybrids exclusively for winter, utilizing ski poles and snow shovels for structure, thus making for lighter travel. Other creative hybrids boast their own insulation, incorporating the sleeping pad and even the bag into one innovative slumber pod with a soft floor and moisture-wicking walls. As their name suggests, hybrids come in all shapes and sizes, with new designs and models arriving every year.

→ SLEEP SYSTEMS

When campers describe their "sleep systems," they're referring to the combination of sleeping pads and bags, and everyone has his or her own preference. The best practice when sleeping on the ground in winter is, essentially, *don't sleep on the ground*. Put as much insulation between yourself and the snow and ice below as possible. Remember when we learned about conduction? When you place your bag or your butt or anything else on the snow, the heat seeps out of that object and into the cold. This is never more of a problem than at night, when you're prone on the ground for hours. Sleep systems combat conduction, isolating your body from the cold using layers of insulation.

SLEEPING BAGS

On a winter trip into the backcountry, sleeping bags are not merely bedtime essentials; they are part of your safety checklist. Your mummy sack quite literally could save your life if you get turned around on a snowy hike and find yourself forced to camp out, awaiting rescue.

The job of a sleeping bag is to capture warm air, retaining as much of your body heat as possible. Outfitters give their bags temperature ratings, identifying a comfort range, so be sure to study a bag's tags and think about how low the mercury is likely to fall wherever you plan to camp. Most winter bags these days feature the "mummy" style, which includes a curve that goes up over your head, leaving only your face exposed. These tend to start off wide at the head and shoulders and narrow considerably at the feet, restricting your movement far more than the rectangular bags of car camping. Most are designed to hug your body and roll over with you, as manufacturers try to reduce the amount of material to save space and lighten the load in your pack. Of course, some hikers prefer to carry a little extra weight for the added comfort of more wiggle room at the end of a long day on the trail.

4

Modern bags utilize all kinds of technology and can be constructed from waterproof or water-resistant materials, ripstop fabric, and denier nylon or lined with polyester. High-end bags even feature wicking inner layers. You'll find yourself considering a whole array of features in new bags. They might have full-length or partial zippers, allowing you to stick a leg out to cool off. Some have hoods with drawstrings. Others feature a pocket underneath your head that you can stuff with a down vest or a fleece to create a makeshift pillow. Some bags incorporate baffles near the face, on seams, or along the zipper to prevent the leakage of warmth. And some have loops on the underside to wrap around the sleeping pad or even pockets underneath in which to insert the pad itself. Manufacturers now make bags specifically for kids and women with smaller profiles. Spend some time thinking about what features you might want. Ask around or search the internet for reviews. Give careful consideration to your bag purchase because: (a) it won't be cheap, and (b) it will be one of the most essential items you'll take winter camping, determining how comfortable you are and how much fun you have.

Many people pair their bag with a liner or even a second bag inside, although the outer bag needs to be large enough so it doesn't crush the inner bag's insulation, rendering it useless. Some clever campers bring an additional puffer jacket to place between themselves and their sleeping pads or over themselves for added warmth. Everyone has their own methods.

WHAT TEMPERATURE RATINGS MEAN

When selecting a bag for your winter camping trip, you'll find yourself perusing a lot of temperature ratings. These represent the lowest temperature at which you'll be comfortable in that particular bag. So if the tag reads +45, you can expect it to keep you cozy as long as the ambient temperature doesn't fall below 45 degrees Fahrenheit. Manufacturers rate bags on the assumption that you're a typical camper wearing your long johns and sleeping atop an insulating ground pad. If you camp only in summer, you usually can get away with a 45-degree bag, though many experts recommend 35 degrees as the cutoff for even the fairest weather. Three-season bags usually range from 10 degrees to 35, and winter bags anywhere below 10 degrees. A good standard is to look for a bag rated 10 to 20 degrees lower than you think you'll need.

Down

Down remains popular in winter sleeping bags. An 800-fill goose-down bag can keep you warm to 20 degrees Fahrenheit, compress to 10-by-8 inches, and weigh only 2 pounds. Down bags often share the design of puffer jackets, using quilted stripes to compartmentalize the feathers. Some feature waterproof baffles to keep the insulation evenly spread. Because it has a lot of loft, creating big pockets of warm air, down is one of the best insulators around. Manufacturers use a certain amount of "fill" in each bag, which is a measure of how many cubic inches per ounce the feathers fill. (An 800-fill bag has 800 cubic inches of down per ounce.) The higher the number, the more fill or insulation. Down bags are soft, extremely light, warm, and they compress well for transport. They also tend to be more expensive, are not generally as rugged as synthetics, and some people are allergic to goose and duck feathers. The worst problem with down, however, is that it loses its ability to keep you warm if it gets wet, and it takes a long time to dry out, which is ironic, since it comes from waterfowl. Some manufacturers have designed waterproof pockets for their down, which go a long way toward solving this age-old problem.

Synthetic

For a variety of reasons, many campers favor sleeping bags constructed of synthetic materials. They're less expensive than down bags. They keep their shape well and retain warmth even when dragged through a puddle. They also dry out fast. Most are constructed from sheets of polyester sewn into the lining of the bag or from polyester fibers made to mimic down. Some of these individual polyester strands are hollow, to allow bigger pockets of space. Outfitters have created their own proprietary designs and trademark names, and options are myriad. Like down, however, synthetics have their detractors. Synthetic bags don't compress as well as down bags do. They're also heavier. Which is better? Depends who you ask. Partisans sleep in both camps, and in either case, the degree with which you take care of your bag is a major factor.

Hybrid Construction

Some manufacturers have created hybrid bags that ostensibly combine the best properties of down and synthetic insulation. The goal is to make them warmer and more compressible than traditional polyester insulation but more water resistant than your typical down bag. These hybrid bags usually have synthetic fill beneath you and down over the top, or at least more feathers on top than underneath. Designs commonly sandwich the down fill between layers of synthetic insulation, keeping it away from the surface and therefore drier. Offset quilting holds everything in place. Some hybrid bags can keep you warm all the way down into the negative teens.

SLEEPING PADS

In winter, you want as much separation from the ground as you can get with your sleeping pad, not only to protect you from protruding roots and rocks but to insulate you from the dangerous conduction of the ground. Sleeping pads provide critical R factor, with values up to 9.5. (R values are the measure of thermal protection insulation provides, the same as is used to differentiate the insulation in your home.) For winter you can get away with a pad with an R value of 4.0, which is good to 12 degrees Fahrenheit, but many people prefer 4.5. Pads come in a variety of styles and divide into two primary types: inflatable and foam. Most winter campers bring two pads: a closed-cell foam pad to lie directly on the tent floor and an inflatable mattress to sit atop it. (One of the main differences between closed- and open-cell foam is the R factor they provide. Closed-cell has a higher value.) And sleeping pads are not just for sleeping anymore. You can use them as seats, keeping you up off the cold snow. You can stand on them when cooking to keep your feet warmer. You can use them in splint construction, in case of an emergency. In some cases, you can even use them as the frame of your backpack. Most manufacturers specify the R factor, the length, and the weight, all of which are things to consider on your winter camping trip.

4

Inflatable

Today's inflatables are not the leaky air mattresses of old. In fact, you wouldn't want an old-fashioned air mattress in cold weather, because they allow frosty air currents to circulate underneath you all night, stealing your warmth. New inflatable mattresses pair insulated air tubes with open-cell foam for firm support, and some even have down or other insulation inside. These mattresses generally self-inflate, which is handy, and you can regulate the degree of cushion by the amount of air you allow in. At truly cold temperatures, however, they might not fully self-inflate, and you might find yourself needing to add a few extra puffs to get the pad to a comfortable level of firmness. Constructed from durable, rip-resistant fabrics, they roll easily and transport well, sliding down the side of your pack or across the top. And they provide excellent insulation. They have their issues, though. Blowing them up by mouth introduces moisture into the mattress, which can then freeze during winter camping. Many people find them too narrow or too short. Some are noisy when you roll over, like sleeping on a bag of chips. They don't play nicely with crampons or other sharp items. The ones that self-inflate and are most compact tend to carry heftier price tags, but there's no denying their comfort when you find one that fits.

Foam

Foam mattresses are light and comfortable and offer a lot of perks to the winter camper. These pads have their own multitude of designs. Some borrow the egg-crate nubbies from those old hospital mattresses; others are flat and hard. Most are rectangular; some have curves. But they all share a few traits. They tend to roll up like a scroll or stack accordion-style. Their closed-cell construction makes them effective insulators, and they fare well when strapped on the back of a pack, mostly impervious to scratches or jabs. Some manufacturers make one side reflective, which radiates warmth back toward your body. Many are customizable, allowing you to cut away a portion to better fit your body or for easier transport. Even the nicest ones tend to be less expensive than inflatables. In the negative column, they're often not as comfortable as their air-filled counterparts, and they don't compress as well.

LINERS

Ever climb into your sleeping bag at the end of the day and find all kinds of dirt at the bottom? Not fun. Liners solve this problem, keeping the interior of your bag much cleaner than a bag without an insert, which helps preserve loft and therefore warmth. In winter, liners offer an additional bonus: They add insulation, sometimes as much as 15 degrees' Fahrenheit worth, which could make your 45-degree, three-season bag comfortable at temperatures below freezing. Made from polymicrofiber, silk, or merino, they wick away moisture as well. Liners are generally inexpensive, compact and light, and you can use them by themselves on warm summer camping trips. Perhaps the one drawback is, when you combine your base layers of clothing, a liner, and a tight sleeping bag, you might feel constricted and uncomfortable.

VBLs

VBL stands for vapor barrier liner, which is a waterproof type of sleeping bag insert that prevents the moisture from your body from reaching the insulation of your sleeping bag. A few wet drips might not be a big deal on a fall overnight, but on a multi-night winter excursion, your nighttime perspiration can compromise the warmth of your bag. VBLs keep your bag nice and dry. The interiors can get a little moist, and most who use them recommend you wear only a base layer for comfort. They also add 5 to 10 degrees to your bag's temperature rating. Some bags have VBLs built in. High-end models feature reflective heat barriers, providing even more warmth. And, of course, their waterproof nature helps if you wake up to find the interior of your tent drenched in spring thaw. Most cost about $2 or $3 and weigh well under a pound.

Fart Sacks

Taking their name from Marine slang, fart sacks are weatherproof covers that fit over a sleeping bag. Not unlike those found on the outside of the government-issued modular sleeping system, these sacks look like big sleeping bags, and they encase your bag and your sleeping pad, keeping any sort of moisture out. Made of waterproof and breathable nylon, they create a mummy sack that can lie right on the snow, if necessary. Weighing in at less than 2 pounds, they can be compressed and carried in the same bedroll as your bag.

➜ CAMP KITCHEN GEAR

Food is critical to winter adventure. Nutrition, of course, is key to any type of outdoor activity, but in winter, when your body is burning thousands of calories just trying to keep itself warm, what you eat—and how much—is more consequential than ever. The promise of a hot meal on a bone-chilling day also provides comfort, helping to entice you out of your sleeping bag in the morning and giving you something to look forward to at the end of a long, cold hike. Few things provide as much comfort in the winter woods as warm sustenance. But first you have to cook it—or at least heat it up. Which means you need the right supplies for your camp kitchen. Depending on where you're going, you may be able to cook over open flames, cowboy-style, or reheat a meal on a woodstove. If not, you'll need a cookstove. Some work better in a deep freeze than others.

4

STOVE TYPES

Besides being necessary for cooking, winter camp stoves fulfill another vital role: They melt snow for water. This is critical if you're not close to a water source, making the selection of a stove a very important consideration. Can you bring your summer stove on your winter camping trip? It depends. Many stoves begin to fail as the temperature falls. This happens for a variety of reasons. Some fuels lose pressure. Others lose the ability to vaporize. The ultralight cat cans (or denatured alcohol stoves, so named because they're about the size of a can of cat food) that have been all the rage in outdoor circles for years do indeed work in winter, but whether they have an adequate BTU output and are big enough to heat everything that needs heating in cold weather is another question.

Most winter campers prefer liquid fuel stoves, which usually means white gas. These stoves perform admirably in temperatures well below zero. They're cheaper to run than propane or isobutane canister stoves, and you can always tell how much gas you have left simply by looking. They're often more stable than canister stoves, a real boon if brutal weather conditions *force* you

➜ **PRO TIP** When melting snow, start with a little water at the bottom of your pot. Melting snow by itself will vaporize the snow before it turns to a liquid.

to cook inside a tent or shelter—which is *never* recommended. If you *must do so*, you *must* take safety precautions, especially against the large flames associated with priming. Some liquid fuel stoves accommodate other fuels, which can help if you're traveling and can't transport fuel. Most must be primed or pumped, however, making them slightly less convenient, and the stoves themselves are often more expensive than propane models.

Canister stoves also work well in winter weather, and if the temperature isn't too low, you can bring along your summer model. There are two primary types of canister stoves for backcountry travel: the upright, or integrated system, with a regulator that screws into a canister base and has tripod arms that hold the burner; and the remote system, which has a fuel line that connects the canister to a burner sitting off to the side. Canister stoves excel at convenience and ease of use, and they're very lightweight. You can set one up in seconds and be cooking in less than a minute, because no priming is necessary. The drawback during winter is the fuel, which doesn't burn well in cold temperatures. Many canister systems use IsoPro, a mix of isobutane and propane, and isobutane works only to about 11 degrees Fahrenheit, at which point it no longer converts into vapor. Propane alone vaporizes all the way down to -43 degrees, so in many cases, winter campers burn off the usable propane and are left with noncombustible isobutane. The trick with IsoPro is to keep the

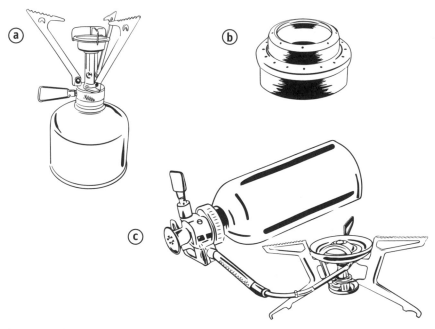

FIGURE 14. Pictured above: (a) a canister stove, which is convenient and easy to use, but whose fuel might not burn well in very cold temperatures; (b) an alcohol stove (a.k.a. a "cat can"); (c) a typical liquid-fuel stove, with the burner attached directly to the fuel source.

canister somewhat warm—by tucking it into your sleeping bag, for example. Also look for stoves with built-in pressure regulators that maintain a consistent pressure, which improves performance in frigid temps and at elevation. Some remote systems allow you to use a windscreen and invert your canister, which helps in winter, but the fuel lines can prove unreliable in deep cold. Propane-only canisters work well in the backcountry, but they tend to be heavier and bulkier and don't fit all stoves. Some campers complain about the stability of the upright stove, which can be top-heavy and wobbly under heavy pots. Others fault the length of the tripod arms on canister stoves, finding them inadequate for larger cookware, but these are issues regardless of the season.

Be aware that, whichever type of stove you go with, you're going to need a lot more fuel in winter than in summer. Some experts recommend 5 fluid ounces per person, per day. You'll be happier to have a little extra left over than to run out, and sleds make fuel easy to transport. In most cases, you'll be boiling snow to provide drinking water, and that alone will burn fuel fast. It's always advisable to set up your stove at home ahead of time, learning its intricacies before it's 20 below, and everyone is waiting for you to make coffee. Take it apart, make sure you understand its components, and light it a few times on a cold day. See for yourself how much fuel it takes to boil snow and do some math to find out what works for you.

4

For more information on which stove type is best for you, check out the chart "Efficacy of Stove Types" on pages 62–63.

KITCHEN KITS

Your three-season cookware—all those backcountry pots, pans, sporks, and spoons stuffed away in your outdoor gear closet—work just fine in the cold-weather months. Refer to Chapter 9 in AMC's *Mountain Skills Manual* for general guidance on setting up your camp kitchen.

The major concern with cooking in winter is keeping your cookstove upright. Cold and stiff fuel lines often make things tippy, and if you build your cooking area on the snow, it will melt as your gear heats up, unbalancing the stove. It's a good idea to have some sort of lightweight, transportable platform to put your stove on. You can purchase several commercial options at a gear outfitter, or you can make your own easily. Winter camping vets have used old avalanche shovels, veneer plywood, hardcover book covers, cutting boards, and a host of other items for this purpose. A couple of simple solutions: a piece of cardboard or a section of an old foam mattress wrapped in aluminum foil, or an aluminum turkey-roasting tray wrapped around a piece of cardboard. These will keep your stove afloat, reflect the heat back up, and weigh next to nothing. As a bonus, they can double as a windscreen or a heat reflector if you find yourself winter camping somewhere where there's a picnic table, rendering your makeshift stove platform unnecessary.

4

EFFICACY OF STOVE TYPES			
Fuel/Stove Type	**Advantages**	**Disadvantages**	**Best Choice For**
Liquid Gas	• Works in all conditions • Inexpensive fuel • Easy to find fuel • Fast boil times • Can handle large or small groups • No disposable canisters	• Bulkier and heavier • Requires assembly, priming, and pumping • Fuel can spill on gear, hands, or food • Generally louder when lit • Needs occasional cleaning of fuel line and burner	• Maximum versatility • You don't mind having to perform occasional stove maintenance • Winter camping, long expeditions, international travel • You want to save money on fuel
Canister	• Easy to light and run • Quieter operation • Smaller and lighter • No fuel spillage	• Canisters less commonly available than liquid fuel • Much costlier than liquid fuel • Disposable canisters create waste problems • Must carry canister, even when empty • Quickly loses efficiency below freezing	• Trips shorter than two days, or with fewer than four days between resupplies • Groups of three or fewer • Weather above freezing • Ease of use is your priority
Hybrid-fuel	• Versatility	• Same bulk and weight as a liquid-fuel stove • Must change stove jet to switch between fuels	• Switching between fuel sources • Good for both very short trips and longer trips • Traveling internationally, where fuel flexibility is important • You don't mind having to perform occasional stove maintenance

EFFICACY OF STOVE TYPES (CONTINUED)			
Fuel/Stove Type	Advantages	Disadvantages	Best Choice For
Pot-stove canister systems	▪ Greatest efficiency for canister stoves ▪ Shortest boil times ▪ No maintenance ▪ Can eliminate one eating bowl	▪ No choice of pots ▪ No frying or baking ▪ Limited capacity for creativity ▪ Most expensive category	▪ Fast and light ▪ Traveling solo or in a group of two ▪ "Cooking" means boiling water
Campfire	▪ Ambiance ▪ Connection with nature and human history	▪ Prone to leaving a big impact ▪ Blackened pots ▪ Not appropriate in alpine environments or high-fire-danger times	▪ Semiprimitive experience ▪ Don't mind blackened pots

4

Windscreens and reflectors are essential in the winter woods. Most campers have at some point attempted to keep their cookstove going in a vicious breeze only to find it constantly blowing out. This won't do in extreme winter, when you're desperate for warm food. Again, you can buy an over-the-counter solution from an outfitter, most of which look like a big foil ring, or you can make one at home using foil or aluminum roasting trays from your local grocery store.

→ GEAR CARE

We've all gone camping with a buddy who discovers all kinds of broken or torn pieces of gear when unpacking his camping stuff from his bag. Sun, water, wind, ice, rocks, cold, dirt, salt: The outdoors is an unforgiving place for gear. Maintaining your kit is a vital part of outdoor adventure, and it's especially important when you're traveling in the winter backcountry, where a missing component can prove dangerous or even deadly. Many outdoorspeople go through their gear piece by piece before heading out on a cold-weather trip, and doing so is a wise practice. Give yourself time to correct whatever problems you may find.

Basic maintenance is neither difficult nor expensive, and it can save you a lot of money and hassle in the long run. All it really takes is time and maybe a little work now and then. Routine and organization prove key. Many hardcore campers buy big plastic totes to store their gear in. This not only keeps everything together; it also protects equipment from moisture and mice, the two archenemies of camping gear. Get a bin for each of your basic needs: shelter, sleeping, cookware, and clothing. Make a list of the items in each one, and check off your lists as you repack post-adventure.

Make sure to stock new batteries, replace duct tape, check expiration dates, and refill whatever stores you depleted so you'll be ready when your friend invites you on a spur-of-the-moment trip. Don't forget to buy new fuel and store it in a safe place.

The single biggest gift you can give your gear is simply to dry it out. Make sure your sleeping bag is clean—if it isn't, consider washing it following the manufacturer's instructions—and then hang it to dry. Do the same with the liner. Once it's had a day or two to air out, hang it in a closet. (Leaving it compressed for long periods crunches the down, lessening its life.) Drape your tent and make sure the interior is free of dirt. Use paper towels or a soft sponge to very lightly scrub any muddy spots. Reapply seam sealer if you feel doing so is warranted. When the tent is ready, pack it away in its sack, making sure not to roll it the same way every time, as this can create creases and wear spots. Unfold your tarp and sweep it clean, allowing it to dry before refolding.

Wipe moisture off headlamps, avalanche beacons, and GPS units and remove the batteries. Towel off your stove components, and wash your pots and pans and dishes, allowing them to dry before tucking them into the storage tote. Rinse out your water bottles with warm water and a tablespoon of baking soda. As with all your gear, make sure they're moisture-free before packing them away.

HOW MUCH SHOULD YOU SPEND?

You don't have to spend like an investment banker on new gear. Many of the items we take into the woods can be purchased used or inexpensively. In some cases, it might even make sense to rent items rather than buy them. If you go winter climbing every couple of years, you can get away with renting an ice ax and crampons rather than shelling out pocketsful of cash. Do the math and see what make sense for you. You can easily save money on many items from thrift shops or discount outdoor retailers. Dry bags, compression sacks, liners, headlamps, and even sunglasses (as long as they provide proper UV protection) can be areas where you save a few bucks.

Squirrel money away for items on which you really shouldn't skimp. Investing in a nice sleeping bag and sleeping pad, for example, will improve every trip for years to come. Rest is crucial in the outdoors, when you're working your body hard day after day, and a good night's sleep is priceless. A solid pack, one that fits your body well and is comfortable for extended use, is also a place where it makes sense to pay more. Whether you decide on a tent, a mid, or a bivy sack, your shelter should be an investment, especially in winter, which places such high demands on gear. Waking up under a heavy snow load because your tent poles snapped is not only unpleasant; it's hazardous to your health.

➜ **PRO TIP** Bring extras. One of the easiest fixes in the field is simply to swap out a broken piece of gear for a working one. When traveling with a group, it's a great idea to bring backup camp stoves, for example. Even if none breaks, you can melt snow faster.

MAINTAINING YOUR GEAR

It has been widely publicized that many manufacturers build their wares to last just a few years so you'll have to buy them again. Still, there are plenty of ways to make your gear last. Simply washing and keeping things dry goes a long way. Treating leathers with oil, polishing aluminum and chrome, applying waterproofing, and resealing seams can easily extend the life of your outdoor gear. Here are a few other ideas.

- **Patch your neoprene boots.** You can extract a few more years out of your pack boots by patching holes with neoprene repair kits, which are easy to find online.

- **Fix tarps and tents with nylon ripstop tape.** Several manufacturers make waterproof adhesive tapes that work great for minor repairs on tent walls, dry bags, and inflatable mattresses. Some even do the job on sleeping bag holes. Make sure to apply tape in warm weather and look for brands that specifically mention hardiness in cold temperatures. Some feature GoreTex's proprietary fabric.

- **Repair sleeping bag zippers.** If your zipper breaks, you can buy new closures online that slide onto broken zippers and bring the teeth back in line. These have adjustable tensioners, which allow you to dial in as much or as little grip as you need. Some local dry-cleaning establishments may be able to repair your zipper for a fraction of the cost of a new bag.

- **Re-stuff your bag with down.** If you find you've lost a lot of stuffing due to a hole in your bag, you can buy replacement down and use gear tape to cover the hole.

- **Replace broken backpack buckles.** Most of the buckles used on packs are easy to replace. Figure out the size, order a new one, and rethread it. You might even be able to repurpose one from a piece of gear you never use.

- **Fix your stove.** Many of the components in camp stoves—fuel lines, O-rings, ignitors—break down over time. Fortunately, they have straightforward fixes. You can find how-to videos on many manufacturers' websites.

- **Remove mold from your tent.** Even though you put your tent away dry, basement air can cause mold to grow. What to do? Several companies sell spray-on products designed to remove mold, and many work well. Or you can make your own using diluted bleach or lemon juice.

- **Fix broken tent flies.** Commercially made grip clips allow you to affix your tent's guy line to the fabric without sewing.

4

HOW TO ADDRESS MALFUNCTIONS IN THE FIELD

Stuff happens in the outdoors. That's why they call it adventure, right? Your headlamp breaks down, leaving you in the dark. The stove won't light. Gas canisters fail. Poles break. And on and on. Fortunately, there are many fixes you can do on the fly and even more ways to prepare for mishaps and malfunctions. Just like we carry first-aid kits for people problems, we should carry kits for injuries to our gear. A standard kit should include:

- **Extra batteries.** Make sure you have plenty of battery power for your head-lamps, GPS units, and other electronics. This is a no-brainer, but you'd be surprised how many people forget their AAs. Lithium models are a better option than water-based alkaline batteries in winter.

- **A roll of paracord.** Paracord rivals duct tape in its nearly limitless uses. Tie stuff to the back of the pack when a buckle lets loose. Lash down a tarp. Compress a bag. Set up a line for drying out gear. Paracord's potential uses are too numerous to mention, but it always comes in handy in a pinch.

- **Duct tape.** Not even going to bother to introduce this indispensable item. Gear tape, the rolled adhesive with waterproofing explicitly designed for outdoor gear, is a wise addition, too. With this stuff, you can patch tents and bags and pads, fix broken poles, and even fashion a splint.

- **Multitool.** Everyone has a preference. Just be sure it has a sharp knife; a skinny, awl-type tool; both screwdriver heads; and a pair of pliers.

- **Extra O-ring.** If your camp stove requires one, make sure you have an extra. A failing O-ring is one of the most common problems in the field.

- **Safety pins and sewing needle and thread.** These can solve all kinds of problems. You can clean most remote stoves by flipping them over and shaking them, activating an internal needle made to keep the lines free. But you may also need to unscrew the parts and manually clean components like fuel lines and jets. Safety pins come in handy here. Push one gently into the jet, cleaning out gunk, and you can fix another common stove problem.

- **A lighter.** No explanation needed.

- **Tent pole splint.** These lightweight metal sleeves slide down over your tent pole, giving it rigidity at the point of a break. Duct tape works in a pinch.

If you find yourself with gear issues beyond your ability to repair, there are an array of outfits online that fix gear. This usually involves shipping your broken item along with payment and waiting for it to be returned in working condition. Though some of these repairs may be costly, they are almost always significantly cheaper than buying new.

CHAPTER 5
SAFETY

→ First-Aid Preparedness   67

→ Environmental Challenges   76

→ The Human Element   86

→ Mental Challenges   87

→ When Things Go Wrong   88

→ Avalanche and Rescue Gear   95

→ Animal Danger   98

→ FIRST-AID PREPAREDNESS

It's amazing how many people venture into the woods without a first-aid kit or any sort of first-aid training. Many don't bother because they won't be out long or they're hiking in familiar terrain or they've been hiking so long without one, they figure they don't need to bother. A foolhardy attitude at any time of year (even if no one gets injured, everyone can use a little moleskin sometimes), it's especially shortsighted in winter.

A basic first-aid kit is an outdoor essential. You can buy a backcountry kit from an array of outfitters or you can go to the local drugstore and put together your own very inexpensively. Everything you truly need can fit into a screw-top water bottle, which will keep the components compact, dry, and buoyant and can double as a water bottle in a real emergency. At a minimum, the kit should include:

- various sizes of adhesive bandages

- medical tape/athletic tape

- tweezers

- moleskin

- ibuprofen and over-the-counter medications for diarrhea and allergies (for example, antihistamine)

- hand sanitizer

- antibacterial ointment

- hydrocortisone cream

- several pairs of medical gloves

- CPR mask
- roll of gauze
- triangular bandage
- safety pins
- paracord
- waterproof matches
- sanitary napkins
- iodine tablets
- sunscreen
- zipper closure bag

These are the basics. Customize at will, including personal medications, aloe vera, tick spoons, or whatever else you think you might find useful. You probably don't need to bring an ice pack this time of year.

WILDERNESS FIRST AID

Imagine a long fall into a stream and breaking bones 10 miles up a mountain on a winter hike—or merely slipping and spraining an ankle. Now think of what it takes to get the medical care you need. Hopefully, you have a group, and someone either can call or go for help. But even if your group leader can get cell service and place a call to 911, it almost certainly will take more than an hour before the local search and rescue (SAR) organization can assemble a team of rescuers and reach you. That's best case, assuming your location is accessible by helicopters or snowmobiles. More likely, it will take hours. It is not uncommon for backcountry rescues to take eight or ten hours or even more than a day, pausing overnight.

Enter wilderness medicine. The basic definition of wilderness first aid is medical help administered more than an hour away from definitive care. Rescuers call this the "golden hour," because it's often a crucial, pivotal period in a patient's treatment. Although people have been rendering aid in the backcountry since time immemorial, wilderness medicine became a recognized discipline in the 1970s, coinciding with the explosion in popularity of backpacking and mountaineering. Taught in outdoor clubs and organizations, including National Outdoor Leadership School (NOLS), AMC, and Outward Bound, "mountain medicine" borrows many techniques from city emergency medical technicians (EMTs) and from war zones, taking into account the delay in treatment commonly experienced in remote settings.

The overarching principle in wilderness medicine is adaptability to the surroundings, a concept that the outdoor medicine development and teaching group Wilderness Medical Associates calls "ideal to real." We know that in an ideal situation, a patient who falls 20 feet into a riverbed will be extricated by a team using the latest protocols for a spinal injury. But we also know that, in a real situation, there's a good chance no one has been able to contact rescuers, the river is rising, and the patient likely will drown or die of hypothermia before help arrives, unless he or she is removed from the waterway. In wilderness medicine, rescuers work with the tools and training they have, doing the best they can in prolonged-care situations amid difficult environments.

Wilderness first-aid courses teach you how to deal with situations like the one above, and the advice in this book is certainly not a substitute for such a course. Classes are now commonly available through outfitters, outdoor clubs, and other organizations, and they make a whole lot of sense if you spend a lot of time exploring outdoors. There are multiple levels of certification in wilderness medicine, ranging from simple first aid, to the 70-plus-hour Wilderness First Responder, to Wilderness Advanced Life Support or Wilderness EMT. The following list provides a good sampling of places where you can find wilderness medicine training. SOLO (Stonehearth Open Learning Opportunities) offers many classes in wilderness first aid in partnership with AMC; visit outdoors.org/activities to find a course near you.

AdventureMed
637B South Broadway, Suite 339
Boulder, CO 80305
970-444-4001; awls.org

NOLS
284 Lincoln Street
Lander, WY 82520
800-710-6657; nols.edu

SOLO
623 Tasker Hill Road
Conway, NH 03818
603-477-6711; soloschools.com

Wilderness Medical Associates
1 Forest Avenue
Portland, ME 04101
1-888-WILDMED; wildmed.com

COMMON WINTER MEDICAL ISSUES, INJURIES, AND AILMENTS

No matter how well prepared, smart, savvy, and experienced you are, accidents happen in the outdoors, especially in winter. You may not be able to prevent them, but with a bit of common sense and know-how, you can mitigate the damage and get back home safely.

The most common medical issue to arise in winter is exposure. Cold kills, plain and simple. Just standing outside in below-zero weather with inadequate clothing and gear will do you in—and quicker than you think. Although hypothermia poses the most basic threat, many other medical issues arise in winter. All the same problems we see in summer—dehydration, blisters, chafing, slips, trips, and falls—also happen in cold weather, and the presence of ice and snow makes terrible tumbles more common. Winter should make us watch our step and use more caution than ever.

Trauma

With crampons, ice axes, poles, and slippery slopes, winter hiking makes traumatic injury even more likely than during other times of the year. In medical terms, trauma is a physical injury (as opposed to an illness or a medical condition). But for most of us, "trauma" connontes an issue on the serious end of the spectrum. Trauma in the winter woods might mean tripping on a rock and breaking ribs, impaling oneself on a ski pole, being burned by a cookstove, or falling down a steep slope and hitting your head on a rock. These are the kinds of accidents you'd call the ambulance for back home. The winter setting makes them all the more likely to occur and exacerbates them when they do. For information on what to do in such situations, check out the section titled "When Things Go Wrong," on page 88 of this chapter.

Hypothermia

You know when you go to the beach and spend too much time in the water and emerge with blue lips and a serious case of the shivers? That's actually a mild case of hypothermia. It's much easier than you think to cross the threshold into this low-body-temperature ailment; more people become hypothermic at temperatures above freezing than below. As a matter of fact, according to the *Washington Post*, more cases happen in summer than in winter, when more people are outdoors and unprepared for cold. (Causes include capsizing in cold water or getting chilled by rain on a cool day.)

How is that possible? The answer is that any time your body's core temperature drops to 95 degrees Fahrenheit or lower, you've become hypothermic. When your body reaches hypothermic levels, it has several ways of compensating. First, it shivers in order to generate energy and warm you up. If that doesn't work, it begins to shunt blood away from your extremities in an effort to keep your core—and your vital organs—as warm as possible. Finally, it begins to shut down, with heart failure the end result.

Hypothermia begins with signs and symptoms you can easily spot: shivering and blue lips, fingers, or toes. Other early signs are decreased fine motor skills, along with what we in the outdoors call the "umbles": mumbles, grumbles, fumbles, and stumbles. When your body is shutting down and your brain is getting cold, your speech becomes slurred, you become irritable, and you have difficulty with coordination. Other signs include rapid breathing and pulse, poor judgment, sluggishness and apathy, and pale skin that is cool to the touch. You know the situation has become deadly serious when shivering stops and the patient has a faraway look, seemingly unable to form coherent thoughts.

The key to beating hypothermia is to identify and treat it early, because once it advances, it becomes extremely difficult to counteract in the field. In any case, the first step is to halt the cooling process. Remove patients' wet clothes and get them into a shelter of some sort. Dress them in dry clothes; feed them hot liquids and sugary, easily digestible food (like warm lemonade or Jell-O); and get them moving to regenerate body heat. Running in place, calisthenics, or any other physical activity helps.

If patients are incapable of warming exercise, they're likely in the moderate phase of hypothermia, when the body temperature dips into the 91- to 94-degree range. Moderate hypothermia is characterized by violent shivering, confusion, lethargy, and reduced consciousness, and many patients become incapacitated. At the lower end of the temperature range, shivering may stop altogether—a very bad sign.

When patients reach this level, it's virtually impossible for them to warm up through exercise. It would take more than 24 hours of concentrated physical activity to raise the body temperature by the required 4 to 7 degrees. The best way to warm and protect patients from the cold is to place them in what is called a "burrito wrap" (see Figure 15 on next page). Making a burrito wrap entails wrapping patients in a dry, wicking base layer covered by a warming layer of insulation and then folding the entire body, including the head, in several additional layers. First, gather warm water bottles, chemical heat packs, heated rocks, or whatever other heat sources you can come up with that won't burn the patient, and place them where the major arteries come closest to the skin, namely the groin, neck, and armpits. Then put a garbage bag around the patient to prevent any urine or sweat from wetting the other layers. Place the patient in a sleeping bag and wrap that with a space blanket, which prevents heat loss and radiates warmth back to the patient. Finally, enclose everything in a tarp, tent, or other windproof/waterproof cover. When you're done, it should look like the patient is inside a mummy bag or wrapped like a burrito. Administer warm liquids and whatever sugary food the patient can get down. It's crucial the patient is well insulated from the ground while you're doing this. Stack as many layers of sleeping pads underneath as you can.

The situation has gotten severe if patients becomes rigid, their pulse slows dramatically, or they lose consciousness. In severe cases of hypothermia, the body temperature falls below 91 degrees Fahrenheit. You should check the pulse and respiration for at least a minute at a time, because both become very slow and shallow as the body shuts down. You'll be tempted to get the patient to professional help, but unless you're near the trailhead and rescue, you may do more harm than good. A severely hypothermic person can go into cardiac arrest if moved too vigorously. The best course of action generally is to hold tight until rescuers can arrive and evacuate the patient gently. This is a scenario where the real versus the ideal comes into play; hypothermia merits urgent but gentle evacuation, and depending on the speed of response, you must use your best judgment.

5

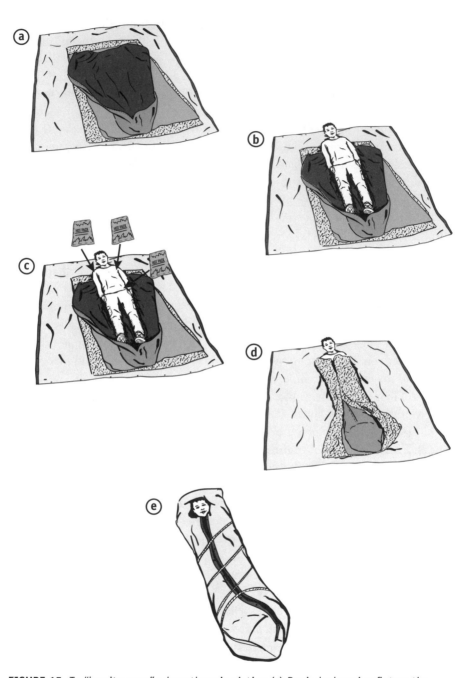

FIGURE 15. To "burrito wrap" a hypothermia victim: (a) Begin by layering flat on the ground a garbage bag, sleeping bag, space blanket, and tarp/tent/waterproof cover, all on top of as many sleeping pads as you can gather; (b) next, have the person lie atop the layers; (c) add any available heat sources, such as hand and foot warmers, that will not burn the victim; (d) wrap the person in the layers; (e) secure the end result, which should look like a mummy bag or a burrito, with rope or bungees.

Staying warm outdoors is the best approach to preventing hypothermia, but there are other ways to keep it at bay. Eat and drink. We know that the body burns a minimum of 2,000 calories per day, just trying to stay warm outside in winter, so you need to eat twice as much as you normally would. Staying hydrated helps, too, but avoid alcohol and caffeine, which cause your blood vessels to expand, making you lose heat through your skin faster. Also watch out for sheer exhaustion, which can limit your tolerance for cold. People with poor circulation, diabetes, severe arthritis, Parkinson's disease, or those who take certain medications are also at higher risk for hypothermia.

Frostbite

Frostbite often sneaks up on people, but when it is profoundly cold, frostbite occurs within minutes. According to the National Weather Service, at 10 degrees below zero, with the wind blowing 5 MPH, the skin and its underlying tissue freezes in just half an hour. And contrary to popular belief, frostbite doesn't attack only exposed skin. Even toes in boots and fingers in gloves can succumb without sufficient insulation. (Boots that are too tight is a common catalyst, because they restrict blood flow to the feet.) Many who have frostbitten tissue don't even realize it, thinking they're just cold because it's so, well, cold. Sometimes others have to point it out to them, so, in deeply cold temperatures, keep an eye on the exposed skin of everyone in your group.

5

Like its big brother hypothermia, frostbite occurs in stages. The first is the relatively innocuous frostnip, when skin just begins to freeze, numbing and turning red. Frostnip does no permanent damage. If you don't rewarm, however, superfi-

WINDCHILL																		
TEMPERATURE (°F)																		
calm	40	35	30	25	20	15	10	5	0	-5	-10	-15	-20	-25	-30	-35	-40	-45
5	36	31	25	19	13	7	1	-5	-11	-16	-22	-28	-34	-40	-46	-52	-57	-63
10	34	27	21	15	9	3	-4	-10	-16	-22	-28	-35	-41	-47	-53	-59	-66	-72
15	32	25	19	13	6	0	-7	-13	-19	-26	-32	-39	-45	-51	-58	-64	-71	-77
20	30	24	17	11	4	-2	-9	-15	-22	-29	-35	-42	-48	-55	-61	-68	-74	-81
25	29	23	16	9	3	-4	-11	-17	-24	-31	-37	-44	-51	-58	-64	-71	-78	-84
30	28	22	15	8	1	-5	-12	-19	-26	-33	-39	-46	-53	-60	-67	-73	-80	-87
35	28	21	14	7	0	-7	-14	-21	-27	-34	-41	-48	-55	-62	-69	-76	-82	-89
40	27	20	13	6	-1	-8	-15	-22	-29	-36	-43	-50	-57	-64	-71	-78	-84	-91
45	26	19	12	5	-2	-9	-16	-23	-30	-37	-44	-51	-58	-65	-72	-79	-86	-93
50	26	19	12	4	-3	-10	-17	-24	-31	-38	-45	-52	-60	-67	-74	-81	-88	-95
55	25	18	11	4	-3	-11	-18	-25	-32	-39	-46	-54	-61	-68	-75	-82	-89	-97
60	25	17	10	3	-4	-11	-19	-26	-33	-40	-48	-55	-62	-69	-76	-84	-91	-98

WIND (MPH)

Frostbite Times: [   ] 30 minutes   [   ] 10 minutes   [   ] 5 minutes

$$Windchill\ (°F) = 35.74 + 0.6215T - 35.75(V^{0.16}) + 0.4275T(V^{0.16})\ where\ T = Air\ Temperature\ (°F),\ V = Wind\ Speed\ (MPH)$$

This windchill chart, used by NOAA and the National Weather Service, illustrates how wind speed impacts windchill, or how cold the air temperature actually feels.

cial frostbite sets in. During this phase, the skin becomes whiter and starts to feel slightly warm, as the layer of tissue just beneath the epidermis begins to freeze and harden. The affected area then begins to sting and swell. When frostbite gets to the deep stage, it involves the dermis, epidermis, and subcutaneous tissue. The skin turns white or gray, and any sensation in the skin numbs and fades. If frostbite occurs in the hands and feet, you may lose the use of them, as the underlying joints and muscles refuse to work. Tissue that remains frostbitten for an extended length of time turns black and dies. Infection becomes a major threat. Other complications include gangrene in the surrounding area, tetanus, and nerve damage.

Frostbite tends to occur at temperatures of 5 degrees Fahrenheit or lower, but it can set in any time the skin stays too cold for too long. Windchill exacerbates the problem. Many of the same risk factors for hypothermia raise your chances of getting frostbite, including diabetes, alcohol, drugs, exhaustion, poor circulation, and dehydration. Frostbite also increases at elevation, because the body prioritizes the core and vital organs when there is a lack of oxygen.

Treatment in the field is tricky, and although frostnip almost always can be safely rewarmed onsite, with frostbite, it's best to rewarm in the field only if the patient is more than two hours from definitive care. Walking on frozen feet is a better option than beginning rewarming if you aren't certain you can fully rewarm the affected area before refreezing occurs. Package the area in insulating materials to stop the danger and splint it, if needed, to minimize use.

If you must rewarm in the field, administer pain medication to the patient first. Many of our nerve endings sit near the skin, making frostbite famously painful as the area rewarms. Because of that extreme pain, people often cut short the process, but you must complete it or risk the loss of more tissue. When the frostbite is superficial, or first-degree frostbite, the usual field rewarming method is to hold a warm body part over the frostbitten area. In other words, to hold the slightly frostbitten fingers in a pair of warm hands. If the case is more severe (that is, second- or third-degree frostbite, in which the skin turns reddish or blue), treatment involves soaking the affected tissue in water warmed to about 100 degrees. Large blisters commonly appear on the skin after the rewarming process, so do not be alarmed to see those. Never use a fire or a cookstove to rewarm frozen areas due to the risk of severe burns.

As with so many other ailments, prevention is the best cure for frostbite. Make sure you cover any exposed skin with enough insulation to keep it warm. Wear boots and gloves that fit properly and are designed for the temperatures at which you plan to recreate. Perhaps most importantly, understand the dangers. Many people enter the winter woods far too cavalierly and without the proper respect for the hazards therein.

Immersion Foot

Also known as trench foot, this ugly-sounding condition was named during World War I, when soldiers sat in wet, muddy battlefield trenches, wearing sodden boots. It occurs when the feet are exposed to cold water for extended lengths of time—we're usually talking days—causing them to lose circulation. Many of the symptoms are similar to frostbite: red or blue feet that become numb and begin to swell. If left alone long enough, blisters form, sores become infected, and gangrene sets in. Like with frostbite cases, when the feet are dried and begin to rewarm and heal, they hurt something fierce. The condition can happen at temperatures as high as 60 degrees Fahrenheit and within a half day, though it typically takes longer. The key to preventing trench foot, like so many other hazardous conditions, is to remain well fed, hydrated, and prepared, with appropriate footwear that will keep your feet warm and dry.

Snow Blindness

Photokeratitis: It's a painful thing. That's the formal name of the unfortunate winter ailment known as snow blindness, which is essentially sunburned eyes. Among outdoor adventurers, this most often occurs above treeline in open snowfields, on days with brilliant blue skies and full sun, but it can occur whenever you spend too much time playing in the snow on sunny days without eye protection. Bright white snow is a very effective UV reflector, sending back about 80 percent of the sun's UV rays, and the problem grows worse at elevation. Because the atmosphere thins as you climb, UV radiation intensifies by about 4 percent with every 1,000 feet of elevation gained.

Symptoms of snow blindness include pain, tearing up, itchy eyes, blurriness, swelling, and a sensation of grit in the eye, often compared to sand. Luckily, treatment is simple: Protect your eyes from the UV radiation. If you wear contact lenses and

> **➜ PRO TIP** If you don't have access to snow goggles or sunglasses, you can fashion improvised goggles by poking little holes in paper and wearing those over your eyes in an emergency.

5

FIGURE 16. With nothing but paper and string, you can make yourself a pair of effective and stylish snow goggles, as shown above.

can see well enough to travel without them, it makes sense to remove them if your eyes become sunburned. A wet cloth and ibuprofen can provide some relief from the pain, and the eyes typically heal within a couple of days. Again, the best course of action is preventing snow blindness in the first place by wearing sunglasses with adequate UV protection, or better still, glacier glasses, which protect the peripheral vision as well.

Headaches

Another consequence of the bright light is headache. This ultra-common ailment is brought on by tension in the neck muscles and dehydration—yet another reason to keep hydrated on the trail. Treatment is the same in the woods as it is at home. Drink water, take ibuprofen, and try to relax. And maybe take a look at the way your pack sits to make sure it's riding right.

➔ ENVIRONMENTAL CHALLENGES

In January 2016, a backcountry skier from Brunswick, Maine, was climbing a slope in Mount Washington's famous Tuckerman Ravine when things got ugly. According to the *Portland Press Herald*, Kaj Huld was ascending the Chute, a steep bowl in the White Mountains, where he'd been skiing for five years. Huld told a reporter he noticed a pair of climbers about 600 feet above him who had turned around because of unstable snow.

They were right to be wary.

In an instant, winter's fury broke loose: "It came from every direction and burst over everything," Huld said. "The avalanche was traveling 35 to 45 MPH, and it seemed to be about my height. It all happened in the blink of an eye."

Huld, the two climbers, and another skier were bulldozed by a 100-foot-wide avalanche and propelled down the mountain. Huld said his biggest fear was being pushed over a precipice. "Everywhere I looked it was coming at me . . . and fast. I got swept away and pummeled down."

The white wave carried him about 200 feet and delivered a savage beating in the process. When it stopped, he was waist-deep in snow, with an injured leg and lacerations to his face. According to the report, Huld freed himself from the snow, but his skis are still buried somewhere on the side of Mount Washington. An avalanche-safety class that was underway in the bowl began rescue procedures. One of the climbers escaped with minor injuries. The other was taken away by ambulance. Everyone survived, but they were lucky. According to National Geographic, about 150 people die in avalanches every year.

Avalanches are but one of the many environmental hazards found in the winter woods. Thin ice, crevasses, slippery slopes, falling ice and rock, trees collapsing under the weight of snow—the dangers are many. But dangers follow us everywhere we go, whether riding a bicycle or flying in a plane. Many of the things we do in life pose existential threats. Like anything else, the backcountry in winter requires due respect and caution, and we can mitigate the risks by being prepared and using good judgment.

WHAT LURKS ABOVE
Avalanches

For many of us, winter adventure means peaks and summits, whether for skiing, climbing, or snowshoeing. And anywhere there is a steep incline, there's the potential for avalanche, or massive waves of snow hurtling down the mountain at speeds of up to 120 MPH. Beautiful, fearsome, and deadly, these white walls are not something you want to witness up close.

Many popular locations prone to avalanches now have teams dedicated to educating people and minimizing the potential for harm. Some ski areas out West hire explosives experts to blow up snow masses that might prove a danger. In the Northeast, areas like the White Mountains boast both an Avalanche Education Foundation (wmaef.org) and the Mount Washington Avalanche Center (mountwashingtonavalanchecenter.org), run by the U.S. Forest Service, where you can pick up tips, read up on snow conditions, and even take classes on avalanche safety. The American Institute for Avalanche Research and Education is another great source for information (avtraining.org). The Mount Washington Avalanche Center's site has a color-coded avalanche forecaster that points out areas of danger, rated from low to extreme. Although predicting avalanches is no certain science, they do tend to follow patterns. A little education goes a long way. People who get caught in slides are often responsible for triggering them by recreating on unstable snow.

Anatomy of an Avalanche

Avalanches most commonly happen on inclines between 30 and 45 degrees, not-so-steep areas where snow doesn't immediately slide off and is able to collect. The danger comes in several types, the most common being loose-snow avalanches and slab avalanches. In a loose-snow avalanche, large piles of snow accumulate on slopes until something triggers their release. This might be warming conditions, something falling from above, or an unlucky explorer stepping on the wrong spot. Slab avalanches occur when snow deposits pile up (some sticky, some loose), usually over several different storms. With these stratified snows, the heavy, icy, upper layers can sit on top of drier, fluffier snow, waiting to be released, like a sledder on a hill. These are the avalanches where you see big fracture lines.

The terrain has a lot to do with avalanche danger. Bowls allow snow to collect en masse. Windswept ridges can trap big deposits. Snowpack on convex slopes is under tension and more likely to shift suddenly. Ravines, gullies, and slides not only aim the snow like a gun barrel; they often prevent routes of escape. Avalanches tend to occur on exposed, north-facing slopes that don't receive as much sun, which helps melt and adhere the snow together. South-facing slopes, where the sun hits all day, thaw and freeze, compacting into a more solid base. This is true until the warming temperatures of late winter and spring arrive, at which point south-facing inclines can prove more hazardous, as the snow melts quicker and becomes less stable. East-facing slopes are often the most dangerous of all due to wind slab loading, from prevailing westerly winds. In these cases, blowing gusts push the snow over ridges, where it collects into unstable piles.

Wind and weather also play a role. Avalanches tend to happen within 24 hours of a storm, most commonly after a large snowfall of a foot or more or a warm rainfall. Big blows often move snow around, taking it from a place of stability and stacking it somewhere precarious. Dramatic temperature swings can also create an unsettled snowpack.

When in Avalanche Country

If you're in an area known for avalanches, proceed with utmost caution. Examine the snowpack for layers and load. Look for signs of previous avalanches, such as big piles at the edge of gullies and trees that have snapped or lost branches on the uphill side. And consider an alternate route. If you decide to cross a steep slope, try to do so at the highest point possible. Tread carefully. Don't dillydally, taking pictures and enjoying the view; just get across the pitch. Travel one at a time rather than in a big group. Study the terrain and look for escape routes, into forests or across ridges.

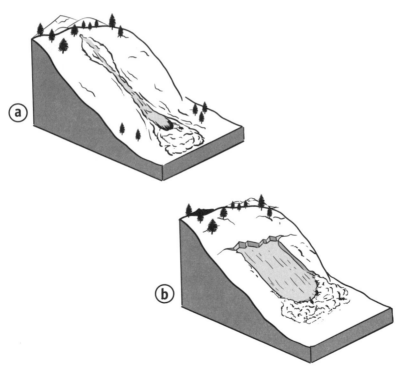

FIGURE 17. The two most common avalanche types are: (a) loose-snow avalanches and (b) slab avalanches. In a loose-snow avalanche, large deposits of accumulated snow slide downhill when triggered by warming conditions, by something falling on them, or by other disturbances to the snowpack. In a slab avalanche, snow builds up over several different storms. The resulting combination of heavy and fluffy snow can lead to large slabs breaking off from the snowpack and sliding downward.

Conversely, look out for hazards below, including precipices you could be swept off and fissures in the snow where a slab might let go.

What to Do in an Avalanche

If an avalanche lets loose above and you have the time, the best course of action is to try to get out of the way. Sometimes a quick dodge to the left or right can be the difference between life and death. If there are immovable landscape features, like rock walls or glades of trees, you can attempt to shelter behind them. If you have time, remove your skis or snowshoes and chuck your poles, as they'll only become hazards. Leave your pack on, however, because it can provide buoyancy. Yell to your group, letting someone know you are in danger. And, of course, make sure your avalanche beacon is on whenever you're hiking in avalanche country.

When there's no escaping, turn your back to the avalanche and crouch. Just before the snow hits, take a deep breath, like you would before jumping into water. Try with all of your might to pull for the surface, kicking your legs and swimming with the current of the snow. If possible, make for the edge of the avalanche, pushing off anything solid you come in contact with below. When movement begins to slow, thrust your arms out and around your face, creating an air pocket. Wriggle, kick, and punch at the snow around you to build as much space as you can. Reach up as high as you can to try to get a hand above the snow. If you're buried and disoriented, you can get an idea which way is up by spitting, because gravity will carry your gob down. Unless the snow is very shallow, you'll have a hard time digging yourself out. Keep reading this chapter for what to do and the gear you'll need if someone in your group does fall victim to an avalanche.

5

Cornices

Cornices are the sculpted faces of windblown snow that hang several feet off ridgelines. These snow formations drape delicately off the crest, resembling a breaking wave, and although they are beautiful, they can also prove extremely hazardous to hikers. Cornices can collapse underneath a climber crossing a ridgeline, and they can trigger avalanches when they break off in big chunks and fall. Cornices form when gusts blowing 15 to 25 MPH move the snow across the peak. Higher winds tend to push the snow completely over, whereas lower breezes don't shift enough of the white stuff. Many of the same factors that create avalanche danger make cornices unstable. These include rain; wide swings in temperature; and wet, heavy snowfall landing on dry-powder snowpack.

When crossing a ridge, be on the lookout for cornices. Keep an eye peeled to the leeward slope of the ridge, the side that gets less of the prevailing winds in the area. (In the Northeast, this is usually the east side.) Be aware that cornices are much easier to spot from below and the side and not as easy to see when they're right below you, especially in blowing or foggy conditions. The most hazardous part of the trail, unfortunately, is the crest of the ridge, which is where cornices usually fracture, although they can fracture well back from the ridge crest. If you must cross a cornice, take the

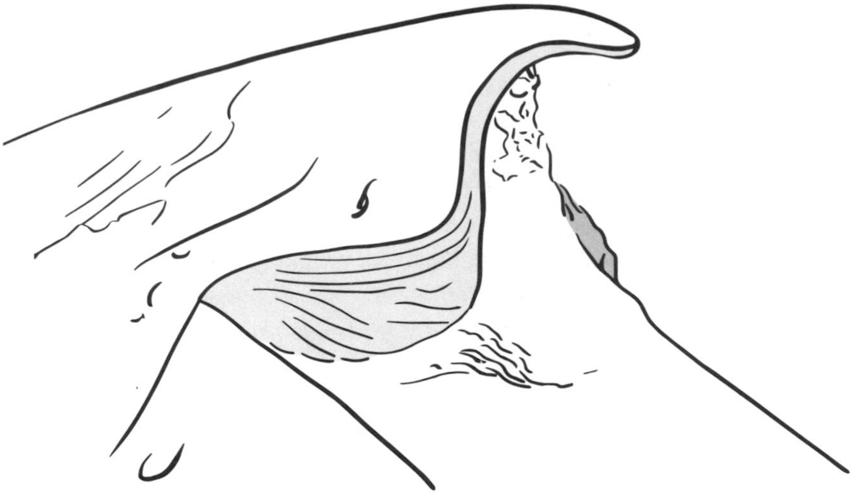

FIGURE 18. Wind blowing snow along ridgelines can form cornices. While beautiful, these unsupported buildups of snow can be dangerous, with the potential to collapse under hikers and to break off, triggering an avalanche.

5

same steps as you would traveling in avalanche country: spread out your group, move quickly, and be quiet, so you can hear any rumbles or groans beneath you.

Rock and Ice Fall

Many winter explorers wear helmets on their winter adventures and for good reason. Snow is not the only thing that falls in winter. Rocks and ice are major seasonal hazards underneath cliffs and even trees. Shifting snow can take down whole sides of a mountain, rock and all, and it often loosens debris. It's wise to be aware of what's above you, whenever you're traveling in the backcountry, and even wiser to put your helmet on when you're moving beneath precipices or snow- and ice-covered trees. People have been killed by falling icicles, which can reach speeds of up to 80 or 90 MPH. The dangers increase whenever the temperatures warm. Baxter Park closed Katahdin's Abol and Dudley trails in 2014 and 2016, respectively, because massive slides of snow and ice shifted the underlying granite, moving boulders the size of compact cars from their usual locations and creating unstable slopes.

WHAT LIES BELOW

A pristine blanket of snow draped across a field or forest is one of nature's great concealers. Just as water disguises dangers, such as submerged rocks, snow hides similar hazards. These might include boulders on a backcountry ski slope or open water below a trail. Skiers can stay safe by skiing packed trails or investigating a route on the climb up. Hikers can test the snow ahead with their poles before putting their feet down.

Tree Wells

Most people never have occasion to climb underneath the tree skirt of a conifer, but if you do—perhaps when nature calls—know that you might have trouble getting out. Tree wells are the depressions that form at the base of evergreens, thanks to the lower branches funneling soft snow into a doughnut around the trunk. Another term for this condition is "spruce traps." These hazards are usually encountered by backcountry skiers who ski too close to a conifer after a big snow and become trapped, as the walls of the well collapse around them. Tree wells are second only to avalanches in immersion deaths, and they've claimed dozens of lives over the years. If you do find yourself falling into one of these depressions, try to keep your cool. Just as in quicksand, struggling and thrashing only exacerbates the problem, causing you to slide deeper in. Instead, do like you would in an avalanche, using your hands to create a breathing space and then wriggling and rocking to loosen the grip of the snow. If you have an avalanche beacon, make sure it's on; likewise, if you can reach your cell phone, dig it out. Yell to other members of your party or nearby skiers.

Vegetation Traps

The vegetation of the winter backcountry poses several challenges to outdoor adventurers, especially those on skis. These include thickets that all but wrap their arms around you and hold you in, logs submerged beneath the snow, tangles of underbrush, and areas of krummholz, those gnarly stunted trees that grow just below treeline. In best-case scenarios, these obstacles simply tangle or slow you, but on occasion they can send you flying and break bones. Staying safe often means keeping to packed trails or checking slopes before you begin the downhill.

5

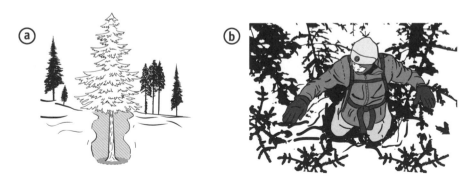

FIGURE 19. Tree wells (a) and vegetation traps (b) can be hazardous, even deadly, for hikers and skiers who aren't paying attention. Always be aware of your surroundings and stay on marked, packed trails as much as possible.

WATER CROSSINGS

Making your way across brooks, streams, and open water carries hazards any time of year. There's always the chance you'll slip and end up in the drink. When it's well below freezing and ice is involved, the dangers multiply exponentially, although there are also benefits. Thanks to ice, we often can cross bodies of water we'd have to go around in summer, which can save a lot of time. And views from the middle of expansive ponds and lakes, with no obstructions to bother you, can be spectacular. But safety, as ever, is paramount.

The first step is to observe the conditions before you. Is there open water? Are there paths where the ice looks solid all the way across? Is water moving underneath the ice? Are there tributaries feeding the body of water or eddies where currents continue to spin? Do you see cracks or fissures, open spots or wetness? Are there a lot of bubbles just below the surface? (Clear ice is generally more solid than ice riddled with air pockets.) Could there be salt in the water because you are near an ocean? (Tidal or brackish waterways do not freeze as solidly as fresh water.)

Ice Color

Remember the venerable saw: "Thick and blue, tried and true; thin and crispy, way too risky." It's a handy guide. You can often judge ice by the hue it takes.

- **Blue or clear:** This is the ice you want, the strongest and likely the thickest. This is the safest ice around.
- **Dark black:** Often very thin. Best avoided.
- **Light gray:** Usually indicates melting ice. Steer clear.
- **White:** It's typically bubbles that give ice a white aspect, and these air pockets make ice less stable.
- **Snow white:** Snow acts as an insulator, and snow-covered ice is generally not as safe as open ice.

Streams and Rivers

Brooks, streams, and rivers pose a conundrum for hikers: They tend to be shallower than ponds and lakes and not nearly as wide, making them tempting to cross, but they also often contain moving water, which doesn't freeze as quickly or as solidly as flat water. Many hikers, even during winter, strip off their boots and wade across shallow, unfrozen waterways. Because your feet are likely heated from hiking, this isn't as bad as you might think, so long as you can get them dry and warm on the far side. If you step out into sticky snow, your feet and boots get cold faster, and you don't want to get any part of your clothing wet, especially if it's windy, so never allow your boots to take a soaking—although it's better to get the outside of fully waterproof boots wet than to rock-hop and risk falling in. If the stream is frozen, take stock of the situation as described above, looking for solid paths across. Stream crossings often require scouting up- and downstream, seeking out the best option. Do you see places where others have successfully crossed? Follow their footsteps. Logs, rocks, or other natural bridges are preferable to ice, wherever possible. Once you've selected your route, use your poles or throw rocks to check the ice. When you feel you've found a safe route, continuously probe the ice ahead with your pole. Traction devices, such as Microspikes, provide better grip on your way across and are recommended when crossing ice. Spread out your group and move single file, as you would in avalanche country, making your way across as quickly as possible. Wearing snowshoes or skis also helps distribute your weight, which could enable a safe crossing of ice that otherwise might be hazardous.

Ponds and Lakes

Crossing big bodies of water requires a little more deliberation than streams and brooks; after all, you'll be out over deeper water longer. But the techniques are the same. Check the ice for safety and look for thin spots or places where the ice looks milky. Always aim for clear ice when possible. Many winter explorers drill holes to check thickness, especially if they're leading a group. If you are crossing a lake in a group, keep the members of your party separated by about 50 feet. As well as being generally useful, rope is a good way to help maintain that distance, with everyone holding on to sections 50 feet apart. Skis and snowshoes can help distribute your weight more evenly across a larger surface. If you're especially nervous, carry your Microspikes in your hand—they'll help you grip the ice if you do fall through.

5

If You Fall Through

If you fall through the ice, keep your wits about you. Most people have one minute to get their breathing under control, ten minutes before their muscles become too cold to be useful, and one hour before they lose consciousness. That first minute is critical. Most people who plunge through the ice into freezing water drown because they start thrashing around and gasping for air, which uses valuable energy and often causes them to slip underwater with their mouths open. If you can pull yourself together, taking deep breaths at the surface and calming down, your chances of survival rise greatly. The next step is to aim yourself at the point where you went in. Presumably, the ice is thick enough there to support you, because it did up to the point where you fell through. Don't attempt to pull yourself out using straight arms and the ice as leverage, the way you would at a swimming pool. Stretch yourself out onto the ice as far as you can horizontally and kick your feet as if you're swimming in an attempt to propel yourself up onto the ice. As you do, dig in your fingers and pull with everything you've got. Once you're far enough out of the water, roll away from the hole and then crawl or walk yourself back to safety. On shore, follow the steps to prevent hypothermia outlined on pages 70–73 earlier in this chapter.

Think about recent weather conditions. Has rain fallen lately or has unseasonably warm weather visited the region? Have there been successive days of deep cold? Even during a cold snap, ice might not be ready for crossing, as deep lakes take longer to freeze than shallow ponds. Keep the season in mind, too. Early winter or early spring ice usually proves less stable than midwinter ice. After considering these factors, use your trekking pole to give the ice a thump. A deep, hollow thud suggests the ice is more than 3 inches deep, the minimum required to support the average hiker, although most experts wouldn't recommend crossing thin ice over deep water or for long distances. If you're traveling in a group, 4 inches is preferred, and older ice, which might have been affected by any recent thaws, should be even thicker, as much as 8 inches. If the sound is more "thwacky" or sharp, take an alternate route, as the ice isn't very thick. Always remember: Just because you stepped on one safe section doesn't mean the whole area is safe to cross. Ice tends to vary in thickness across a pond, lake, or stream.

➜ **PRO TIP** Some winter explorers carry an "ice bag" with them, which includes a flotation vest, an ice pick for climbing out of a hole, and a dry compression sack with a full change of clothes. It might seem like overkill, but if you're traveling through a region with multiple ice crossings and are in charge of the safety of a group, it's a good idea.

5

Glaciers and Crevasses

Although glaciers are receding everywhere due to climate change, they are still prevalent in many recreational areas, and these ice mountains pose a unique set of challenges. Crossing a glacier is unlike hiking a snow-covered granite slope, and you absolutely should either take a class on the subject or go with an experienced guide. Why is it so different from a rocky mountain slope? Glaciers are built of compacted layers of ice and snow, and occasionally these massive ice mounds fracture, creating deep, dangerous fissures called crevasses. These ice holes can get covered by snow, transforming them into natural booby traps. Writers have filled whole books on glacier travel, and it requires a technical skill set, including the use of crampons, axes, ropes, and belays. Take a class or go with a veteran mountaineer before embarking on a glacier trip alone. Actually, never go alone.

Moats, Bridges, and Undercuts

Boulders, logs, and crevasses are not the only hazards concealed by snow. Moving water, warming and freezing temperatures, and certain terrain conditions create an array of challenging natural snow formations. When water flows underneath a mound of snow, it can create bridges and undercut areas where the snow seems solid but has been carved out from below. These bridges can collapse easily beneath the weight of a hiker. Depending upon how high up you are, it might mean a brutal and dangerous fall. Or it might just result in a twisted ankle or knee.

FIGURE 20. Moats (a), bridges (b), and undercuts (c) are caused by moving water and are common once the spring melt sets in. All are potential dangers for winter recreationists. Watch out for them and avoid crossing, if possible.

Bridges and undercuts become more common in the spring, as the melt sets in. That's when we often see a similar hazard develop: moats. These channels appear during the transition between snow and rock. The sun warms boulders, causing nearby snow to melt away and creating a gap between the rock and remaining snow that is not unlike a crevasse and can be difficult to cross.

When hiking through terrain that might contain these conditions, use your poles as you would when crossing ice. Test the snow ahead of you with each step. Roping up with your group is a smart move. Steer clear of the areas where snow and rock meet and try to stay on areas uncovered by snow wherever possible. Listen for moving water and avoid it if you can. If you must traverse a moat, look for areas with the densest snow and try to cross early in the day, when it's colder.

➜ THE HUMAN ELEMENT

One of the many beauties of winter travel is the solitude it affords. Standing miles from the nearest town in a remote and frozen landscape with brilliant white, unbroken snow as far as you can see is a sublime, restorative experience. But winter travel doesn't always match this ideal. You might be taking in the views on a backcountry lake accessed by a lonely trail no one uses, even during the beautiful days of summer, when you hear the roar of an engine echoing off the surrounding peaks. Moments later, a parade of colorful snowmobilers tears by. Wherever you go these days, there are people. Although interactions like this can disturb your winter reverie, they can be a minor miracle if you have an emergency.

Remember: Most people are out there for the same reasons you are—enjoying the winter outdoors—even if they do so in different ways. Keep in mind a few etiquette tips for coexisting in the boreal woods.

SHARING THE TRAIL WITH ATVS/SNOWMOBILES

In many corners of the Northeast, ATVs and snowmobiles proliferate. Maine and New Hampshire, for example, boast extensive highways of trails capable of taking snowmobilers from one end of the state to the other. Many of these trails cross, run parallel to, or join trail networks used by snowshoers and cross-country skiers, so meeting vehicles is almost inevitable—unless you're traveling somewhere, like parts of Baxter or the White Mountains, where they're not allowed in the backcountry.

Snowmobiles are loud. You'll be aware of them long before they notice you. The onus is thus on you to be vigilant when they're around. If you hear a gas-powered vehicle approaching, step off the trail in a spot where the riders can see you. If you're using trekking poles, gather them so they're not a hazard to the driver. Use the moment to rest or have a snack. Look down the trail for additional sleds, since snowmobiles often travel in packs. Sometimes the lead sled holds up fingers to indicate the number behind him, so watch for that signal. Once you're confident all of the snowmobiles have passed, get back on trail. Use the same etiquette when meeting ATV riders.

Happily, the days of snowmobilers battling on-foot recreationists for use of trails seem to be fading. A spirit of cooperation has evolved, with both sides realizing they have more in common than not.

SAFETY DURING HUNTING SEASON

This one is easy: Wear blaze orange. Any time your travels take you into regions where hunters might be pursuing prey, fly the flag of the season. Put on an orange cap, hang a blazing hoodie over your pack, and grab your brightest jacket. Here are some other tips for sharing the woods with hunters.

- **Be aware of the season.** Before heading out, check the state's fish and game department to see if it's open season on any animal. Most big-game hunting is closed during winter, but deer, bear, and moose hunts occur in late fall in some states, overlapping with snow season. Many states allow hunters to pursue hares, grouse, squirrels, bobcats, porcupines, and coyotes and to trap beavers during the cold-weather months.

- **Check the rules of the specific land agency where you're headed.** Some places, like parks and wilderness areas, ban or restrict hunting, although others don't. Find out ahead of time.

- **Look to see if the land is posted with No Trespassing signs.** Landowners, private or public, often close or restrict certain areas to hunting. Keep your eye out for signage.

- **Consider the weekend.** Hunting is closed in many states on Sundays, but not everywhere, so make sure you check before you go.

- **Avoid bushwhacking.** Staying on-trail limits your chances of running into hunters, who roam the backcountry in search of game.

- **Head for the hills.** Most hunters avoid mountains and peaks, seeking easier terrain.

- **Be extra careful at dawn and dusk.** Because animals are on the move at these times, hunters are too.

- **Make noise.** Letting hunters know you're around keeps you safe.

5

➔ MENTAL CHALLENGES

Everyone expects outdoor adventure to be a physical challenge in winter, and it is. Post-holing and trail breaking, weather difficulties, cardio stress, slips and falls, unforgiving landscape—none of it is easy. What many don't anticipate, however, is how much stress dealing with all of that puts on us mentally. Distances can seem longer in winter because we move slower. Loads are heavier. Gnawing hunger caused by an insatiable need for calories can make us irritable. The sun goes down earlier. The constant cold can dampen your spirit. An unexpected soaking or momentarily feeling lost can cause panic and fear.

None of this outweighs all of the good that winter adventuring brings. Science has proven that simply being outside is beneficial for many reasons, from increased vitamin D to greater happiness due to light, and that doesn't stop during wintertime. In fact, getting outside might be even better for you in winter than in summer. Spending time in the sun is such an effective antidote for combating seasonal affective disorder, the depressive malady associated with winter darkness, that many doctors actually prescribe it.

Then there's the rush that comes from setting a goal or meeting a challenge head-on. Winter is undoubtedly a more difficult environment for outdoor pursuits than the other three seasons. Spending a weekend camping in winter, while your friends point out that you're crazy, often feels like a real accomplishment. Hauling oneself to the top of a snow-covered peak or testing one's mettle on an epic nordic ski is hugely satisfying for anyone.

➔ WHEN THINGS GO WRONG

As any ranger can tell you, bad things happen to good backpackers, even people who are careful, experienced, and well prepared. When things go wrong, winter hiking requires many of the same skills as summer adventuring. The number one goal in both cases is to keep your head about you. Sit down, pause for a minute, and think through the options. Panic doesn't help anyone, regardless of the time of year. Whether you break through ice or a party member takes a major fall, you're best served by taking a few deep breaths and making a sensible plan. If you've followed regular preventative protocols, setting up contingencies for emergencies, letting people know where you're going, and preparing evacuation routes, help likely is not far away. Emergencies are scary, but it helps to have a basic idea of what you should do when one arises. The following principles will put you in good stead.

1. **Size up the scene.** The first step is simple situation awareness, taking a moment to consider the scene you're facing and identifying ongoing or additional threats to the safety of the group. In other words, what's the next (hiking) shoe to drop? *Someone was dragged down the slope by the avalanche. Will you all fall over the cliff if you try to reach her?* The first rule of rescue is to stay safe. According to wilderness rescue protocols, the injured individual is the fourth-most important consideration. We must first think of the safety of ourselves, our partners, the broader public, and then the patient. The situation only becomes worse if others are injured in the process of helping the patient.

2. **Assess the seriousness of the problem.** Some injuries cause immediate panic. A head wound, for example, may seem horrific at first. Trauma to the scalp bleeds and bleeds and bleeds. Clean off the wound, however, and

you may find it to be a minor scrape. Conversely, a person who fell several feet might look OK on the outside only to be hemorrhaging blood internally from the impact with a hidden boulder. It's important to get a handle on the severity of the issue at hand. You need to locate the source of a bleed, for example, even if it means removing clothing in the cold. It's also imperative to check the entire body for issues. Sometimes the most severe injury in a fall is the one you don't see.

3. **Determine resources.** Establish how many assets you have at your disposal. Who's the natural leader? Is it the person with the most experience or the individual with the most *medical* experience? Who should you send for help? Should you send *anyone* for help? The natural leader in a sketchy situation may not be whom you think it will be, and the group leader may not be the same person as the medical leader. Has someone completely lost his head in the face of the emergency? Factor that in, as well.

4. **Create a plan.** By their very nature, emergencies are unpredictable, and you have to handle each one in its own way. Not all injuries are created equal; some require immediate evacuation, whereas others can be managed during the remainder of the trip. Think your plan through. You'll feel foolish when the rescue helicopter you summoned arrives for a head injury that turned out to be just a cut. Once you've considered your options, keep the following in mind:

   - **The future safety of the entire group.** Factor in the difficulty of the evacuation and the risk to any responders. Does it make sense to hike out on a dark mountain trail that you don't know in falling temperatures, putting everyone at risk, for a broken bone? Again, further injuries create further problems.

   - **The best interest of the patient.** In many cases, staying put might be a better option than extrication. Make the victim as comfortable as possible. Assign someone to monitor her condition and provide whatever care is needed.

   - **The best interest of the party.** Make sure that if you do hit the trail, everyone stays warm, hydrated, and fed. Try to keep the vibe as positive as possible.

   - **Adapt and improvise.** Remember the "ideal to real" concept from wilderness medicine? What is the optimal treatment for your problem? How can you get closest to that using what you have on hand? You'd be surprised what you can assemble with a little ingenuity, duct tape, webbing, and a backpack frame. And if your solution doesn't seem to be working, you have to come up with something else.

   - **Consider conditions.** If the weather becomes severe, you might have to change your plan and build shelters or a fire for the safety of the group.

5

EVACUATION

Occasionally someone in a party is going to be hurt badly enough to require immediate evacuation. Usually this is due to some form of trauma (injury) or a medical condition (caused environmentally or internally). It might be something as terrifying as a stroke or as innocuous as an unstable ankle. Typically, you have three options: The patient can self-rescue, moving out unassisted; he can walk out with the help of members of your group or external rescuers; or he can be transported out via litter. Sometimes it's a combination of the above. A hiker with an injured knee, for example, might walk miles with a splint but then find it too difficult or painful to continue. She might then require the help of members of the group, who put their arms around her upper body to assist her in walking. But late in the day, when everyone becomes tired and the victim simply can't go any farther, you might call for help.

The first task is establishing what sort of rescue you require. If you think you'll need assistance, get word out quickly. Whether help comes in the form of search and rescue personnel carrying a litter or a helicopter dropping from the sky, it takes time to scramble the required teams. A long, all-day litter carry could involve as many as 40 people, and it is a monumental and prolonged effort to simply get everyone to the scene. Calling for an air evacuation should be weighed carefully, and the final decision will be made above your head. Anytime a helicopter flies, it puts those onboard at risk. Add in mountains, darkness, and unpredictable weather, and the hazards grow dramatically. If there's any possibility of self-rescue, you should wholeheartedly make the effort.

PREPARING FOR HELP

If there is no way to get your patient out safely with the resources you have available, you'll have to request assistance. Before you do so, make sure you have all the information rescuers need to know. This includes:

Location. It seems obvious that rescuers need to know where you are, but so many outdoor groups have a difficult time describing their location with any detail, even when on marked trails. If you have a GPS, provide coordinates, either longitude and latitude or Universal Transverse Mercator, better known as UTM. If not, give as much detail as you can, including the trail (if you're on one), approximate mileage from the trailhead, and visible landmarks. Dig out your map and find your precise location, estimating coordinates and describing your location in relation to bodies of water, campgrounds, peaks, or other landscape features. Be aware that when you call 911, the dispatcher, who could be in a city hundreds of miles away, may not know the terrain.

Problem. Explain what happened and why you need emergency help. Again, be as specific as possible, since it impacts the kind of response you get and the kind of equipment rescuers bring.

Patient. Describe the patient. This includes name, age, sex, height, weight, and medical history. Find out if he or she has any allergies, takes any medication, or has ever had a similar issue before this trip.

Type of Assistance Requested. Do you think you need a litter? Does the patient require certain medication (say, insulin) or first-aid equipment, such as a defibrillator? Consider this ahead of time, too.

Resources. Rescuers need to know how many people are in your group, as well as all ages, conditions, relevant medical experience, relationships to patient (that is, family, friends, members of an organized group).

Plan. What is your plan? Are you moving toward the trailhead or are you staying put? How long will it take you to get to the parking lot?

Weather Conditions and Other Hazards. It's very helpful for rescuers to know if the mountain is shrouded by fog or is being blasted by wind, because that rules out helicopters. The temperature, too, lets them know how much time they might have. Are you in a shelter? Tell them that.

When calling for help, speak clearly, slowly, and enunciate. Take your time, even if you're nervous. This stuff really matters. Taking an outdoor medicine course before you venture out greatly benefits you as well.

5

SENDING FOR HELP

It seems like cell service always cuts out when you need it most. If your communication devices don't work, you'll need to send members of your group down the trail to find help. Make sure they take a note containing all of the above information with them. In some cases, they'll find their phones resume working before they make it to the trailhead, and they can place a call; in others, they'll have to continue to the parking lot. Either way, they need to have all of the details at the ready for rescuers.

When sending for help, select a team of three strong, capable hikers, designating one as the leader. Selecting a trio is wise because it means that even if one of them gets injured, one can stay with the new patient and the other can still get through. Ensure they have food, equipment, first-aid supplies, a map, and bivy gear, in case something goes wrong on their journey. Make sure everyone understands exactly where they are going and insist they stick to the plan. (It's not uncommon for rescues to include long searches for party members who split up or decided to take a shortcut.) Also remember that, while they need to make haste, the safety of their group is priority number one. Hurtling down the mountain to get help and getting themselves injured only creates more problems.

WHEN TO CHANGE YOUR ROUTE

Ah, the best-laid plans. Winter in the woods is unpredictable. Storms come out of nowhere, bodies of water are unfrozen and uncrossable, sections of trail are unstable—any number of factors that can force a group to reconsider its route. You should always have an alternate plan and know potential exits from your current route. As the old saying goes: Hope for the best, plan for the worst.

Weather is probably the single biggest factor in changing a plan. Even with today's modern forecasting, storms change and morph and confound weather prognosticators. You may devise a plan based on a hike up a certain ridge only to find at the base that the mountain got rain when you were expecting snow. Now avalanche danger has heightened and is in the red zone. Or your group may have set out in the sun, only to be blasted by a blizzard that was supposed to track far to the north. Be wary of loops and traverses in winter, as unexpected conditions near the end might force a choice between continuing into dangerous or difficult territory or retracing a long path back to the start. Good hikers are always ready to change their plans. As hikers like to say, the mountain will always be there to climb another day. No objective is worth putting your group at risk, especially in cold weather.

IT'S ALWAYS OK TO TURN BACK

Turning back is often the better part of valor when adventuring in winter, whether you're hiking, skiing, ice climbing, or mountaineering. There is no shame in it; in fact, it's the wise and noble thing to do in many cases. (Ask any ranger.) Turn around anytime the following occurs:

The Weather Changes. Everyone knows you should curtail your trip if a sudden blizzard drops. But what if temperatures warm or plummet precipitously? What if a soaking rain falls? These are the kinds of conditions that often require you to turn for home. If you lose visibility, if the weather renders your gear inadequate or creates any unexpected hazards, it makes sense to turn around or alter your plans.

Injuries Happen. Again, it seems like a no-brainer: When someone turns an ankle or wrenches a knee, you should abandon your adventure. But what about smaller problems? Even a minor injury can grow into a major problem in cold weather if it slows down your group or causes you to make frequent stops. Time is of the essence on a winter trail with limited daylight. If everyone else in the group is standing around waiting, they can begin to chill easily, inviting frostbite and hypothermia. Proceed cautiously any time a member of the party gets hurt.

If You Get Wet. Wetness and winter do not mix. If someone in your group gets wet and is unable to dry themselves through exertion or a change of clothes, you should make for the exit. Cold injuries are insidious, sneaking up on people, and the consequences can be dire.

If You Have the Wrong Gear for the Terrain. This one trips up so many winter adventurers. People strike out on an exciting excursion and do fine for much of the way. Later in the trip, though, the weather or the conditions change, and the gear the group brought with them is no longer able to keep them safe. For example, a light snow turns to a soaking rain, and everyone left their waterproof jackets in the car. Or a group steadily ascends a peak with their Microspikes, only to find themselves on wide-open ice fields above treeline where their little spikes are no longer adequate. The incline and the sheerness of the ice requires crampons, axes, and rope. But they push on because the summit is right there—which is the wrong strategy. Whenever you find your gear is no longer doing the job, you should err on the side of caution.

If Conditions Slow You Down. Darkness comes early in winter, even more so in mountainous and woodsy regions, where the landscape can block the sun. Combined with the slow speeds the season often requires, early dark means sometimes there simply isn't enough time in the day to accomplish your goals. Always be mindful of the hour. Consider how long it's taken you to get where you are. Never move faster than the slowest person in your group. If weather changes or other conditions cause delays, it's wise to return another day.

LOST AND ALONE

There are myriad ways to get turned around in the winter woods. You might step away from camp to see a view you passed earlier and forget the way back. You could lose your bearings in whiteout conditions. Or you may want a break and tarry longer than the rest of your group then are unable to find them. It's always best to stick together when hiking, regardless of the time of year. But things happen, and people inevitably, at some point in their hiking lives, get separated. If you find yourself lost and alone, do your best to keep your head. Many studies have shown that a calm, rational mind and a positive attitude dramatically improve your chances of surviving a difficult situation. Also consider that, despite the cold, winter can help lost persons get found in a variety of ways: You can often track your own prints in the snow to find your way back to camp; others can track you for the same reason. And your colorful clothes contrast with the monotone backdrop, making it easier for rescuers to spot you.

If you're certain you're lost, you can take many steps to help yourself. The following is an easy-to-follow guide for getting yourself found.

Blow Your Whistle. Every hiker should have a whistle for just this purpose. Three short blasts is the universal distress signal.

Mark Your Territory. It's a good idea to make yourself as visible as possible. If you're in the woods, hang brightly colored clothing or stuff sacks or whatever you can spare from trees. These items help searchers spot you. At night, hang cyalume sticks (a.k.a. glow sticks), if you have them. Build a fire (see page 142 in Chapter 8, Campsites).

Not only does a fire provide heat and comfort, it sends up smoke signals during the day and casts a glow at night.

Build Camp. In most cases, it's best to stay in one place, unless you are confident of your navigation skills. The other members of your group are probably already looking for you, and it's likely they are not far away. Keeping an eye on the time and the weather conditions, consider the chance you'll be out overnight. By midafternoon, you should establish a camp, setting up some sort of shelter. If you have your backpack and all of the supplies you need, put up your tent. It's another spot of color, and you'll be prepared come nightfall. If not, start looking for natural shelter. This might mean a spot beneath a dense evergreen, if the conditions are right; an overhang; or a snow den. (See snowcraft on pages 154–157 in Chapter 8.) Try to find some sort of natural insulator to keep yourself off the ground. Boughs are ideal for this. Cut or break off some leafy branches from nearby conifers and arrange them in layers for a bed. If you don't have a sleeping bag, find as much dry, natural material—leaves, moss, etcetera—as you can and fill your jacket with it. Believe it or not, this will keep you warmer. One of the simplest, most effective shelters is a lean-to built of evergreen branches with a fire in front of it.

Walk with a Plan. If you think you are capable of self-rescue, make a plan. Aimless walking only gets you more lost, more tired, and even farther away from your group. Consult your map and compass if you have one. See if you can identify any nearby landmarks. Try to recall how you ended up where you are. Did you cross a trail or see a body of water? Do your best to pinpoint your location on a map and look for logical routes out. If you don't have a map, study the landscape around you. Do you recognize any features? Listen. Can you hear water or a road?

Find Your Way Out. If all else fails, it makes sense to search for a more familiar area by incrementally hiking in each of the cardinal directions. Starting from your base camp, walk five minutes in the direction you think is most likely to bring you to a recognizable place. Mark your way, either by prints, building snow cairns, or using branches arranged in an arrow. Blow your whistle as you go. If you don't see anything you recognize, turn back to your base camp. Do the same in the opposite direction, going for five minutes and creating a path. Again, if you find nothing, turn back for camp. Move out in the other two directions for five minutes each. If you still can't find anything useful, try hiking in the first direction again, going five minutes farther this time. Repeat this grid until you come across a landmark or a trail, always returning to your base camp and always blowing your whistle. Keep your ears tuned for water or human-made sounds. This approach, if performed in a disciplined manner, can help you find your way out of the woods, but it can also get you further lost, so be cautious and keep a clear head. The beauty of the cross grid is that even if you can't find your way out, you've created trails leading rescuers directly to your location.

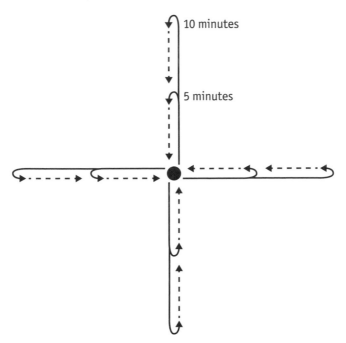

10 minutes

5 minutes

FIGURE 21. To use the find-me cross, build an impossible-to-miss home base out of available materials, such as downed branches. From this hub, walk five minutes in one direction then return to your home base. Repeat in the remaining three directions. If you don't recognize your surroundings, repeat again, extending your walks to ten minutes each. Repeat until you recognize a trail or a landmark.

5

➜ AVALANCHE AND RESCUE GEAR

We all know that we need to switch on our avalanche beacons any time we're in avalanche country, but what do you do if someone's goes off? What steps do you take if you see someone swept under by a big slide? Wearing beacons and carrying transceivers is no help if you don't know how to use them.

If you see someone trapped by an avalanche, you must first focus on the last point where you saw the person and predict the likely course where the individual might be buried. Keep your eye on that region, identifying landmarks that might help pinpoint the person's location. Estimate the distance between you and that spot. Once the avalanche has stopped moving, head as fast as is safely possible to the point where the victim was last seen, remembering that a rescuer's first priority is always one's own safety.

When you reach the site, begin your signal search down the path of the avalanche using the transceiver, which emits a series of beeps that get successively louder as you approach the victim and also displays the distance to the victim's beacon. At first, you're simply looking to find a signal. Sweep your way down the avalanche field, listening carefully to your device. You should aim to make switch-backs to within 30 feet of the edge of the slide, with no more than 50 feet between them. In other words, create a zigzag pattern.

Once you have a signal, begin the coarse search, slowing down and methodically going over the area near the strongest beacon signal. Try to narrow your region of interest to about 10 feet, making sure the signal remains strong. This becomes your fine search area. Bend down so that your beacon is directly on the surface of the snow and focus your efforts on the strongest signal. Get out your avalanche probe and begin probing in concentric circles around this point, checking every 10 inches for the resistance of a body.

When you believe you've located your victim, fix the probe in the snow right there. Set yourself up downhill from the probe, so that you're not packing snow onto the victim's airway, and then begin digging uphill toward the victim. In any deep-snow situation, you want to begin digging 1.5 times the burial depth of your probe. If you have multiple rescuers, one should concentrate on the area imme-diately downhill from the probe and the other 1.5 times the depth downhill. You want to excavate a 6-foot-wide trough, angled toward the subject, and you want to throw your snow to the sides.

After fifteen minutes, the victim's chance of survival decreases by 60 percent, so time is very much of the essence in an avalanche situation. Many alpine and mountaineering organizations offer avalanche safety training that covers the res-cue trinity—beacon, shovel, and probe—and if you are planning on adventuring anywhere avalanche-prone, you absolutely should take a class. Look for AMC offerings at outdoors.org/activities.

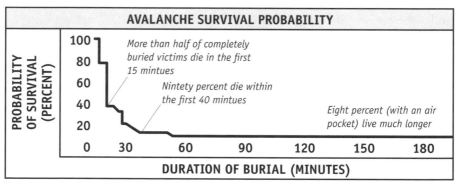

AVALANCHE SURVIVAL PROBABILITY

PROBABILITY OF SURVIVAL (PERCENT)

More than half of completely buried victims die in the first 15 mintues

Nintety percent die within the first 40 mintues

Eight percent (with an air pocket) live much longer

DURATION OF BURIAL (MINUTES)

This chart shows the probability of survival, based on how long someone is buried under an avalanche. After fifteen minutes, the chance of survival is less than 50 percent.

Adapted from a chart by Steven Achelis, which tracks the survival rate of 301 avalanche burials that occurred in Canada between 1981 and 2004.

AVALUNG/AVALANCHE AIRBAG PACK

The leading cause of death among avalanche victims is asphyxiation. People buried beneath the snow use up oxygen in the snow pocket where they're trapped and replace it with carbon dioxide. Once the oxygen is depleted, they begin to breathe the CO_2 they've exhaled and eventually expire. After 45 minutes, the chances of rescue are drastically reduced; only 20 percent are ever recovered. Hopefully, you'll never fall victim to an avalanche, but there are a couple of devices that can help you survive that worst-case scenario, should it happen.

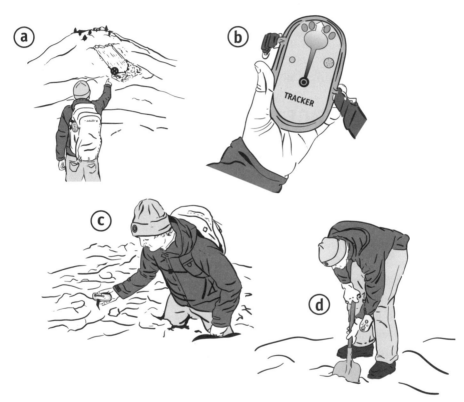

FIGURE 22. When searching for an avalanche victim, there are several key steps. First, begin by (a) surveying the avalanche closely, paying special attention to the last spot you saw the victim and predicting where the avalanche likely left the person buried. Once the avalanche has stopped and it is safe to do so, go to the site where you think the victim might be and (b) begin your search using your avalanche beacon transceiver, which will emit beeps that grow louder as you (c) approach the victim's location, narrowing it down to a 10-foot square and then probing in concentric circles. (d) Once you have found the victim's location, position yourself downhill from the victim and begin excavating snow, making sure to throw all removed snow far enough to the sides that it will not press down on the victim or impede rescue.

One such device is the Avalung, a 9-inch tube with a small mouthpiece that straps to your chest. In a burial situation, it filters the usable air from the snow around you and expels CO_2 well below your face, giving you a greater chance of surviving until someone can dig you out. Some manufacturers claim the Avalung can give you up to an hour of added breathing time. Several experts have challenged the device, questioning whether people really would be able to grab it and get it to their mouths before being pinned by the weight of the snow, but it adds only 9 ounces to your load and, when used properly, could save your life.

Another avalanche safety tool is the avalanche airbag pack. These inflatable packs consist of bladders that expand at the pull of a strap, giving you greater buoyancy in the event of a snow slide, the idea being that your increased volume will help lift you to the surface. You can buy backpacks with air bags installed or purchase bladders to insert into your own pack. Many of the commercial versions allow you to remove the bags for hikes outside avalanche country.

➔ ANIMAL DANGER

In the next chapter, we'll learn how to track animals. If you follow that guide, there's a chance you could catch up to a live one. If so, give it space. Watching wildlife is often the highlight of our wilderness explorations, but animals are not outdoors for our amusement. They are wild beasts going about their business and must be respected. Rangers like to use what we call the "rule of thumb": stick out your arm, shut one eye, and extend your thumb. Can you cover the animal with it? If not, you're too close.

When it comes to animals, the same rules apply year-round. Avoidance is your safest course. Don't feed any creature in the wild, no matter how cute or how hungry it looks. Feeding wildlife disrupts their natural patterns, habituates them to humans, and attracts them to your group. Many people find it entertaining to feed squirrels when camping, but they don't seem so adorable when they're digging holes into your pack to get more of that gorp you gave them earlier. Keep your camp clean and your food in airtight containers outside your tent or sleeping space. Move your garbage away from your camping area and hang it from a tree limb.

Occasionally you'll stumble onto a beast as large as you—or at least one that gives you pause, such as a moose, coyote, or big cat. Bears are less common in winter, since they tend to be hibernating, but they will leave their dens to forage if the temperatures warm and they're hungry. Most want nothing to do with you. Major concerns occur in three situations: when animals are breeding and you step between a male and a female; in the spring, if you step between a mother and her offspring; or if you manage to corner a critter, and it feels trapped.

If you stumble upon an angry beast, make yourself as large and loud as possible, spreading your arms overhead, yelling, and banging noisy items together, and back away slowly, keeping your eyes on the animal while avoiding actual eye contact. Most megafauna are opportunists. If you appear to be more trouble than you're

FIGURE 23. When viewing an animal in the wild, stick out your fist and extend your thumb so that it covers the animal. If you can still see the creature around the edges of your thumb, you're too close.

5

worth, they'll slink off. But bears and moose and big cats that stand their ground can pose real danger to humans. Luckily, the body language of these animals is not difficult to interpret. If they lay their ears back, expose their teeth, or take aggressive postures (lowering their heads and extending their feet toward you or scratching the ground), they feel threatened and mean to attack.

BEARS

Black bears don't tend to be problems in winter, but they can be active any time of year. Although small compared to the rest of North America's bear population, averaging about 250 pounds, black bears can grow up to 400 pounds or more. They are widely distributed across the continent and are particularly prevalent in the woodlands of the Northeast.

Black bears are grazers who must consume 5,000 calories a day most of the year. In the fall, as they're fattening up for winter, they eat as many as 20,000 calories a day. Most calories come in the form of produce, such as berries, roots, grasses, nuts, seeds, and honey. But these omnivores also eat insects, fish, small mammals, carrion, and garbage. They're not picky. They especially love anything left on a picnic table.

The black bears of the Northeast are better athletes than they look. While they might appear fat, slow, and lazy, bears can hit speeds of 30 MPH at a run, and they climb trees very rapidly. They also swim well. Most bears have no interest in humans, and the only glimpse of them we usually get is their rear ends disappearing into the woods. They very rarely attack people and only do so if they feel their young are endangered, they feel trapped, or they're protecting food.

Like most other animals, bears are easy to read. If they don't automatically turn and run, they might feel threatened. It isn't difficult to figure out when they're angry. They tend to be curious animals, though, and they have poor eyesight, so sometimes they might stand and look at you a while before sauntering off into the forest.

Aggressive bears will attempt to make themselves appear large, rearing onto their hind legs or moving sideways. They'll paw the ground in front of them, sway back and forth, attempt to circle you, or even charge a few feet toward you. These bluff charges are meant to intimidate, and they don't always mean the bear will attack.

The most effective defense against a menacing black bear is to make yourself as big and loud as possible. Many people bang pots and pans and scream and holler. Getting your group together and making a concentrated effort to be large and imposing also helps. If you're alone, you still want to seem as imposing and noisy as you can. While doing so, be sure to keep an eye out for cubs or anything else that may have agitated the bear. When mobilizing as a group, make certain to leave an exit for the bear. You won't come across any grizzly bears in the Northeast, but if you're adventuring somewhere they do live, be aware that dealing with them is quite different from encountering black bears, and you should familiarize yourself with best practices for doing so before venturing out.

Most experts caution against throwing things, running, or attempting to climb a tree to escape an angry bear. They are faster and better climbers than we are and may transition from bluffing to genuinely attacking if you pelt them with rocks. Most definitely, do not play dead. If a bear tears into your tent, follows or stalks you, or otherwise attacks unprompted, it wants a piece of you. These sorts of incidents are extraordinarily rare but have occurred at points in the Northeast. If a bear does attack, your only option is to fight back with everything you have, aiming blows, if possible, at the bear's eyes and snout.

MOOSE

A favorite megafauna in the North Woods, moose seldom act aggressively toward people. Unlike bears, they have no predatory instinct, but they will protect their young or charge if they feel cornered. The biggest deer and tallest mammal in North America, moose can weigh 1,500 pounds or more. Their antlers stretch as wide as 6 feet across, and their hooves are massive. Winter finds moose in a precarious state, as their favorite foods are harder to come by. What's more, moose are more easily picked off by predators in winter due to their difficulty moving in snow. They're heavy and sink deep, and they don't balance well on ice.

These big, gentle herbivores typically pose no threat to outdoor adventurers, but they have attacked and even killed people in the past. Like bears, they're also easy to read. Most moose you encounter in the woods give no indication they even know you're there. Their eyesight is famously poor, and they'll often prick their ears when they suspect something's around before returning to whatever they're doing. In winter, that usually means munching on evergreens.

When a moose detects trouble, however, it will turn, lower its head, lay back its ears, and raise its hackles, much like a dog. This is a sign you need to turn and run. Moose are faster than you are but generally won't chase people far. Try to put a tree trunk or another large object between yourself and the animal. In the unlikely event it knocks you down, don't attempt to fight it. Curl into the fetal position and cover your head. If you flail around, scramble to get away, or attempt to kick or punch the moose, it will stay angry and keep kicking you. If not, it will usually step away, feeling the battle has been won. Remember: Moose don't want to eat you and will turn and leave when they sense the danger is gone.

OTHER LARGE MAMMALS

You have little to fear from any big creatures in the woods of the Northeast. Besides moose and bear, the only other animal known to attack humans is the eastern cougar, but they've been considered extinct in the region for the past century. Occasional talk rears in outdoor circles that someone's spotted a cougar in Maine or Vermont or Pennsylvania, but it's rare. The Cougar Network (cougarnet.org) reports confirmed spottings in Massachusetts, Maine, New Brunswick, and Quebec, but as of now, big cats are no concern to Northeastern outdoor lovers. Their kitty cousins, lynx and bobcats, have healthy populations in the Northeast but don't tend to tangle with people.

The coyote is another large mammal that haunts this corner of the continent, but it almost never bothers humans. According to the Humane Society, popping champagne corks and stray golf balls account for more injuries than these canids.

TICKS

Although you might think these little parasites would not be an issue in winter, you'd be wrong. Statistically, ticks pose more of a threat to humans than bears and moose—by some magnitude. When the temperature warms enough, ticks become active, even if there's still snow on the ground. These disease carriers do not present as much of a threat to people as they do in summer, but they are famously hardy. They survive winter by crawling under leaf litter and using snow cover as insulation. Tick season in the Northeast is usually considered to be April through November, but thanks to warming winters, ticks can and do become active any time of year. Be wary of the smaller varieties, especially the deer tick, which are about the size of a pencil dot, because they transmit disease to humans. Whenever you're in tick country, even in winter, check your group regularly, paying close attention to armpits, groins, scalps, ears, necks, toes, and navels. If you find a tick, pull it off

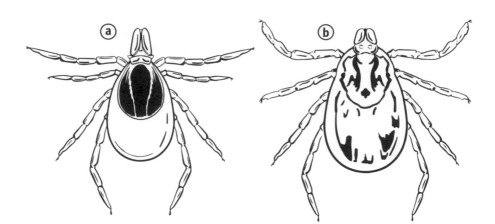

FIGURE 24. The deer tick (a) is the notorious carrier of Lyme disease, while the dog tick (b) is far less hazardous to humans. Deer ticks can be as small as a pinhead, while dog ticks are much larger and easier to spot.

5

with a slow, steady tug using a pair of tweezers or, better yet, a tick comb. Make sure to grab the tick by its head, as close to the skin as you can get, and try not to jerk or twist. Draw a circle around the spot and monitor it to be sure it doesn't grow red or infected or develop a ring around it—possible signs of Lyme disease. If you suspect a tick was embedded for more than 24 hours, see your doctor.

If your group does come across a dangerous animal in the wild, be sure to let rangers, wardens, or other local officials know. Animals that venture near humans could be acting uncharacteristically due to rabies or another illness, and these creatures could prove a hazard to the hikers who follow you.

CHAPTER 6
NAVIGATION

Maps	104
Compasses	108
➜ Route Finding	112
GPS	115
Smartphones	119
Celestial	120
Additional Navigation Tools	121
Setting Your Pace in Winter	123
➜ Tracking Animals in Winter	124

When it comes to finding your way in the woods, winter is a season unlike any other. Everything depends on the conditions. Some days it's remarkably easy to pick your route and stay found; you leave a trail everywhere you go, a literal line on the ground that points the way home. Other days getting lost seems inevitable, with signs and trail blazes covered by snow, reduced visibility, and falling flakes filling in your footsteps as fast as you can make them. Some days you'll have excellent reception for your phone and signal for your GPS; other days you'll see the atmosphere closed to cell service. And, of course, the consequences of getting lost are exponentially greater in cold weather.

All of which means you should understand how to navigate before venturing into the backcountry. Today's smartphones are extraordinary tools but should never be relied upon for route finding in the woods. Simply put, batteries die, and the cold drains them more quickly than usual. You might be ten hours into a hike in unfamiliar terrain, put your hand into your pocket for your trusty phone, and find it dead. Some phones also suffer in the cold from the moisture collected while in your pants, rendering them useless. Service can be intermittent in many popular hiking areas, especially deep in the backcountry. As many rangers will tell you, mountains and ridges and hollows conspire to block signals.

GPS units are fantastic for navigation, too, but suffer many of the same ailments, and they require practice to be used effectively. A map and a compass, however, rarely let you down—provided you know how to use them. Therein lies the key. So many people venture into the woods without knowing how to use these age-old partners. They seem so simple—a needle that shows you direction, a piece of paper that explains a region—that many would-be adventurers shove them into a pack pocket without any real understanding of how they work together to give you your bearings and a route home. (The Maine Warden Service, which oversees the state's famous Registered Maine Guide licensing program, has seen so many people fail their oral exams on the map and compass segment, they do it first, so as not to waste everybody's time.)

Don't let this be you. Make sure you have a handle on navigation before you head into parts unknown. This chapter serves as an orientation to orienteering, setting you on the path to learning how to decipher all those squiggles on a map and figuring out what the pointing red needle really is telling you.

➜ MAPS

Maps are indispensable for outdoor adventure, especially in winter. Not only can you establish a route, but you can also learn a lot about the territory, details that may keep you safe. The names of peaks and streams, elevations, water sources, alternate routes, nearby attractions, potential shelters, exits for safety—a good map shows it all. Many even feature written descriptions of trails and landmarks on the back that give you an idea as to what you're getting into. Whenever you venture into country you don't know, especially in cold weather or inclement conditions, it's vital you have a map with you.

And we're not talking any old map. You can pick up cartoony little hiking handouts at the trailhead or get your hands on tourist guides that show you the major features of an area. Then there are large state maps and travel atlases. None of these will do. You need a chart of the actual region you're planning to explore, one that includes detail down to a scale of 1:24,000 or better, and you want it to be topographic.

Topographic maps show an area's features in three dimensions, using contour lines to represent landscapes rising off the earth. The United States Geographical Survey (USGS) produces a series of topographic maps that have become ubiquitous in the outdoors. Available online at usgs.gov and at many outfitters, these maps cut the nation into quadrangles of 49 to 70 square miles, showing features at the 7.5-minute level. This measurement means each map charts an area of 7.5 minutes of latitude and 7.5 minutes of longitude. The USGS quadrangle series uses a scale of 1:24,000, where each 2.5 inches on the map represents a mile.

The 1:24,000 scale allows for great detail. You can easily make out features, such as rivers, streams, woodsy areas, roads, and bridges. You can judge the steepness of inclines by studying the density of contour lines. These maps pair well with compasses, and you can easily find one for just about anywhere in the country you want to go. The only real drawbacks of the USGS maps are their size—they're as big as posters—and the fact that they're not weatherproof. Many outdoor lovers photocopy them in color and fold them into zipper closure bags, folding the specific region being

➜ **PRO TIP** Just like milk, maps go out of date. Grab the wrong one, and you might find yourself stumbling around looking for a trail that no longer exists or searching out a bunkhouse that was torn down years ago. Make sure yours is current.

traversed on the outside, so it shows through the bag. Some people also complain that obvious landmarks—like, say, a fire tower—are not always included on USGS quadrangle maps, nor do they usually feature up-to-date trail information.

These are not the only useful maps for exploring backcountry areas, of course. Many cartographic companies make great maps, often of popular places to hike. National and state parks, recreational areas, and outfitters all sell or distribute free maps of their areas. If you have some familiarity with basic cartography, a great resource is caltopo.com, where you can create custom maps of any region to virtually any scale. You can make satellite hybrid maps, add slope angle shading, and export to a GPS if you want. For the rest of us, the Appalachian Mountain Club publishes backcountry trail maps of the East Coast, including Maine's 100-Mile Wilderness, Acadia National Park, the White Mountains of Maine and New Hampshire, and other hiking, biking, and paddling regions in the Northeast. Find them at outdoors.org/books-maps.

Indeed, you can find handy maps all over. And don't disregard those free trail-head maps. Although many may not be adequate for accurate navigation, they often have plenty of useful local information. You can find ranger stations, camping areas, old trails and logging roads, water sources, and other resources that might be useful in winter, if you find yourself in a bad way.

HOW TO READ A MAP

6

Map reading is not as straightforward as it looks, as many people find to their personal detriment. In many cases these days, you can't even trust the colors. You might expect that green means vegetation, blue indicates water, and brown represents elevation, but cartographers may need to use multiple shades of green to distinguish, for example, between the bulk of a national forest and an area within it of special ecological concern, which may have extra restrictions, such as no camping or fires. Becoming literate, map-wise, is a skill, and it takes a bit of time and some familiarity with typical features. These strategies will get you started.

Check the scale. The scale of a map represents its level of detail, as mentioned above. This measurement is typically presented as a ratio. For example, the popular USGS Quad Series scale is 1:24,000, where 2.5 inches equals 1 mile. You'll also see outdoor maps with scales of 1:62,500, where 1 inch equals 1 mile, or 1:100,000, where 1.25 inches represents 2 miles. Whatever the scale, it's important you familiarize yourself with it, so you can accurately grasp distances.

Know the colors. It seems elementary, primary even, to understand the colors of a map, but it's very important to do so. Not all maps feature traditional colors, and the colors may tell you things. Blue may represent water on maps, but darker blue often denotes deeper pools. Dotted blue lines often show seasonal or temporary water bodies. Likewise, where green represents vegetation, darker green often indicates thicker vegetation or areas of special concern, as described previously. Black usually represents human-made features, such as buildings, roads, and bridges. Trails are often dotted black lines, but some maps use red for trails and boundary lines and brown to indicate buildings, camping areas, or picnic shelters. Whatever the case, read the map legend and make sure you understand what all those pretty colors are telling you.

Consider the contours. The squiggly brown lines you see running parallel on a topographic map are what make it topographic. These represent the third dimension, showing elevation. The closer the contour lines, the steeper the slope. Mountains and ridges, for example, appear as areas with very little space between the lines. At summits, you'll typically find circles and rhomboid shapes. Contour lines correspond to the scale of a map. Most maps in 7.5-minute scale feature contour intervals of 40 feet, but some maps can get down to 10 feet.

When you look at your map, make sure you understand the distance between each contour line. Reading between the lines will help you pick routes appropriate for your group and avoid walls, cliffs, and drop-offs. Counting contours and doing some elementary math can give you a good idea of an area's elevation. Many cartographers simplify this by making every fifth contour line a heavier brown, called an index contour. With 40-foot contours, this gives you the ability to count by 200s, figuring out your elevation that much quicker.

Orient the map. Orienting the map is where many newbies go wrong. The goal is to make the map and the compass work together to give you information you can use on the ground, and to do that, these two tools have to be facing the same direction. Most maps have an arrow or compass rose indicating north. Use that to align your map with the landscape so that the terrain ahead corresponds with the map. This means that north on the map and north in real life are in the same direction. When the map tells you to head west between two nearby hills, you'll know you need to walk to the left, and you should probably be able to see the notch in question. Orienting the map is a critical step when it comes to using the map to find your bearings in real life—so important that some game wardens bump your map to disorient you during the Maine Guide test, to see if you check it twice before route finding.

Match the map to the land. Orienting the map makes the map and the real world agree, but it's also important to pick out landmarks shown on the map, giving you a real-time feel so that when you're looking east, you see the big mountain that's supposed to be there. Rivers, streams, lakes, ponds, roads—these all make good landmarks that will help you situate yourself in relation to your map, pinpointing your location. Be cautious about using anything indicated in black to orient yourself. These are generally artificially constructed features that may or may not be

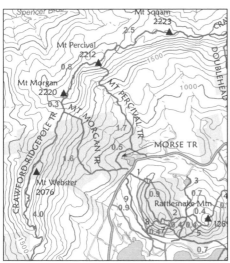

LEFT: **FIGURE 25.** An example of summits (Squam, Percival, etc.) from AMC's *White Mountains Trail Map 3: Crawford Notch–Sandwich Range.*

MIDDLE ROW, LEFT TO RIGHT: **FIGURE 26.** An example of a saddle from AMC's *White Mountains Trail Map 2: Franconia–Pemigewasset.* **FIGURE 27.** An example of a drainage from AMC's *White Mountains Trail Map 3: Crawford Notch–Sandwich Range.*

BOTTOM, LEFT TO RIGHT: **FIGURE 28.** An example of a ridge from AMC's *White Mountains Trail Map 1: Presidential Range.* **FIGURE 29.** An example of slopes and cliffs from AMC's *White Mountains Trail Map 3: Crawford Notch–Sandwich Range.*

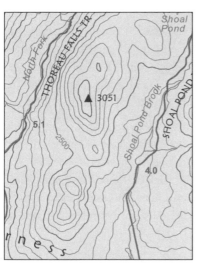

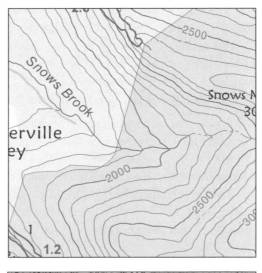

6

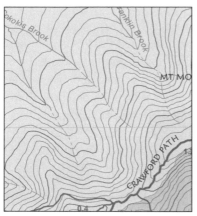

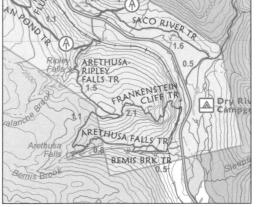

present in real life, depending on the age of your map. Trails close, buildings burn, and bridges get swept downstream.

Calculate distances. When you learn to read a map correctly, you gain the immeasurably useful ability to estimate distances. Using the map scale and the inch measurements on your compass's baseplate, you can get an accurate sense of the mileage between points A and B on a map. Trails don't always follow straight lines, of course, so your measurements will only be approximations. But they should give you a good idea what to expect. You can substitute just about anything if you don't have a compass. String's pliable nature, which allows it to snake along trails, makes it an ideal measurer. Sticks, blades of grass, a pack buckle, your multitool's ruler—you get the idea. Many modern maps, including AMC's, indicate the lengths of trail segments in red. These distances are almost always measured to the tenth of a mile. (It's a fun game to compare map distances to those you find on trail signage, which sometimes differ.)

Look for obstacles. It's important to search out any impediments to travel when you're reading a map. These might include rivers and streams, deep valleys, or impassable mountain cliffs. Note the difference, too, between ridges and drainages. V-shaped contour lines might indicate either one. If the "V" points toward lower elevation, it's a ridge. If it points upward, to a higher elevation, it's likely a drainage, which might be an uncrossable water flow. Concentric circles represent summits, which, unless you're planning to climb a mountain, tend to get in the way of things.

Keep your map at hand. It seems obvious, but it's wise to keep your map readily available. If it's tucked deep inside your pack, you're less likely to dig it out and consult it. Many people place it in a zipper-closure bag in an exterior pack pocket. Others strap it to the waist belt or even put it on the back of the point person's pack, so it's always plainly visible. Maps are not only useful navigation tools; they inform a hike, pointing out all the various features of an area. It's always entertaining to sit atop a peak and identify everything you see.

→ COMPASSES

Compasses are the map's best buddies, their cosmic BFFs. This primitive aid has been showing travelers the way since the Chinese discovered the tool's usefulness more than 1,500 years ago. Compasses take up little space, don't need batteries or recharging, are not reliant on reception, and have very few parts and pieces to go wrong. Once you understand how they work, they'll almost always point you in the right direction. Many new technologies are finding their way into backpacks these days, but few can improve upon the utility of a simple magnetized needle.

Compasses come in all sorts of configurations but there are two primary types used in the outdoors: lensatic (a.k.a. military or engineering) and baseplate. We won't dwell

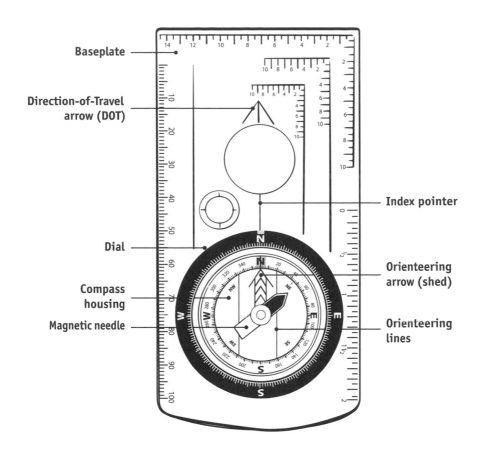

FIGURE 30. The parts of a baseplate compass.

6

on lensatic compasses, which have a viewing window and a sighting wire, because it's the latter kind you'll most often find in the pack of your average winter explorer. Part of the reason for this is the simplicity with which baseplate compasses pair with maps.

The see-through nature of the baseplate compass allows you to place it on a map and align or orient the map, calculate bearings, and draw route lines, all of which we'll get to later. Invented by the founder of the Silva compass company, baseplate compasses consist of a translucent plastic rectangle, with a round compass making up the bottom half. Extending through the center of the rectangle is an index pointer ending in a red arrow, which shows the direction of travel. The compass itself is ringed by a dial with degrees. In its center is the orienteering arrow ("the shed" of the doghouse we'll learn about later), which can align with the red, north-pointing, operative end of the magnetic needle. Most baseplate compasses also feature rulers on one side, which help calculate distances.

HOW COMPASSES WORK

Forget what you know about compasses, because it's probably wrong. Technically speaking, a compass needle points toward Earth's south magnetic pole, not north, for example. A large field of magnetism surrounds the Earth, and it is strongest at the poles. Compasses feature a magnetic needle floating in a suspension that is attracted to its opposite, in this case the globe's south magnetic pole, which is located at the apex of the northern hemisphere. If that isn't confusing enough, the magnetic pole is not at the geographic North Pole but about 1,000 miles south, in the wilds of Canada, last seen near Ellesmere Island and drifting toward Siberia. That's right: It moves, shifting with Earth's magnetic field. According to scientists, it has traveled about 620 miles toward Russia's famous wintry province in the past century and, as of 2019, was moving at a faster rate than ever. All of this makes it hard to take instructors seriously when they teach you to trust your compass.

But you should. The beauty of the compass as a navigational tool is that it's able to account for all this. Cartographers have incorporated the idea of a magnetic declination, which is the difference between the magnetic North Pole and the geographic, or true, North Pole. Most quality maps list the current declination, along with arrows representing true and magnetic north, for the region's location. Because the Earth is round and maps are flat, and because the angle between the two poles grows or shrinks depending upon how far you are from the poles, every region has its own declination adjustment. If you have an older map, it makes sense to check the NOAA Declination Calculator online (ngdc.noaa.gov/geomag/calculators/magcalc.shtml) to ensure you're working off the right declination before you venture into the wilderness. In the East, say in Acadia National Park, the declination is in the 16- to 17-degree range to the west. In the western United States, it might be as much as 20 degrees to the east.

Looking at your compass, you'll see that 16 to 20 degrees is a big chunk of the dial. If you don't get your declination right, you can easily land miles from your destination, so take this part seriously.

HOW TO USE A MAP AND COMPASS

The first step to using these two tools together is to orient the map. To do this, find the declination of your map and adjust your compass accordingly. If you're hiking in Maine, for example, you'd likely move your bezel 17 degrees west. To do this, turn the degree dial 17 degrees to the left. Then align the edge of your baseplate with the true north line at the edge of the map and slowly rotate the map until the compass points north. Or, as orienteering instructors like to say, until Red Fred (the needle) is in the shed (the red orienteering arrow).

➜ PRO TIP When using a compass, make sure you're not holding it in proximity to anything metallic that might compromise your reading. Cars, keys, knives, multitools, and some carabiners often have enough metal in them to confuse your compass.

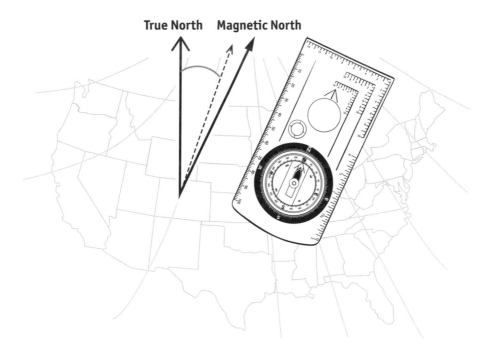

FIGURE 31. "True North" points to geographic north, a fixed point, while "Magnetic North" points to the North Pole, which changes over time.

GETTING YOUR BEARINGS

Once you have your map oriented, you can use your compass to take bearings between points. Determine point A and point B on your map and use the baseplate to
connect them. (Make sure your direction-of-travel arrow is pointing the right way.)
If the points are too far apart for your compass, lightly draw a line between them
with a straightedge and use that to line up your baseplate. When you've done this,
rotate the degree dial until Red Fred is in the shed, being careful not to move the
map or compass. The index pointer will indicate your bearing.

To follow your bearing, leave your degree dial where it is. Turn the compass until
the needle points north then walk following your direction-of-travel arrow. You're
not following the north needle, mind you, but the pointing arrow at the operative
end of the baseplate. This will eventually land you at point B (assuming, of course,
you're starting at point A).

Following a bearing gets many people in trouble. Some set off in the direction
of the north needle. Others attempt to follow the direction-of-travel arrow exactly,
taking every step with the compass pointed north. Depending upon the terrain,
this can be quite arduous, taking you through rivers, puckerbrush, and over drop-
offs. Instead, pick a notable landmark in your direction of travel. Then make your
way to *it*, by the most convenient path possible. Once there, orient your compass to
your bearing, and do the same again, "leapfrogging" your way to point B.

You can use your compass to find field bearings, as well. Say you're on the side of a lake, and your group wants to explore some ice fields you see on a nearby peak, but there are woods between you and the peak. You know that once you get into the woods, you'll no longer be able to see the vast sheets of ice that intrigue you. If you take a bearing on the ice from your viewpoint, you can follow that bearing to your ice fields. Here's how: First, face your landmark. Point your direction-of-travel arrow at the landmark. (Many instructors suggest dropping to one knee and using your upright knee as a base on which to put your compass.) Rotate your degree dial until Red Fred goes back to his shed. Double-check that your direction-of-travel arrow is still pointing at the landmark. The index pointer line will give you the bearing you need to reach your target.

When you're using bearings, you always know the way home. If you want to return to point A from point B, you can simply reverse your steps, putting the white/south end of the needle in the shed, rather than Red Fred. Another option is to turn the whole compass around, pointing the direction-of-travel arrow at yourself and putting Fred back in the shed.

➜ ROUTE FINDING

Maps and compasses provide our bearings, but it is up to us to select routes that are appropriate and achievable for our party. Nobody wants to hike for half a day only to find themself at an impassable wall. It makes sense to spend time ahead of your trip reading the map and looking for a route everyone will be comfortable with. Figure your mileage, mapping out reasonable days. Familiarize yourself with landmarks, which will keep you oriented onsite, making sure to mark water crossings, steep ridges, swamps, and other landscape features that might make your hike a slog. Find the kind of terrain you feel is appropriate for your group. Maybe people want to bushwhack or are looking for serious elevation gain. Or perhaps they'd rather keep to marked trails and go for long lowland hikes. In many places, more than one trail ends at the same location, creating the possibility of loops. One of these loops may be much easier than another, and some may even be closed during winter. Conservative route choices often provide better options for less-experienced hikers.

MACRO AND MICRO ROUTE FINDING

When you're mapping out your route, consider both the big picture and the little picture. In other words, look over the general area, direction of travel, starting and ending points and get an idea about the overall landscape. We call this the macro route. Then consider the minutiae: landmarks, landscape features, and details, such as whether you need to turn right or left at a junction or cross a stream once or twice. Keeping in mind the macro route will help you track where you are in the greater landscape; following the micro route will help you stay on the right trail, taking the safest, most efficient path.

ON-TRAIL

Many popular hiking areas boast exceptional trail networks that do the route finding for you. Hikers often assume these marked trails will be easy to follow, even without a map, but be aware that snow can cover the trail signs, cairns, and blazes you were expecting to find. It's a good idea to spend some time with a map, even when traveling to well-marked parks, taking mental waypoints. Look for streams, ridges, bridges, and other features that will help keep you oriented when you come across them on your hike. Focus especially on landmarks that give you general directional sense; for example, *If I stand with my back to the pond, the mountain should be to the north.*

OFF-TRAIL

AMC generally encourages hikers to stay on-trail whenever possible. Not only will this help if you get lost and need to be found; it prevents you from tumbling off precipices and lessens the environmental impact of groups trekking through wilderness areas. Snow cover changes this equation somewhat. Big piles of flakes soften the impact of our travels. Sensitive vegetation hunkers far below the surface, protected by several feet of winter wonderland. Hiking off-trail, otherwise known as bushwhacking, can be a great adventure, but it brings its own risks. Like getting lost. Or walking off a cliff. Or getting scratched to bits by densely packed vegetation. (Hint: Remember those goggles!)

Most of the same rules for route finding apply, whether you're on- or off-trail. Pore over your map, finding the best route to wherever it is you want to go. Consider vegetation, elevation, and impediments, like stream crossings or granite walls. Select several landmarks to keep you oriented. We always like to look for "handrails," or what we call natural features that run parallel to the direction we're hiking, and "backstops," the same idea, only perpendicular. These might include streams, long lakes, mountain ridges, roads, train tracks, or power lines. If you keep a handrail in sight while hiking, you can't really go wrong. Backstops are less reliable, as you can't always see them, but they still can help you pinpoint your location. You might know, for example, that if you walk far enough in the right direction, you should come to an old logging road.

An off-trail trick when using the macro and micro system is to pick out a point person who is the micro route finder. (It's always best, when hiking in groups, to have a point person at the front to find the way and a sweep person at the back to make sure everyone gets to the end of the trail safely.) The point person hikes a few minutes ahead of the party, making sure to always stay in sight of all party members, and picks out the best pathway through the woods, looking for the easiest, most efficient, most micro route.

When planning a bushwhack, it is key that you locate potential exits. Where can you get off the trail in case of an emergency or if someone in the group is not

6

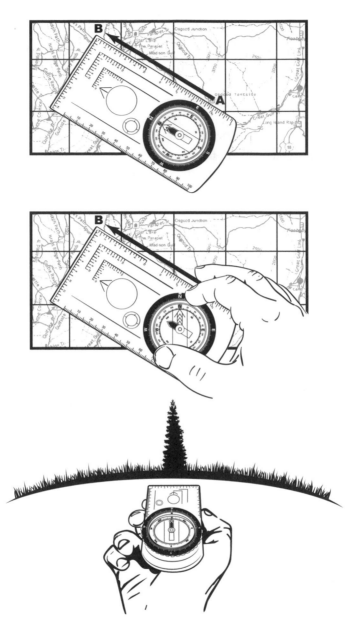

FIGURE 32. To orient your compass to a map: (Top) Lay the compass on your map, aligning the baseplate edge from A, your starting point, to point B, your destination. Make sure the orienteering arrow is at 0 degrees. (Middle) Now align the orienteering arrow with the meridian lines on your map to get an accurate reading without moving the baseplate. (Bottom) When you are sure you have the compass pointing north, remove the compass from the map and, holding the compass, turn your body until the red end of the magnetic needle moves into the orienteering arrow. Follow this direction to get from point A to point B.

feeling up for the hike? You should find at least a couple of exits to give yourselves options. Although you should always let someone know where you're going ahead of time, doing so is paramount when bushwhacking. If you get lost or injured in some remote backcountry locations, you might never be found.

→ GPS

What did we do before GPS, the Global Positioning System? In a word, we got lost. Scientists at Johns Hopkins University's Applied Physics Laboratory first conceived of GPS after the launch of Sputnik in the late 1950s. They found that radio signals coming from the Russian spacecraft grew more pronounced as it got closer and faded as it moved farther away. The light-bulb moment happened when they realized they could track satellites from the ground by the wavelength of their radio signal. And, conversely, they could figure out the location of receivers on Earth by how long it took for those receivers to retrieve signals from space. That experiment, in essence, explains how modern GPS works. Receivers pinpoint their location, elevation, and rate of travel by the time it takes to fetch radio signals from at least four satellites cruising through space.

The military quickly saw the applications for this navigational aid, and by the 1970s, the U.S. Department of Defense developed GPS technology for its own use. By the 1980s, the government opened GPS to civilians. Today, the Air Force runs the Global Positioning System, and it's available to anyone with a GPS radio receiver that can connect to four or more GPS satellites. These receivers have made their way into our cars, planes, boats, computers, and even our tablets, phones, and dog collars. Modern GPS coordinates can be accurate to about 9 feet with a strong signal, which, considering Earth's size, is impressively precise. (If you activate a feature on your device called the Wide Area Augmentation System [WAAS], which was developed by the aviation industry to enhance accuracy, you can often get that down to 3 feet, roughly the length of your arm.)

The Global Positioning System has three component parts: the user (that is, you and your phone/car/dog collar); ground control (ground-based stations that monitor and correct satellite transmissions); and the satellites orbiting above and linking the user to ground control.

THE USER

GPS devices are incredibly useful in the backcountry. Not only do they help keep us found; they also provide us with a whole lot of data. Many show topography, distance hiked, speed of travel, elevation, even sunrise and sunset. Many outdoor adventurers wonder why they need a dedicated handheld GPS when they already have GPS capability in their phone, but there are myriad advantages, including better reception, improved accuracy, waterproofing, and batteries that can be changed in the field.

6

What to look for in a GPS? Today's units have an array of handy features. The list of possibilities is extensive. You can get GPS with touchscreens, two-way radios, personal locator beacons (PLBs), onboard commercial maps, wireless connectivity with your phone and computer, expandable memory, texting capability, electronic com-passes, barometers, altimeters, cameras, weather stations, even geocaching features. Some are about the size of a large cell phone, others as big as an old Handy-Talkie. Some have rudimentary black-and-white displays; other boast colorful, sunlight-read-able screens. As a general rule, the more complex the GPS, the more battery power it requires. Simple units, like old AM radios, can last a long time without the need for battery replacement. Regardless, you should always carry extra batteries (ideally lithium batteries) if you intend to rely on a GPS for navigation.

➜ **PRO TIP** Learning to navigate can be tricky. Until you feel comfortable and have some experience, try route finding while on-trail, so that if something goes amiss, you won't be lost. Don't just read this book then head straight out on an epic off-trail adventure!

The price of a good handheld GPS varies widely according to the number of fea-tures it sports. For winter use, you might consider one that's waterproof, with but-tons to navigate, rather than a touchscreen, which can be a hassle to operate while wearing gloves. Sunlight-readable screens help in snow glare. Built-in weather sta-tions can be useful in the cold-weather months. Most major brands do fine in cold temperatures, with some Alaskan users reporting success down to -55 degrees Fahrenheit. And make sure you factor in battery life.

The key features in a GPS, of course, are reception and navigation. The former can be improved by a better antenna, so you might want to prioritize that over less crucial items, like cameras and altimeters. Keep in mind that quad-helix antennas, the most popular in commercial use, offer better reception than flat-patch anten-nas, those square and rectangular types that mount to flat surfaces when you're not holding the unit upright in the palm of your hand. Also remember that GPS works using the line-of-sight principle. In other words, if you are beneath a rock overhang, in an ice cave, or have deep forest cover overhead, your signal will not be as strong.

GROUND CONTROL

The Air Force's GPS Operational Control segment tracks, monitors, and repairs satellites, as well as sending up commands and corrections. The system consists of a master command station at Schriever Air Force Base in Colorado, plus eleven com-mand-and-control antennas and sixteen monitoring sites spread across the globe.

SATELLITES

The Air Force maintains about 31 satellites in its Global Positioning System, orbiting Earth like a giant constellation. The network requires at least 24 active satellites at any given time, which provides sufficient coverage for any place on Earth to hit four satellites at once.

USING YOUR GPS

Like their antique navigational cousins, the map and the compass, GPS units don't do you much good if you don't know how to use them, so it's a good idea to spend a little time in the backyard getting acquainted before departing for the backcountry. Especially in winter. And, because we cannot stress this enough: batteries, batteries, batteries! If you're going to rely on an electronic device for your navigation, you better be darn sure it remains in working order. (Many devices have a feature that allows you to conserve battery charge.) And just in case, most seasoned outdoors adventurers still carry a map and compass. Some even put a compass and a GPS to use at the same time, finding bearings on the GPS and following them using the compass. Regardless, you need to understand your unit before depending upon it.

The key steps in understanding your GPS unit are to read the owner's manual, to familiarize yourself with the user interface and controls, and to set up the device long before you plan to travel. Among the most important decisions you'll have to make is on the position format and map datum you want to use. When it comes to coordinates, most GPS units can speak a lot of languages. You can format longitude and latitude using degrees, minutes, and seconds; degrees and decimal minutes; and decimal degrees. Or you can set up your device to display the UTM, or Universal Transverse Mercator, format. Both show your location on the face of the Earth, but they present the same information in different ways. For example, if your device was to give you the coordinates of Maine's highest peak, Katahdin, you'd get: 45° 54' 16" N, 68° 55' 17" W in degrees-minutes-seconds; 45.904362, -68.921392 in decimal degrees; and 506097 E 5083425 N, Zone 19 in UTM format.

The important thing is to ensure that how you format your GPS agrees with your map or guidebook. You'll find it easy to change settings back and forth. The USGS, for example, considers the decimal degree system the de facto standard. USGS maps use the 1927 North American Continental United States Datum. They also list UTM coordinates and feature UTM grids.

Longitudinal/Latitudinal Coordinates

To gain a basic understanding of these languages, you first need to understand how to read coordinates. Modern navigation relies on latitude and longitude, those long, arcing lines on a globe. Latitude is the horizontal set of lines. The equator represents zero degrees, and each pole sits at 90 degrees. The North Pole would be represented as 90° N. Longitude divides the Big Blue Marble the same way, only vertically, with the Prime Meridian, a line that connects the North and South Poles (passing through England, France, Spain, Algeria, Mali, Burkina Faso, Tongo, and Ghana), as the center. Your latitudinal position is written as east or west of this line.

So, the Empire State Building in New York would be 73.9857° W, for example. When latitude and longitude are put together, you get a very precise location. The Empire State Building would be 40.7484° N, 73.9857° W.

UTM Coordinates

Most people consider the metric-based Universal Transverse Mercator system easier to use than the latitude/longitude system, and most military forces have been using it since shortly after World War II. The UTM system divides the globe into 1,000-meter squares, using x–y coordinates, like a street atlas. The x coordinate is the east–west measure, known as "easting," and the y coordinate is the north-south measure, known as "northing." UTM uses distance from the equator in meters to determine the northing value and the distance to the eastern border of the particular 1,000-meter square that one is in for the easting value. The farther north or east in the grid, the higher the number. USGS maps include the UTM zone number at the lower left, and your GPS will automatically show you your zone once you set it for UTM.

When reading UTM coordinates, you read easting first then northing. (The old saying goes: "Read right, then up.") The same order holds when you write your coordinates, which always turn into seven-digit figures for entry into a GPS. UTM coordinates for Katahdin, then, would be 19T (which is the UTM zone) 0506097E 5083425N. With maps that are pre-gridded for the UTM format, like USGS topographic maps, it's very simple to pinpoint a location on the map using the UTM GPS coordinates. If your map does not come pre-gridded, you can draw out your own UTM lines to locate yourself.

The USGS topographic maps show UTM grid coordinates in the upper-left- and lower-right-hand corners. Each grid is marked by 1,000-meter increments across the x-axis and y-axis. The Katahdin map begins in the upper left, with 501000E and 5094000N, for example. The map highlights the second and third digits of the easting value and the third and fourth digits of the northing value, which correspond to the 1,000-meter scale of the map boxes. Thus, the x-axis starts at 0 and goes to 10 across the top, and the y-axis begins with 80 and ends with 94 at the top.

HOW TO FIND YOUR LOCATION USING UTM GPS COORDINATES

Read right, then up. Look at your GPS coordinate, which will always be a seven-digit figure for UTM. For the easting coordinate, the GPS adds a zero at the beginning, totaling seven digits; for example, 0506097E for Katahdin. You read to the right, searching across the grid until you come to the column beginning 05. Knowing the peak is 5083425N, you then read up, looking for the row beginning at 83. Somewhere in that grid, within those 1,000 square meters, you'll find Maine's highest mountain and the northern terminus of the Appalachian Trail.

NORTH AMERICAN DATUM

Not only do you need to have your individual coordinates correct when using a GPS, you have to make sure the datum is set to correspond to the map you're using. *Datum* is a term for a system of coordinates, and GPS receivers have a datum setting with myriad options. The UTM grid in the United States is typically referred to by the years 1927 and 1983, which was when corrections were made to the UTM grid. Most maps, including the USGS topographics, list the datum year, and it's easy enough to enter it into the unit settings page. It might look something like "NAD27 CONUS," which translates to North America Datum 1927, Continental United States.

Your GPS has a handful of basic jobs: showing your location, setting up a route, showing you where you've been, and showing you the way home—or what outdoor pros call "breadcrumbs." Once you have your datum set and you understand coordinates, GPS units are intuitive. Most take a few minutes to calibrate upon startup, acquiring a signal from the heavens. The more open the sky is above you, the easier it is for your unit to track. If you are under tree cover or someplace that may interfere with reception, check the signal strength, which is typically indicated by bars, like a cell phone. This will give you an idea of how much you can trust your GPS.

Using your map or guidebooks, you can often lay out your trip ahead of time by setting waypoints. These are GPS locations you intend to visit. Many online topographic maps have preconfigured routes and waypoints for popular areas that you can simply transfer to your GPS. With a pre-programmed route, once you arrive at the trailhead, your unit will know which way to take you. Your GPS will provide you with bearings and update itself constantly as you hike. If you find certain places you'd like to visit again while in the field, you can mark them as waypoints and save them for your next trip. Likewise, you can set waypoints for water sources, gear caches, good campsites, or any other place you might want to return.

→ SMARTPHONES

You can't go anywhere without seeing cell phones these days, even deep in the backcountry. Hikers have them, rangers use them, wardens carry them—they're everywhere. They can be very useful tools, with compasses and GPS capabilities, map apps, fitness trackers, flashlights, cameras, emergency tips, and the ability to call for help in a pinch. But this all assumes you have a signal and a working battery, which is why most professionals will tell you that you should never rely on your phone in the outdoors. Phones fall out of pockets and into streams and outhouses. Batteries invariably die when you need them. They can't connect due to atmospheric conditions or because you don't have any data left. And often you're just plain in a place where no signal can be found.

If you insist on relying on using your phone as a navigational tool, consider getting a waterproof case and an external battery pack. Confirm your carrier plan is up to

6

date before you head out and that it includes the terrain you're heading into. (It's no fun to arrive at the trailhead only to find out you're "roaming.") Look for map apps that work without a signal or download maps you might need ahead of time. In other words, know which aspects of your phone you can rely on and which you can't.

→ CELESTIAL

Travelers have been navigating by the stars for centuries, and we're not the only ones to do so. Several bird species, from the arctic tern to the indigo bunting, use the night sky to direct their migration. Even dung beetles use clues from above, so it can't be that hard. Many more animals, from sea turtles to monarch butterflies, find their way by utilizing the sun as a reference.

The sun's daily journey across the sky can provide basic orientation. We know it rises in the east and sets in the west and is at its highest point around noon. If you wear a watch, you can use it as a very basic compass by holding it horizontally and pointing the hour hand in the direction of the sun. Halfway between that hour hand and 12 o'clock on your watch dial is south. (If you're exploring after daylight saving time begins in March, you'll need to find that halfway point on the dial between the hour hand and 1 o'clock.)

The North Star is a more precise reference point. It always hangs in the sky above the North Pole, while the heavens rotate around it. One of the night's brightest stars, most people can find it easily. Simply look for the Big Dipper. The two stars in the front of its ladle aim directly at the North Star, otherwise known as Polaris. Measure the distance between those two stars and draw a line approximately five times its length, and you'll always find the North Star. The constellation Cassiopeia—five bright stars in the shape of an M or W—is another reliable pointer and is helpfully situated about the same distance from the Big Dipper on the other side of Polaris, making it visible even when the great astral ladle is obscured by trees.

Once you find the North Star, you know the direction of true north, wherever you are in the northern hemisphere. With this in mind, you can walk in the direction you want to go, as long as you bear in mind which way is north. You can also get an approximation of your latitude using Polaris as a guide. Assuming the horizon is 0 degrees and the zenith or highest point of the night sky is 90 degrees, estimate the angle at which the North Star sits. The mariners of yore used a sextant to calculate this measurement, but you can use your fist, aligned with your thumb on top, with each fist-length counting for roughly 10 degrees when outstretched. That angle is your latitude.

Celestial navigation is a nifty skill to have in your tool bag, but it's all very approximate, and you'll have a difficult time trying to get yourself to an exact location. And you're out of luck if cloud cover is obscuring the stars. It's best used as a rough guide, helping to aim you toward a road, river, ridge, or some other large, long landmark—or as a last resort in case of emergency.

6

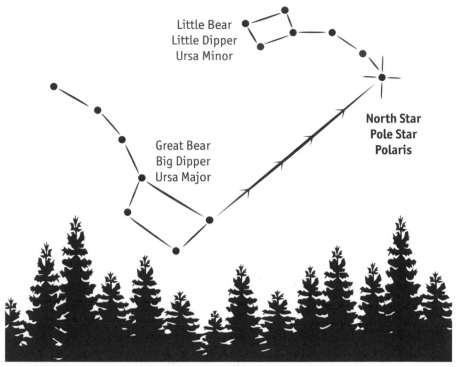

FIGURE 33. To find Polaris, or the North Star, look for the constellation commonly known as the Big Dipper. Locate the star that serves as the top-right corner of the Big Dipper's pot then trace a line from it to the last star in the Little Dipper's pot handle. This dim star in a dark patch of sky is Polaris.

6

➔ ADDITIONAL NAVIGATION TOOLS

Slope meters. These gadgets can come in handy when you're traveling in avalanche country. These inclinometers give you an inkling as to how steep a slope is and whether it is likely to present an avalanche danger. Resembling little protractors, these devices have grooves to fit onto ski poles and allow you to measure the angle of a particular hill. Most feature a danger zone marked in orange and red, which stretches from 30 to 45 degrees. Some even have grids on the reverse side to measure snow crystals, which helps to further assess the avalanche potential of an incline. Avalanches happen under a variety of conditions, and nothing predicts them perfectly, but slope meters provide a better idea about hazards.

Binoculars. When weight is not a consideration, it's never a bad idea to have a pair of binoculars with you to aid in navigating. They allow you to pick out distant landmarks; to spot approaching weather; and some models have compasses and range-finding tools built into their lenses. Those with onboard compasses allow you to take bearings on faraway landscape features. Range finders help you calculate distances to objects and even gauge the height of cliffs and peaks.

Field Communications. Two-way radios, used by alpine rangers everywhere, are a good idea when traveling with a group. Those sold for civilian use come from consumer bands, so you violate no FCC laws, and they allow you to keep in contact for as much as 40 or 50 miles when you're out of cell phone range. Some have a group feature that lets you communicate with everyone at once. Most are 4 or 5 inches long, making them easy to tuck into a pack pocket; are rechargeable at home or in a vehicle; and have handy features, such as NOAA weather radios. Many are waterproof. Plus, you get to use cool ranger lingo, giving yourself code names and ten-fouring each other.

Beacons and Probes. No one wants to think about disasters in the winter woods, but you have to when planning a cold-weather expedition. Avalanche beacons make a heck of a lot of sense when traveling in "av-prone" country. About the size of a small cell phone, these transmitters send out a pulsing signal in the event that you go under. Good ones have a 65- to 70-yard range, which should make it easier for searchers to find you. Before heading out into avalanche-prone terrain, everyone should make sure their beacon is switched on and worn properly, strapped over the shoulder, underneath the outermost layer, or zipped into a snow pants pocket. Avalanche beacons are useless if they're buried deep under your sleeping bag in the bottom of your pack. Search and rescue personnel carry receivers that provide an audio signal and a visual display with distance and direction indicated; carrying a beacon can be the difference between life and death.

Probes help rescuers find you if you ever get submerged in snow. Long poles with receivers built in, they pair well with beacons. Rescuers drive them 10 feet or more into snow at various intervals when searching for avalanche victims. Much of this technology now has Bluetooth built in, making it easy to download the latest upgrades.

Probes and beacons often give winter travelers a false sense of security. Don't let this be you. You must still use caution, avoid dangerous slopes where avalanches are likely, and change your route if need be.

InReach. The logical extension of GPS technology, InReach transmitters allow you to send out emergency messages in the backcountry. They resemble your basic GPS but have additional communication options. You can pair them with an app on your smartphone and send texts via satellite, sending out communications and sharing your location. Some come with subscription services that work similar to how OnStar does in cars, connecting you to dispatchers who know instantly where you are and possibly even providing your medical history to rescuers.

Personal Locator Beacons. Personal locator beacons, or PLBs, are similar to InReach devices, and are among the best options for sending out distress signals from a wilderness area. About the size of a small GPS, PLBs work just about anywhere, have no subscription fees, and use batteries that last for years—although you should still double-check them. Most do one thing and one thing only: send out SOS signals via satellite. Just remember that once you push "send," there is no undo button. If you ever need to use a PLB to call for help, stay put. Many people have a tendency to try to get themselves "unlost" and end up making life difficult for rescuers.

Spot Devices. Also known as satellite messengers, spot devices are small, satellite-synced gadgets with tiny keyboards that allow you to stay in contact with family and friends, wherever you may be. They transmit and receive text messages using orbiting satellites, requiring a monthly subscription fee for the privilege. They also enable direct communications with search and rescue personnel in the case of an emergency.

Cell Phones/Sat Phones. Again, cell phones are handy tools in the backcountry for many of the reasons we've listed previously, but they should not be relied upon for emergency communications. They have failed too many people too many times to be the sole option if things go bad. If you're insistent upon having phone capability, a satellite or "sat" phone is a far better option. These look like clunky, old-fashioned cell phones and give you the option of making calls and sending and receiving texts, no matter where you are on Earth, because they utilize satellites rather than cell towers. They are also expensive and bulky. Some companies allow you to rent sat phones. But keep in mind that no communication device is effective 100 percent of the time, making it especially important to possess the knowledge, skills, and gear to be self-sufficient at every experience level, from beginner to expert.

➜ SETTING YOUR PACE IN WINTER

When using technology to plan your route and estimate distances, remember that, for the most part, we all travel much slower in winter. If you've ever tried running in snow, you know your pace is different than it is when the ground is bare. You'll need to adjust your expectations. Whereas most reasonably fit hikers can keep up a 2.5-MPH pace on moderate ground in summer, doing so is far harder on snow cover. On snow, we sink in, making every step less effective than it would be on hard ground. And that's when we're not post-holing, which can slow a group to a crawl. Snowshoes help keep us afloat, but they're nowhere near as quick to hike in as a pair of lightweight hiking boots.

Not only is it more difficult to walk, we tend to carry a lot more weight in cold weather, filling our packs with sleeping bags, extra clothing, more food than usual, and emergency supplies. We wear heavier boots. We might pull sleds, which literally creates drag. We travel at a pace that allows us to cover ground but not so fast as to really sweat, which can be dangerous in cold temperatures. Everything we need for safety and travel in winter conspires to slow us down. Experience will give you a sense of your own pace, which may be 50 percent slower than in summer, so you'll need to factor your speed into time and distance estimates.

There are exceptions, of course, such as skiing and crossing frozen ponds. If you're on cross-country skis and are lucky enough to be traveling largely down-hill, you'll be able to move faster than you would in summer. If you can make a

6

beeline across an iced-over body of water rather than walking all the way around it, you can also shorten your travel time.

➜ TRACKING ANIMALS IN WINTER

Winter makes us all trackers. The white stuff provides an ideal surface for animal impressions, and even a cursory inspection in a snowy acre reveals hundreds of tracks going in all directions. Given how quiet and still the winter woods can seem, it's intriguing to see these signs of life and to think critters might have been running about just moments ago. Tracking is an art, but there are a few simple principles that will get you going.

CONSIDER WHO'S AWAKE AND AROUND

Remember that certain species migrate and others hibernate in winter. Don't expect to find groundhogs, who famously slumber for long periods, or chipmunks, who fill their cheeks—and their burrows—with food for the big sleep. Bears, too, are well known for falling fast asleep in their dens.

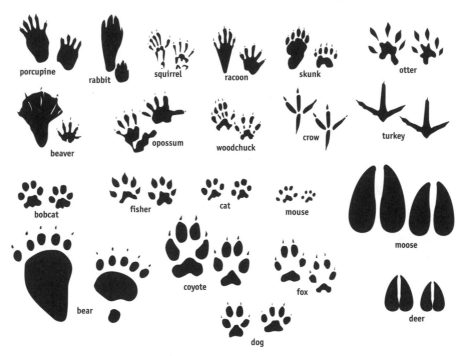

FIGURE 34. Snow provides an excellent base for animal tracks, but be aware that melting snow can make tracks look larger than they are. Above are some of the most common tracks you are likely to see in the Northeast.

With that in mind, most of the Northeast's megafauna go about their business as best they can during the cold-weather months. Deer, moose, lynx and bobcat, weasels, coyotes, and turkeys all spend the season in an unending search for food.

CONSIDER THE SURROUNDINGS

Are you in the woods or a meadow? Is water nearby? Do you see evidence of digging or tamped-down snow, where an animal might have curled up for a nap? Is there any scat or yellow snow or even blood? If there are trees nearby, look for nibbled branches or scratched trunks. All of these signs give you a picture of the animal you are tracking and what it might have been doing. It may seem obvious, but you have to follow the tracks for a while to get a sense of what's making them.

LOOK FOR THE MAIN TRACK

Study the main track. What is the pattern of movement? There are three primary types. Big animals—moose, deer, dogs, and us—tend to leave alternating prints in a long line. Tracks that show two prints close together are common among mice, squirrels, and weasels, which hop from their back feet to land near the prints left by their front feet. The third major pattern is made by animals, such as rabbits, that bound, landing with all four feet together.

CHECK THE FEET

Look at the size of the print, keeping in mind that tracks in snow are often larger than those in mud, and they grow bigger as they begin to sag in the sun. Consider the depth, too; larger animals sink deeper into the snow. The two types of mammalian prints are either hooves or paws. If it is a paw print, look at the number of toes and the pattern of the pads. Remember that cats have retractable claws and canids do not.

If you find tracking intriguing, there are innumerable guides available that provide extensive detail.

6

CHAPTER 7
HEALTH AND HYGIENE

➜ **Your Body in Winter**   126
➜ **Water Sources**   129
➜ **Water Filtration Methods**   130
➜ **How to Keep Water Liquid**   133
➜ **Nutrition**   134
➜ **Hygiene**   137
➜ **The Restroom**   139

➜ YOUR BODY IN WINTER

The human body has a remarkable capacity to adapt to various climates. When people dispersed to various corners of the globe, their bodies adjusted wherever they went. Some, of course, made homes in the cold-weather areas of the north, and their bodies became shorter and stouter, giving them more mass to generate heat and less surface area to lose it. Their basal metabolisms sped up, they ate lots of rich and caloric foods, and they grew an insulating layer of fat around their vital organs.

Thanks to modern technology, we don't have to shrink or put on fat to enjoy the winter outdoors. But we can take a few lessons from climatic anthropology: When we're outside in cold weather, we need to insulate and we need to eat. Simply standing around outdoors all day in cold weather burns the 2,000 daily calories your body requires just to keep warm. Which means that if you're moving—hiking, skiing, climbing, and so on—you need to double your usual intake. That's a lot of gorp. One of the beauties of outdoor adventuring in winter, not unlike hiking the Appalachian Trail, is that you can eat pretty much whatever you want without worrying about expanding at the waistline.

CALORIE BURN

In winter we must feed our internal furnaces. Not only do we need to double our calories for a normal day outdoors, but we typically ask our bodies to work harder on a cold-weather hike than we would on a summer one. Slogging through snow is more difficult than skipping down a summer trail, and we have to carry more gear for the sake of safety in winter. All of that effort requires even more calories. Keeping well fed and hydrated is crucial for hikers, never more so than in wintertime.

There is no one precise figure or equation, but the typical, moderately active adult needs to consume about 1,500 to 2,000 calories in a normal day. You may require a little more or a little less depending upon your gender, size, and metabolism, but 1,500 to 2,000 makes a rough average. If you're going for a winter hike, you'll likely use 2,000 to 3,000 calories in addition to that initial allotment. In steeper terrain or if you're breaking trail, you'll need more still. Sleeping in the cold demands another 1,000 calories, as your body works to keep itself warm in slumber. Add it all up, and you're looking at 3,500 to 5,000 or more calories per day.

HYDRATION

The human body is truly a wonder of the world, and it's amazing to think of all the uses it has for water. Good old H_2O cushions our spines. It lubricates our joints. It helps create neurotransmitters in the brain. It aids cells in their growth and survival. It distributes oxygen, flushes waste, detoxifies our interiors, and regulates body temperature. The simple chemical compound in our water bottles really is quite an incredible elixir.

We've all heard by now that our bodies are largely composed of water. The adult human body consists of about 60 percent water. It makes up a significant portion of many of our most important parts, including the brain (90 percent), bones (22 percent), blood (83 percent), and, crucially for those of us who like to explore the outdoors, the muscles (73 percent).

Yet many people don't come close to drinking enough water during the average day, let alone when working hard on the trail. We lose vast quantities of water through perspiration (sweating) and aspiration (breathing). The average athlete sweats out about a liter an hour of water during exercise. When you step out into the morning air on a winter adventure, enjoying views of the snow-draped hills and excited about a day on the trail, you see your breath as little clouds in front of you. That's water vapor leaving your body. Some studies suggest we emit another 400 milliliters (13 ounces) simply exhaling all day.

The cold of winter alone causes us to lose water. To keep itself warm, the body shunts fluid from the extremities, keeping it around the core. This causes blood pressure to rise as the heart pumps the same amount of blood through a smaller space. The kidneys try to compensate, reducing the amount of fluid and producing more urine, a phenomenon called cold diuresis. We pee more when it's cold and lose more water that way, as well.

All this water needs to be replaced for our bodies to function properly. When it's cold out, we often don't recognize

7

➜ **PRO TIP** Check your group regularly for signs of dehydration. Headaches, fatigue, cramping, dry mouth, and lack of appetite are all clues that someone hasn't been drinking enough. Try to pay attention to the frequency your group makes "pit stops," as well.

the need to drink; we don't feel thirsty the way we do on a hot summer day, despite the fact that we're perspiring due to exertion. In winter, by the time you realize you're thirsty, you're already beginning the process of dehydration. You may have lost as much as 2 percent of your body's water content and 10 percent of your muscular effectiveness. Dehydration is a major concern among outdoor lovers, leading to problems both small and large. In winter, one of the biggest concerns is hypothermia, as inadequate body hydration leads to decreased circulation and thus poor thermoregulation.

The solution to dehydration couldn't be any more straightforward: Drink more water. Just as we graze all day on the trail, it's wise to drink at regular intervals. Keep your water bottle handy, preferably in a side pocket of your pack, so that you don't have to take off your pack. We recommend using an old-fashioned water bottle over dromedary-style hydration bladders, because those are not as effective in winter, since their parts—the bite valve and hose, especially—are prone to freezing. Some hikers elect to use them anyway, blowing back into the hose regularly to keep it clear of ice and wearing the bladder next to their body, rather than carrying it in their cold backpack.

On a winter hike, aim for a minimum of 4 liters of water per person a day, although many people feel they need more. A lot of hikers find that drinking 1 liter in the morning, drinking every time they stop for breaks, and downing another liter with dinner works well. Just remember that the human body can absorb only 1 liter per hour. As with grazing, it's better to take a lot of small drinks than one big guzzle.

How much you need is determined by the weather, your body size, your pace, and the topography. If it's a warm March day, you're a big person, and you're climbing a 4,000-footer in the sun, you'll want more water than a diminutive hiker trekking along level ground on a cool February afternoon.

Simply drinking isn't enough, though. You need to be sure what you're drinking is helping you stay hydrated. Conventional wisdom recommends against drinking alcohol and caffeine in outdoor settings because both are diuretics, causing you to urinate more frequently, thus having the opposite effect you're looking for. There are several studies that contradict this wisdom, however. And many outdoor lovers find that the positive hydrating effects of avoiding caffeine are offset by the headaches and other issues people face when they don't get their coffee in the morning. In moderation, both alcohol and caffeine are probably fine. If you need your morning shot of coffee, just make sure you chase it with a couple of cups of water. The same goes for a celebratory beer at the end of your hike.

7

➜ **PRO TIP** There are a couple of little tricks you can use to tell if your body is losing water too rapidly. First, pinch the back of your hand. If the skin returns to normal quickly, you're fine. If it takes a split second, you need something to drink. But your best bet is to check the color of your urine. If you're peeing out a steady stream of light or clear fluid, you are well hydrated. If your urine is the color of light beer or darker, you need to drink a pint or more of water.

RECOMMENDED DAILY WATER INTAKE ACCORDING TO BODY WEIGHT	
Body Weight in Pounds	Water Intake in Liters (34 oz.)
100	3
120	3.6
140	4.2
160	4.8
180	5.4
200	6

Source: The National Outdoor Leadership School's Wilderness Guide

➜ WATER SOURCES

Be prepared to treat your water, even in winter. Many winter campers assume that bacterial nastics, such as *Giardia lamblia* and other waterborne parasites, die off in the deep cold. Not so. They merely go into suspended animation, ready to warm back up in our intestines and go about their business, causing cramps, diarrhea, and fatigue. Anyone who has suffered through a gastrointestinal battle with a microorganism knows the little parasites always win, and the convenience of scooping water out of a pretty stream is not worth the risk.

Water sources in areas with a lot of human use also can be contaminated with flu viruses, hepatitis, or bacteria—like the dreaded *E. coli*. Outbreaks of *E. coli* in frozen foods have proven this hardy bug can survive freezing. Likewise, scientists have discovered influenza in frozen Siberian lakes. Drinking untreated water any time of year is a big no-no.

Water is all around us in the cold-weather months in the forms of ice and snow. Pop some snow in a pot, melt it, and fill your bottles. This is what many winter newbies think until they actually try to melt mass quantities over a cookstove and burn up all of their fuel. It's more straightforward, of course, to use open water, already in liquid form, but that isn't the easiest to come by this time of year. Streams still run in winter, but it can be difficult getting to them. The second choice, lakes and ponds, also pose certain difficulties. There's always water under there, but drilling down to it when there's a foot of ice can prove a daunting task.

There are plenty of handy tricks when it comes to water acquisition. You can turn your trekking pole into a fishing rod by tying a piece of para-

7

➜ **PRO TIP** If you cut a hole in the ice of a lake or pond, be sure to mark it in some way: a bough stuck into the snow, something colorful left nearby, etcetera—both so you can find it again later and so no one accidentally falls through.

cord to your water bottle and dunking it into a stream or lake while you stand safely back from thin ice. Be careful with your bottle, though; the plastic strap holding the cap can weaken over time. If you tie the paracord to the strap, you can lose your bottle in the drink, so we'd recommend securing your cord around the lip.

You can use an ax to cut a hole in lake ice, but an ice pick or a chisel works even better, if you have one handy. Commercial ice saws are ideal but are too large to carry in the average backpack. Know that any hole you create will refreeze before long, so if you're staying in one spot, you may want to go give it a whack every few hours.

If you find yourself someplace where open water is impractical, you can melt mass quantities of snow over a wood fire using a pillowcase or sheet. Fill the pillowcase or sheet with snow and hang it over the fire, being careful not to hang it too close to the flames. Place a pot underneath to catch the runoff. Or simply put the snow into a pot. When you're selecting snow, find the densest flakes you can; this results in more water, and ice produces even more—but always keep an eye out for yellow spots. After you get the fire going, put a little snow or ice in your pan to keep it from scorching and add small amounts to the pillowcase or sheet. Doing so is more efficient than trying to melt big chunks.

→ WATER FILTRATION METHODS

One of the advantages of melting snow for water is that you can consider the resulting liquid clean and safe once it has been boiled. (All water, even when collected from a perfectly white snowfield, should be treated.) There are numerous ways to do so, but bear in mind that cold weather negatively affects many of the most common methods of filtration. (See Appendix D: Drinking-Water Treatment Methods on page 197 for more information.)

PUMPS

Pump filters are often a pain in the winter because they can ice up, clog, and crack. These devices draw water in when you pull up the handle, sucking it through a filtration system big enough for water molecules but too small for bacteria or spores to get through. Their narrow hoses and small valves can freeze in winter, however, rendering them useless. Some winter hikers persist with them, putting pumps in sleeping bags at night or burying them in down pillows inside backpacks, but even so, pumps are prone to failure in deep-cold conditions.

ULTRAVIOLET

Ultraviolet filters, including the SteriPen, are very convenient and work fine in winter, using UV rays to kill bacteria like a laser gun—that is, if their batteries hold. The company recommends avoiding alkaline batteries in winter and switching to

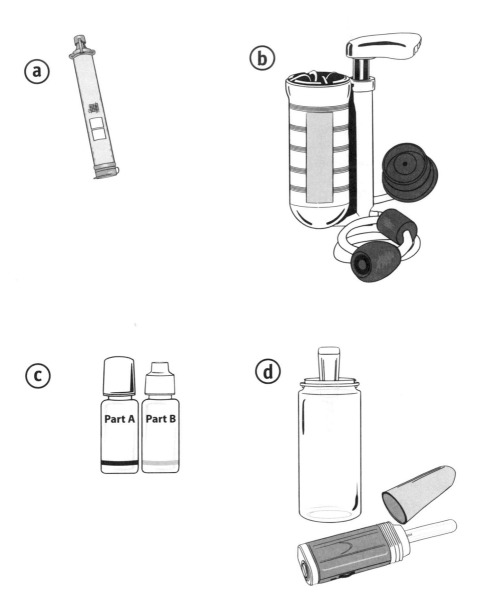

FIGURE 35. Backcountry water-treatment methods include: (a) a filter straw, which allows a backpacker to drink directly from a water source but can freeze if packed away with water inside; (b) a pump system, which pumps water directly from a source and through a filter, all made of parts that can ice over and crack; (c) a chlorine dioxide solution, also known as a chemical treatment; and (d) ultraviolet radiation, which uses a UV light in the water container to inactivate pathogens, although the batteries that power UV filters drain more quickly in cold weather than in warm weather.

7

lithium batteries, although in profoundly cold temperatures, even lithium batteries can lose a good deal of their discharge power. If you do choose to use a UV filter in winter, bring extra batteries and keep them wrapped in your pack to protect them against low temperatures. Some users like to wear their sterilizer pens inside their jackets to keep them warm, which prevents them from freezing and helps prolong battery life. Remember, too, that although UV treatment kills bacteria, it doesn't remove dirt or grit or protect you against chemical contaminants. These magic wands also occasionally fail for other reasons, such as a bad internal element, so carrying some sort of backup is wise.

CHEMICAL FILTRATION

Chemical water treatment tablets are another option in the cold, though they are not fail-safe, either. Some bleach-based liquid drops can freeze and fail. Tablets tend to work better, but chlorine dioxide often requires more time to act and can lose some of its effectiveness in cold water. Some military studies have shown you might need to carry more tablets and increase the dose to get the same level of treatment you would in summer. Iodine tablets work well but definitely require more time, three or four times longer in winter than in summer. This can mean as much as a couple of hours. (If you object to the taste of these chemical methods, add a bit of powdered drink mix to mask the flavor.)

STRAWS

Straw-style water filters, such as LifeStraw, have grown extremely popular among backpackers over the past decade. These plastic tubes are small, light, and very efficient at filtering water as you drink, purifying up to 1,000 liters at a low cost before they need to be replaced. Like other filtration units with tubes and small parts, they are susceptible to freezing if you put them away with any water left inside. Many hikers wear their straws around their necks to keep them warm and use them to filter from their water bottles.

BOILING

Which brings us back to boiling. This is a fail-safe and effective method for treating your water, but it requires a lot of fuel. An alternative, as mentioned above, is to use a campfire to purify mass quantities of water, perhaps while everyone is sitting around the fire in the evening. The rule for boiling has always been to allow the water to boil for five minutes, but the EPA recommends a rolling boil for just one minute. Best to be safe.

7

WATER TREATMENT TIPS

- **Find the cleanest source possible.** The more sediment you can eliminate at the outset, the better off you are.

- **Let water sit a while before you filter.** This allows sediment to settle at the bottom. You then can scoop water out or draw from the water at the top.

- **Use a coffee filter.** No matter what filtration system you're using, pouring your water through one of these strainers and into a bottle filters out a lot of impurities.

- **Let your filter dry.** If you do use a pump, straw, or UV pen, allow them to air out someplace warm after use. If you store them wet, they can crack and/or get funky.

- **Combine systems.** Many outdoorspeople conserve fuel by heating water until it's warm then putting it in a bottle and using a straw, a pen, or even a chemical treatment.

- **Pour water back and forth.** When you've purified your water, you can improve the taste by pouring it between two clean vessels, be they bottles or pans.

- **Improve the taste of water by adding a pinch of salt per liter.** You can also use a powdered drink mix. Some of these contain vitamin C, which helps fight colds.

- **Watch out for yellow snow.**

➜ HOW TO KEEP WATER LIQUID

Because of these difficulties using the hunter-gatherer method of water acquisition, many people elect to simply pile a few gallons onto their sleds. On really cold days, they'll turn to their water for cooking after making camp and find a frozen block. There are dozens of ways to keep water from freezing. Many hikers use an insulated case for their water bottles. (If you do this, turn the water bottle upside down at night; this keeps the cap from freezing tight.) Others wrap their bottles in wool socks, a piece of old sleeping bag foam, or bubble wrap, which is a very effective insulator. Some people put their bottle inside their jacket, hanging from a cord around their neck, and use body heat to prevent freezing. At night, many outdoorspeople keep their water bottles in the tent or, on especially frigid nights, in their sleeping bags. Heat the water before you turn in and you'll have both a warm bag and drinkable water in the morning.

7

If it's not too cold, you can leave your water in the tent as you sleep. Body heat will warm the space enough to keep it from freezing. Some people sink their water bottles into the snow—nature's insulation—at night. Large volumes of group water can be covered with a foot or so of snow and won't freeze overnight. Just remember where you put your stash! If it looks like it will snow or you're concerned you won't be able to find your water in the morning, place a ski pole, a tree bough, or some other marker upright at the site where you bury it.

→ **PRO TIP** A classic trick for keeping the contents of your thermos warm longer is to fill the insulated interior with boiling water and screw the top back on. Let it sit for six or so minutes. Quickly empty the water out and add whatever hot liquid you choose. This preheating can add an hour or two of heat to your trip.

→ NUTRITION

Many outdoor adventurers struggle to eat as much food as they require during a day of vigorous winter hiking, but it's necessary. A simple method is to double what you would bring on a warm-weather hike. If you usually eat a big breakfast before a long day on the trail, by all means, have a big breakfast. And bring along a second breakfast for an hour or two into the hike. If you typically eat an energy bar for a snack, bring a second one. If you eat one sandwich at lunch, pack two. This is one of the big bonuses of winter camping: You can eat whatever you want. Revel in your options. You're more likely to lose weight on a cold-weather expedition than you are to put on a single ounce.

GRAZING

Most nutritional experts recommend grazing during a day on the trail. This means having a ready supply of easily accessible foods you can munch on at regular intervals. On a winter hike, you're using calories almost as fast as you eat them. Everybody's favorite, gorp (good old raisins and peanuts) makes for a perfect grazing snack. Throw in a bag of M&Ms or big chunks of chocolate, if you want. If you graze steadily during the day, your body will always have the calories onboard to stay warm and energized. Eating this way also makes it easier to avoid long lunch stops, so you can push on through instead of stopping and standing around in the cold.

PROTEINS, CARBS, AND FATS

When planning meals and snacks for a winter outing, be sure to include a mix of proteins, carbs, and fats, as each serves its own purpose in fueling our excursions. Simple carbohydrates serve as a source for a quick burst of energy. These sugary foods—think fruits and sweets—readily transform into blood sugar, which is immediately available for the body to burn. More complex carbohydrates—breads, vegetables, and beans—take an hour or more to digest and don't release energy until then. Proteins, such as meats, take days to fully process and serve as building blocks for the bones and muscles that drive us forward. Fats store energy for future use. A fit, active person should combine all three in roughly these proportions: 55 to 60 percent carbohydrates, 25 to 30 percent fats, and 15 percent proteins.

Together, these three fuel types deliver the balance of energy we need while adventuring in winter. Carbohydrates give us the short-term benefit of a sugar rush, but that rush is generally followed by a crash as your body devours this blood sugar then craves more. Combining fats with your carbs when out on the trail can help prevent this carb roller coaster. Tasty options include adding some coconut chips, nuts, and cheese to your pack. By eating fats both before you head out and along the trail, your body can better regulate the amount of blood sugar in your system during periods of exertion. Bringing along any type of meat jerky, some tuna in a bag, a stick of pepperoni, or some cheese sticks can provide a bit of protein on the trail.

MEALS

Traveling in winter is like going camping with a refrigerator: You can take pretty much whatever you want, pulling it on a sled rather than carrying it on your back. Meal planning for the winter woods is not only easy but fun, and you can make breakfast and dinner the highlights of your day. These two meals are your biggies, since you want a lot of high-calorie foods to prepare for a long day on the trail and for overnight hibernation. A typical excursion's meals might look like this: a big, one-pot breakfast; hearty snacks all day long; a lunch on the go that doesn't require cooking; and a full spread to look forward to at dinnertime. Hot comfort foods for dinner almost always go over well. For wholesome backpacking recipes weighed by gram and ounce and calculated by calorie, see AMC's *Real Trail Meals* (AMC Books, 2017).

Your menu obviously depends on the size of your group, your mode of travel, and your cooking setup. Grilling over an open fire is a much different prospect than heating stew on a woodstove. Dried foods pair better with backpacks than dense or heavy foods, although you can transport the latter more easily on a sled. And don't forget to consider how below-zero temperatures will affect your menu. Pre-slice meats and cheeses so they're ready when you arrive at your destination. (When they're frozen, they're much harder to cut.) Many other foods, including eggs, fruits, and vegetables with high water content, cream-based foods, and soft cheeses don't respond well to a deep freeze. Prevent them from freezing by wrapping them in bubble wrap or stowing them between fleeces in your pack—or select something else.

➜ PRO TIP Today's freeze-dried foods are far more inventive and delicious than the options available even twenty years ago, better for nourishment than punishment. At most outfitters and many supermarkets, you can find a wealth of dried foods that you'll look forward to after a rugged day's walk, from beef Stroganoff to curries to chicken fajitas to Thai veggies.

7

Keep a permanent marker handy when repackaging food. It can be hard to tell the difference between powdered milk and powdered cheese when working by headlamp. When doing your pre-trip shopping, keep preparation time in mind. You don't want foods that take a long time to cook, since the rest of your group likely will be standing around and cold. Appetizers like cheese and crackers can buy you only so much time before the campers get restless.

When planning meals, take the opportunity to be creative. People tend to be conservative when laying out camping eats, but there's no real reason to be, especially if you're toting a sled in winter. You can find an array of ideas online, from fresh-baked bread and doughnuts to breakfast burgers, rolled pizzas, chili and biscuits, grilled enchiladas, chicken pot pie, fennel-stuffed fish, and countless delicious stews.

One- or two-pot meals are ideal for both morning and evening. They are easy to prepare ahead of time, feed multitudes, are ready all at once, and are straightforward to clean up. For breakfast these might include spiced oatmeal, grits, cinnamon rolls, breakfast burritos, scrambled-egg tacos, skillet quiche, or banana pancakes. In the evening you could treat your party to hot-pot pork chops; fish fillets; quesadillas; bacon, beef, and bean casserole; or virtually any soup or stew. When planning these meals, remember the key ingredients for winter camping: fats and carbs and warmth. Your dishes should include a lot of butter or oil; milk powder, bouillon, or some other sort of base; meat, if you eat it; veggies that can handle the cold; and starches like pasta and potatoes. This time of year, think hot, rich, and hearty.

We also recommend preparing your meals ahead of time, as it both simplifies the cooking process and gives you more time for adventure. It also reduces weight and waste in the woods. Much of the prep work can be done before you leave, and many outdoor cooks prepare almost everything in the kitchen at home, sometimes assigning dishes to various group members. They bake desserts, roast meats, and whip up casseroles and soups into one great portable potluck. It's well worth a few extra pre-trip hours in the kitchen to have a delicious, filling, home-cooked dinner at the end of a frigid and tiring day of hiking.

Some winter wanderers even make their own gooey snacks for the trail, combining butter, peanut butter, chocolate, and honey into a sweet, mushy mess. Roll this into a wax paper tube, put it in the freezer, and it's like a homemade, high-calorie energy bar. In a pinch, you could subsist on it for days.

SAMPLE MENU

Breakfast Day 1
Oatmeal, peanut butter bagels, granola bars
Coffee, tea, or hot cocoa

Lunch Day 1
On-trail sandwiches
Jerky, cheese, pepperoni
Gorp and similar snacks
Water and more water

Dinner Day 1
Beef and cheese chili or hearty vegetarian minestrone
Bannock bread
Choco-banana melt
Coffee, tea, or hot cocoa

Breakfast Day 2
Potato, bacon, and cheddar quiche
Cheddar and potato quiche for vegetarians
Bannock bread
Coffee, tea, hot cocoa

Lunch Day 2
Jerky, cheese, dried fruits, nuts, peanut butter bagels, and goo
Chocolate
Water

Dinner Day 2
Spinach lasagna
Hot buttered rolls
Pineapple upside-down cake
Coffee, tea, or cocoa

7

➜ HYGIENE

Keeping clean in cold weather is a serious challenge. We push our bodies extra hard to get where we're going, forcing our wicking layers to soak up a lot of moisture, and then we crawl into our smelly bags at the end of the day, no shower in sight. It's all too easy to find yourself stuck wearing your sweat for days in a row.

But hygiene is very important. Sickness travels fast in winter, as anyone with schoolchildren can attest. Although we may not be able to maintain our ritual cleanliness on cold-weather excursions, we can still take care of basic maintenance. Here are some suggestions.

- **Take a warm bath.** With a little bit of biodegradable soap and a hand towel, you can do a pretty good job of giving yourself a bath using water warmed on the cookstove. Make sure to dispose of the used water at least 200 feet from any water source.

- **Wet wipe it.** Commercial baby wipes, hand-thawed in a tent, can wash the most common trouble areas—face, pits, groin, and behind—if you can't heat water. In small quantities, they warm easily. Just be sure you don't let them freeze into a giant block.

- **Powder up.** A little baby powder in these same areas helps prevent chafing and reduces odors. Many outdoor lovers swear by anti-chafing lubricant sticks, which reduce the rubbing that can happen as you sweat.

- **Wash your hands.** We all touch common items during a day of winter camping, sharing spoons, stirring ladles, ski poles, and fire pokers. Germs travel from one person to the next this way, and by the end of a trip, a whole party can come down with the same illness. Handwashing is critical, especially during meal prep. A tiny bit of water and a little antibacterial soap is one of the most effective methods of preventing the spread of germs. Liberal use of hand sanitizer also nips camp contagions in the bud. Just make sure it doesn't have too much alcohol, which evaporates quickly and leads to frostbite. Keep reusable cleaning cloths and hand sanitizer near your toilet area so that members of the group can clean up after use.

- **Keep your contact lenses clean.** An extra pair of glasses is also prudent if you can't function without corrective lenses. The cold, dry winter air is a notorious contributor to parched contacts. Bringing remoisturizing eye drops helps as well. Saline doesn't freeze well due to its high salt content, but another trick is to sleep with your lens case to keep contacts from icing up. This is obviously not a problem if you wear multiday lenses.

- **Take your meds.** Many people forget to tuck their prescription bottles into their pack. Nothing's worse than being many snowy miles from home only to find you don't have your medication.

- **Wash your bowls, cups, and utensils.** Doing dishes with hot water disinfects your cookware for reuse.

- **Keep your nose clean.** Always bring extra tissues or even a hankie to clean your nose periodically. Postnasal drip goes wherever exercising people go in winter. If anyone has a cold, it can spread fast unless the group practices nose and hand hygiene.

- **Change your socks and underwear.** Even in the wilderness, you should put on new smallclothes daily. If you run out of clean pairs, make sure you remove and dry them, at least. Air out your feet, too. Applying foot powder can help prevent odors and blisters. And don't ever hop into your sleeping bag at night with wet socks or underwear.

- **Feminine hygiene.** Consider cotton or merino underwear. Both do a good job preventing the spread of bacteria, although cotton doesn't wick as well as merino. Some women forego underwear in their sleeping bags to allow air to circulate. Leave No Trace principles require women to pack out their used hygiene products. The best way to do this is by bringing a menstrual bag: two gallon-sized zipper closure bags work well. Include baking soda or crushed aspirin to minimize odors and zip one bag inside the other. Treat this bag the way you would food or garbage while in camp, as the smell of blood can attract animals. Some women prefer to use menstrual cups in the backcountry, which don't require changing as often as other hygiene products. Dispose of the contents in a cat hole away from camp, just as you would other body waste.

- **Bring lip balm.** A bit of salve on your lips before you go to bed and before you head out in the morning helps protect them from the brutal cold. Don't share.

- **Brush your teeth.** Dental hygiene is straightforward in the woods. Use a little less toothpaste and water than you would at home and spit in a bag, packing it out with the trash. Your floss goes in here, too. Some campers like to bring along mouthwash in a plastic bottle, but it adds weight to your haul.

➜ THE RESTROOM

We've all heard stories of people who refuse to go to the bathroom in the outdoors. This is a very unhealthy practice and can make you uncomfortable, at best, and seriously ill, at worst. People have been pooping and peeing outdoors since the dawn of time. The cold adds a few wrinkles to the process—there's nothing like freezing wind on sensitive body parts in the middle of the night—but there are a variety of ways to ease the chore of doing your business while winter camping.

The simplest option is to visit the outhouse or latrine if you're staying in a park or wilderness area that has them. If not, set up a "bathroom" in camp, making it far enough away that people feel a sense of privacy but not so far that they won't want to use it. Some people build a snow wall for added seclusion; others locate it somewhere well out of view. There are a variety of toilet options. For years, outfitters have used the classic toilet seat on a 5-gallon bucket. This works well, and the screw-top lid keeps everything where it belongs until you can empty it responsibly. Government-issued ammunition boxes available at army-navy stores or online serve the same purpose, and you can purchase commercial inserts: plastic containers

7

➜ **PRO TIP** Many campers carry individual personal hygiene kits: little double-bagged, zipper-closure bags. Packed with toilet paper, wet wipes, and hand sanitizer, they keep things sanitary.

designed to fit inside 20-millimeter ammo cans. As grim as it sounds, it's best to pack out your solid waste at the end of a trip, including toilet paper. Some people prefer to use double- or triple-bagged garbage bags or commercial waste bags (a.k.a. wags). To cut down on your solid waste, many adventurers use snow as toilet paper, as it is very effective at cleaning, and you can chuck it somewhere out of the way. Still, it's a good idea to bring extra toilet paper just in case.

Urinating is far more straightforward. Again, find someplace away from the trail and camp and go for it. Urine is mostly water and leaves a minimal trace. Men can avail themselves of the opportunity pretty much at will, so long as they're mindful of others. Marking territory is for animals. Be sure you're not leaving a minefield of yellow snow for someone else to see and always scoop a handful of snow over your leavings. Women can use snow to wipe up or pack out toilet paper. On long excursions, some ladies like to carry a rag for this purpose, rinsing it out between uses. Commercially made "female urination devices," essentially silicone funnels, are also growing in popularity.

Getting up to hit the latrine on a frigid night is something many of us like to avoid. Some campers keep a "thunder jug" in their tent or cabin for just that purpose. This is generally a largish—and very well marked—bottle with a screw top. Men can typically focus their efforts; women may like to use a pee funnel. Dispose of the contents during the day, well away from camp.

7

CHAPTER 8
CAMPSITES

➜ Siting Your Camp   141
➜ Fire Building   142
➜ Permanent Structures   150
➜ Backcountry Camping   152

A comfortable camp can make all the difference on a winter backpacking trip. After a long, cold day on the trail, the comforts of "home" mean even more than they do in summer. It's a chance to warm up, change into dry clothes, sit by the fire, eat hot food, and let go of worries: everything you need to be safe and happy in the winter woodlands.

Most of the backcountry skills you use in your three-season trips will serve you well on a cold-weather expedition. But there are a few winter-specific skills you need to know. Selecting your campsite, for example, is more important than ever. It must be somewhere safe but as protected from the elements as possible. Water sources are often difficult to come by. Firewood also becomes a critical concern—sometimes you need the heat of a fire for emergency purposes—in a way it isn't in summer.

In other senses, though, campsite building is easier in winter. You don't have to worry about sleeping on roots and rocks, and you have one of nature's great building blocks at your disposal. With snow, you can erect walls to protect yourself from wind. You can level depressed areas to create a perfectly flat surface for your tent. You can make benches to sit on or build your own custom kitchen and half bath. Dedicating a little extra time to creating a welcoming bivouac pays dividends when you return from an exhausting day of winter adventuring.

➜ SITING YOUR CAMP

When picking your campsite, keep the following tips in mind.

- **Avoid avalanche country.** Obvious, but people do it.

- **Camp behind windbreaks.** You'll be warmer, you'll sleep better, and it is easier to cook if you find a location out of the wind. A ridge, a copse of trees, or a human-made snowbank between your site and the bracing breeze can make all the difference.

- **Watch out for lows.** Cold air sinks, so you want to avoid setting up in hollows or depressions.

- **Look up.** Take a glance above you before staking out your tent. You don't want to set up beneath dead boughs or swaying snags that can break in a breeze or snow-laden branches that can let go and bury you.

- **Site near water.** It's a good idea to locate as close as possible to a usable water source. It beats melting mountains of snow. Of course, you need to follow the Leave No Trace guideline of siting 200 feet from any water source.

- **Avoid trails and outhouses.** Just stay away. They're busy and stinky. Unless, of course, you're in a commercial area where the sites are located by these camping staples.

- **Consider feng shui.** Think about the flow of the site, where people will be, and the relationship among sleeping, cooking, fire, and bathroom areas. Remember, too, that the whole site will get tramped down, and you don't want to be situated where doing so will damage sensitive areas.

- **Take advantage of snow.** It's always a good idea to camp on top of snow rather than on open ground, if you can. The snow makes a great cushion under your tent, protects against trampling vegetation and causing erosion, and is often warmer than camping on bare ground.

- **Enjoy the sun.** The more of it you get, the warmer and more content you'll be. Think about the sun's daily circuit through the sky and orient your camp to maximum advantage. If you must choose, give preference to morning sun. You may not even be back from a day of hiking to enjoy the sun in the afternoon, and a bit of brightness helps to get everyone going in the morning.

- **Give yourself extra time.** Remember that setting up camp, especially if you're building a fancy bivy with a dining room, kitchen, storage cabinets, and a three-walled outhouse, takes a lot longer in winter than it does during the other three seasons.

- **Don't forget about critters.** Especially in late-winter camping, pests can find their way to your camp. String up your food and garbage.

→ FIRE BUILDING

8

Rangers at Baxter State Park often marvel at how many people struggle with lighting a fire. It's one of the most important and elemental life skills, something humans have been doing for millennia. Yet thanks to our current urbanized existence, with its climate control and one-touch heat sources, many campers can't figure out how to kindle a blaze. In the winter woods, this is need-to-know stuff, literally the difference between life and death in an emergency situation. It's worth practicing in a high-impact area, like a frontcountry campground, so long as you have permission.

A hot fire is a camping tradition and the highlight of many a winter trip. Campfires provide myriad benefits for a group, serving as a focal point of camp, a place to come together and talk, tell stories, and create lasting bonds. These crackling blazes have an ability to restore us at the end of a long day, a way of making people slow down and reflect, looking inward and relaxing before turning in. They also serve the more practical purpose in winter of thawing out cold campers and drying out wet gear.

Not every winter camping area allows fires, however, and in some places, permits are necessary. Leave No Trace principles recommend avoiding campfires where possible, because in the wrong hands they can scar the land. The first step in campfire building is to determine whether a fire is allowed, whether you need permission, and whether your group really needs or wants one.

FIRE PRINCIPLES

Once you understand how fire works, you'll have no problem constructing one. Fire has three main ingredients: a heat source, fuel, and oxygen. If any one of these is missing or compromised, you won't be able to ignite a blaze.

Heat

Heat sources include matches, lighters, and flint and steel. Matches are the most basic, and they work well most of the time, as long as you keep them dry. Waterproof matches are a little tricky, because their coating makes them a little more difficult to strike. It's a good idea to practice with a few at home before trying to strike one in the field with frozen fingers. Lighters are straightforward, although it's wise to check that they have fuel before relying on them, and windproof designs are worth exploring if you plan to use lighters to start your cookstoves and campfires. Flint and steel or fire strikers require a bit of skill, and you should definitely practice with them at home before venturing into the outdoors with them.

Fuel

For a campfire, fuel consists of tinder, kindling, and large chunks of firewood. This is where many people fall down in their fire building: selecting wood that's too wet or too big, and using too little tinder or kindling.

Tinder

Tinder can be anything from balled-up newspaper to cotton balls soaked in wax to strips of birch bark to shavings made from a dry piece of wood. Many campers bring tinder from home to simplify fire starting. Some simply grab steel wool or dryer lint, which ignite easily. Others soak cotton balls in petroleum jelly or coat twine in paraffin wax. Newspaper rolls work great, too. The key to all of these is dryness. Cotton balls, lint, steel wool, and twine all fit nicely into a tiny lidded food container or an old film canister, if you still have some of those lying around. In the field, you can find or create your own tinder. Fire builders have used birch bark for eons. It's easy to strip away pieces of the papery outer skin to find the dry interior layers, and the bark has natural oils that are flammable. Always use dead and downed wood, in keeping with Leave No Trace. It's also quite simple to find a dry stick (remember: dead and downed wood) and shave it with your knife, whittling off thin, papery curls. Gathered together into a little nest, these shavings burn well. You can even leave them on the stick, peeling back sections until you have a twig with a lot of fine curls.

8

Kindling

Your selection of kindling largely determines whether your fire sparks into a blaze or remains a forlorn pile of logs. Kindling is where the action happens. Many newbies fail at the kindling phase, choosing wood that is too wet or too big or using the wrong amount. As a general rule, softwoods make better kindling, whereas hardwoods are far superior as logs once the fire is going. You'll find few better sticks than cedar or hemlock to start your conflagration, although pine, balsam fir, and spruce also work well. As with tinder, always source your kindling from dead or downed wood. Many winter campers collect wood as they travel, pausing to pick up good-looking dry sticks and putting them on their sled. Otherwise, some groups create a wood-gathering, fire-building detail once they arrive in camp, while the rest of the group begins dinner preparation or sets up tents.

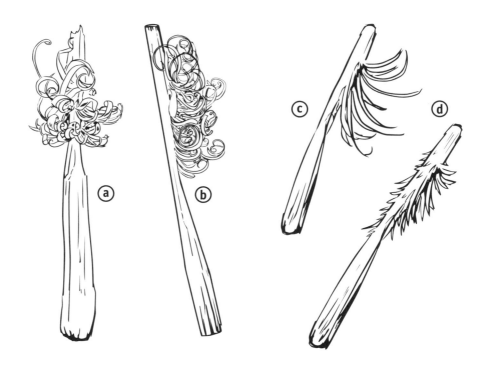

FIGURE 36. Don't be lazy when preparing tinder. Putting in the effort pays off, and the activity alone will help warm you up. For good tinder: (a) Repeatedly shave one end of a downed twig; (b) thereby creating lots of curls that will easily ignite. Examples of poor tinder include: (c) thicker, less delicate shavings; and (d) short, stumpy shavings that won't ignite as easily or burn as long.

Wood

Just remember the "five Ds" for the wood-gathering process: you want wood that is downed, dead, dry, dinky, and distant.

1. **Downed.** Just as it implies, you want sticks that are on the ground. Many parks and wilderness areas require it, prohibiting the cutting or maiming of live trees (which don't make good firewood anyway).

2. **Dead.** Green wood, or wood that is still alive, is filled with moisture and burns poorly. The wood you're looking for should be long dead, old, and dried out. One way to tell: If it breaks easily, it's good and dead and has little water content left inside. If it bends, it's still too green. Watch out for rotten wood; although technically dead, it has begun to decompose and is no good for burning.

3. **Dry.** Firewood must be dry to burn well. Look for sticks that are leaning up off the ground or are on the upper half of deadfall, away from the wet earth. If you can't find anything that seems dry, you can often cut away the soggy exterior with a knife or an ax to reveal dry inner layers. The snap test works in this case, too. Wood that is nice and dry will break with a snap.

4. **Dinky.** Wood that is too big takes a long time to light and often doesn't burn all the way through, leaving behind ugly husks. Leave No Trace principles suggest using no wood larger than your thumb.

5. **Distant.** If you've ever camped in a heavily visited park, you've probably noticed that there's not much firewood to be found near your site, with everything dead and down already scavenged—one reason why you should gather your wood a good distance away from your camp. Doing so also reduces your impact on the area.

Oxygen

Just as we need oxygen to live, so does fire, but many frustrated fire builders don't give old O_2 its due. They pile a bunch of big logs on top of each other, without allowing space for air to circulate, and end up with a smoldering mess. Fires need that space so that they can breathe. (This is why woodstoves feature dampers, which regulate the air flow.) Keep circulation in mind when constructing your fire. A good sign that a fire is not getting enough air is smoke. If you're working with good, dry wood, and the fire is putting out big gray clouds, it's probably not oxygenated enough, and you need to spread out your fuel.

8

CAMPFIRE TECHNIQUES

There are a wide variety of effective ways to build your campfire. Conventional wisdom has always held that you put your tinder and kindling under your logs because heat rises, but there's an array of inventive methods used by fire builders today.

Tipi Fire

Tried and true, the tipi method has been taught to generations of scouts and soldiers.

1. Place your pile of tinder in a nest.

2. Lean your kindling sticks against one another above the tinder nest, making a tiny tipi. Make sure to use several handfuls of very small sticks.

3. Place a few larger logs around your kindling, leaning one against another in a conical shape.

4. Ignite your tinder.

5. If needed, fan the flames during the tinder phase to supply more oxygen.

The tipi method works because it allows for great air circulation. As the flames grow larger, they rise into the next layer of fuel, until all of the upper layers are involved. Once the fire is going, the logs collapse on themselves, and you can add more atop them. Initially, your "logs" should be only an inch or so in diameter, but as the fire gets going, you can add larger pieces. The main drawback of this type of construction is that the logs occasionally fall away from each other in different directions, spreading out the fire. Some people, too, find it difficult to keep the logs upright during the building process.

Lean-to Fire

Not unlike the tipi, the lean-to places sticks and logs over the tinder, utilizing the upward flow of heat.

1. Place one of your largest pieces of wood flat on the ground.

2. Make a pile of tinder in front of it on the downwind side of the log.

3. Lean kindling against the log, over the tinder.

4. Light the tinder, fanning gently.

5. Once the kindling has begun to burn, add thicker wood, keeping the shape to give the fire a channel of air.

8

One of the primary advantages of the lean-to method is it protects the tinder from the wind, making it easier to light and more likely to continue burning. It also creates a tidy pile of centralized wood.

Log Cabin Fire

The log cabin technique borrows the stacked log construction of its namesake.

1. Make a nest of tinder.

2. Place logs on either side of the pile, running parallel.

3. Put another pair of logs perpendicular across the first two, creating a square around the tinder.

TOP: **FIGURE 37.** Named for its shape, the tipi fire builds from thinner, faster-igniting layers at the base to thicker layers above that will burn for a longer time. The tipi eventually will collapse, and you can add larger logs to the fire.

MIDDLE: **FIGURE 38.** To create a lean-to fire: (a) Plant a large, downed branch in the soil to stabilize your fire; (b) build a frame using thumb-size downed branches, fold your bundle of kindling in half to increase its density, and cover your frame with pinky-size downed twigs; (c) continue adding twigs until the kindling is protected on three sides, leaving one side accessible.

BOTTOM LEFT: **FIGURE 39.** This fire type is named after its shape, familiar to anyone who played with Lincoln Logs as a child. By essentially building a box around the tinder, you protect it from the wind, allowing the fire to catch and grow more easily.

BOTTOM RIGHT: **FIGURE 40.** The Leave No Trace-friendly fire-pan method borrows from other fire-building practices but requires you to carry a pan.

8

4. Continue building upward by adding layers, essentially making a box around the tinder.

5. Balance kindling between the logs over the tinder.

6. Strike your match and apply to tinder.

Like the lean-to, the log cabin creates a wind barrier, protecting the tinder.

The Leave No Trace Fire

The primary idea behind Leave No Trace is to tread as lightly on the landscape as possible so that it can be enjoyed by others, leaving the bare minimum of evidence from those who've visited previously. Campfires, of course, do exactly the opposite, leaving ugly dark scars on the ground and charred wood lying around. To compensate for this, Leave No Trace recommends: using only a cookstove; using only existing fire rings; or, if you must build a fire, doing so in a way that leaves nothing behind, not even a black smudge. The snow cover of winter makes the last option much easier. One of the more popular methods of Leave No Trace fire building is to construct your fire on top of a cookie sheet or fire pan, using any of the above methods. Oil pans and animal feed trays also work well. Then you simply enjoy your fire, ensure that it's out when you're done, clean the pan with some snow, disperse burnt wood far and wide, and you're good. Be aware that the fire will sink as the snow beneath it melts, so it's helpful to set your pan on rocks or boughs close to the ground.

BACKCOUNTRY COOKING

Many outdoor adventurers cook over a campfire in winter. It allows you to melt snow for drinking, boil water for purifying, cook and grill for a group, and it transitions into a living room hearth for the evening's entertainment. Others prefer to use a cookstove. Whichever way you go, you'll need to establish a comfortable camp kitchen. The first step to this is siting your kitchen. Which way do the prevailing winds blow? You'll want to set your cooking area in the biggest lee you can, sheltered from the wind. Will you use a campfire or a stove? If so, you'll need to avoid low-hanging branches and tree cover. The kitchen is a high-traffic area, especially if it is near the campfire. You'll want to make sure it's not too close to trails, tents, or the latrine and that it doesn't impede access to any of these places.

One of the many advantages of winter camping is that you can build your ideal camp kitchen out of snow. You can form counters, food-prep islands, benches, windbreaks—you name it. With a shovel and a sense of fun, you can design the custom kitchen you've always dreamed of.

8

KITCHEN TIPS

- When building a custom kitchen, it's easier to build down rather than up. In other words, dig out a space rather than trying to collect and mound snow. Use your shovel to sculpt and your feet to pack down.

- Dig two deep rows, forming a table in between them. Shovel more shallowly on the outside of the trenches to create benches.

- Insulate your benches using foam sleeping pads. This turns your kitchen into a comfy lounge.

- If you want to prevent everything from getting wet from falling precipitation, tie a tarp over your kitchen area—though not above your campfire.

- Dangle a headlamp from your tarp for a chandelier.

- When laying out your kitchen, create logical stations for handwashing, food prep, and dishwashing. Keep hand- and dishwashing away from your cooking and prep area.

- Store your kitchen supplies in a single box or tote, keeping everything handy. Put it in your sled and slide it right to your site.

- Don't forget a station for brewing hot drinks. Some camp baristas like to shovel out their own bar for this purpose. A ready supply of hot water for cocoa, tea, or coffee improves many a mood.

- Remember that your cookstove will melt the snow beneath it, so place some form of shelf or insulation under it. Keep the fuel off the snow, too. The blade of your shovel or bottom of your sled works well for this.

- Bring or build a windbreak for your cookstove. Cold breezes make your stove work harder and your fuel burn faster. You can solve this problem by digging out a shelf for your stove below the surface of the snow, protecting it from the wind.

- Assign crews. Many groups create cooking, cleaning, and fire details.

- Trash your trash. Leftovers should be saved for breakfast or, if no one wants them, placed in the trash. Pick out as much of the large garbage as you can and use snow to pre-clean the dishes. Then wash your dishes in hot water.

- Watch your gas. Liquid fuel almost instantly takes on the exterior temperature if it spills, and it evaporates quickly. This can lead to frostbite if any lands on exposed skin.

- Store your food away from your tent. Although bears are unlikely to be a major problem, rodents might be about. Hanging your food and trash from a tree limb at night prevents any issues. (See Figure 41, next page.) Stainless steel "rat sacks" help keep even those pesky pine martens from getting at your tasties.

8

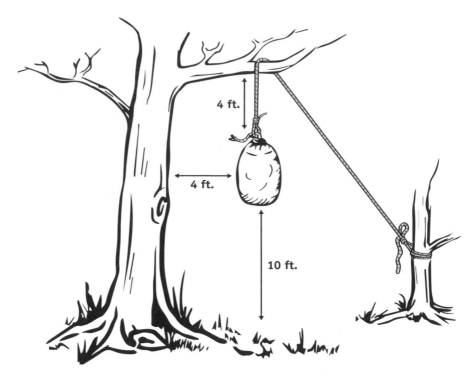

FIGURE 41. A traditional bear hang keeps food at least 10 feet off the ground and at least 4 feet in all directions from any trunks or branches.

→ PERMANENT STRUCTURES

Many parks and recreational areas rent cabins, huts, or yurts all winter long. Consider trying out winter camping in one of these dwellings before going all in on a back-country tent expedition. They offer a great try-before-you-buy opportunity if you're unsure about this whole fun-in-the-cold business. Most have bunks and woodstoves, which allow you to hang your gear and dry it all out at the end of the day. In some cases, meals are provided, lightening your load and preventing the hassle of having to prepare meals in the cold while you're starving from a day spent outside. If you do have to cook, at least you have a structure around you, protecting you from the wind, and you can stay warm as you wait for the pot to boil. You'll also have the comfort of knowing that staff are around, in the case of an emergency. Camping in a building may seem like cheating, but it's a good introduction to cold-weather adventuring.

LODGES

The Appalachian Mountain Club and other organizations maintain lodges in the frontcountry. More like rustic hotels, these often come complete with private rooms or bunkrooms and baths, plus a family-style dining room. They make great bases for exploring a backcountry area, with the knowledge that dinner and a bed will be waiting for you at the end of the day. Some rent or loan gear and offer guides as well. You can drive directly to most of them, which gives you an easy bail-out option if you decide winter camping was a big mistake.

HUT TO HUT

Hut-to-hut networks now exist in several Northeastern states, including AMC's eight huts just off the Appalachian Trail in New Hampshire and three sets of lodges and cabins in Maine's 100-Mile Wilderness. These provide another great way to spend the whole day outdoors in some of the most pristine country in the nation without having to haul a lot of food or a tent. They work this way: You hike, snow-shoe, or ski for roughly four to six hours, moving from one of these little hostelries to the next (or up and back from a trailhead), and sleep on a bunk at the end of the day. Accommodations vary between locations, but most provide meals and hot showers. Some shuttle you back to your car if you end at a different place than you started. Some allow you to tent nearby, enjoying the best of both worlds. You can have part of your group stay inside, eat hot meals together, and dry out gear before returning to your private camp at night. Many provide bag lunches for the trail; some allow you to use the kitchen to cook for yourself.

CABINS

You can find remote cabins in parks and wilderness areas across the country. Some are primitive, vintage sporting camps, built from logs and heated with woodstoves; others are new construction and "cabins" in name only. They might have caretakers and offer meals, like AMC's properties in Maine, or be unstaffed, like those in and around Baxter State Park, which require you to bring everything you would on a backpacking trip, save the tent. The level of creature comforts varies widely. Many are drafty and difficult to heat. Others are tight and cozy. Some have baths, others outhouses. All offer the advantages of a roof over your head, a heat source, and an opportunity to dry out your gear.

8

YURTS

Yurts are the round, impermanent structures used by the Mongols back when they ruled most of Europe and Asia. No longer made of animal skins, they're mostly canvas-walled now. They've become quite popular in the last fifteen years among outdoor lovers and are scattered across the Northeast. Some are full-service sporting camps, with kitchens and even dishwashers, and charge about what you'd pay for a hotel. We're talking full-on glamping. Others are more primitive and akin to a remote cabin.

BUNKHOUSES

Some parks and recreational areas are home to bunkhouses. These are essentially cabins shared hostel-style, where you pay for a rack rather than a room. (Some will let you rent the whole thing out.) Bunkhouses have their advantages: an inexpensive roof over your group; heat and gear drying; and the camaraderie of meeting other like-minded outdoor lovers. But they also have their drawbacks, specifically a lack of privacy. Most bunkhouses feature outhouses, whereas others have interior bathrooms. You need to bring all of the cold-weather equipment you would tent camping, minus the tent, and cook for yourself. But you have an escape if the weather turns or there's an emergency.

LEAN-TOS

Often referred to as Adirondack-style shelters, these wooden structures consist of three walls, a roof, and a sleeping platform, with an opening at the front. As the name suggests, they are common in upstate New York, as well as in state parks and camping areas across the Northeast. Many campers like lean-tos because these shelters feel more primitive than a cabin, since you're still exposed to the elements, but they get you up off the ground and put a roof between you and whatever might be falling from the sky. Again, you need to carry whatever you would tent camping, except the tent. Experienced lean-to campers know to bring a tarp to hang across the shelter's open face, to block the wind and most of the snow. (Check to make sure you're allowed to do this in the area where you're camping.) There's no heat, of course. Most lean-to sites feature fire rings and picnic tables and are inexpensive compared to cabins and huts. They also tend to be in spectacular settings, their open faces looking out at lakes and mountains.

TENT PLATFORMS

A few camping areas still provide tent platforms, or wooden decks that lift your bivy off the cold, hard ground. They don't offer much advantage in winter, because they're likely covered in snow anyway. And since cold air is often trapped underneath the platform, they can even be colder than sleeping directly on the snow. But most have fire rings and picnic tables, which simplifies grilling and kitchen creation.

➔ BACKCOUNTRY CAMPING

Perhaps all of this lounging in permanent structures is not for you. You want to get out into the deep backcountry, where you can have the snow and sky all to yourself. This requires a tent or some other sort of shelter. As discussed in on pages 51–54 in Chapter 4, Backpacking Gear, the options are virtually endless, from commercial walled tents to tiny hammock mids to snow quinzees and tarp lean-tos that you construct yourself. Think about your personal needs. Do you want the comfort of being zipped into a structure built for winter camping or the adventure of building your own snowy fortress of solitude? This depends on how much you want to carry. A 16-by-20-foot canvas-walled cabin with a collapsible, stainless-steel cookstove will weigh you down a lot more than a 16-by-20-foot tarp and a shovel. Just as with any other form of camping, you have some decisions to make.

SETTING UP YOUR TENT

Once you've located a safe campsite, it's time to put up your tent. Again, it's wise to give yourself at least a couple of hours to set up camp, as establishing your campsite in winter takes longer than it does in summer.

When you select the location for your tent, you can easily pack down the snow using your boots or, better yet, your snowshoes. Tromp out an area about twice the size of your tent. Once you level the site as best you can, let it sit and harden for fifteen minutes. Next, go stomp out pathways to the other parts of camp, so you don't have post-hole on the way to the bathroom at night or wear snowshoes everywhere. You can then make any adjustments you want with the blade of your shovel. Just as you can create a custom kitchen, you can make your master bedroom to your liking. Many campers like to hollow out a shelf in front of their tent for a mudroom, giving them a place to sit and put on their boots in the morning. Others build a wall to protect the tent opening from the wind, whereas some make a walled city. Many winter tenters create a vestibule for their gear, whether the tent has one or not.

Setting up your tent in winter is slightly different than during the other three seasons. Due to the potential for high winds and heavy snows, it is imperative that the tent be taut. A saggy tent will luff like crazy in the wind, keeping you up all night, and it will stretch and wear the fabric. If it's windy when you're establishing camp, you might need several people to put up the tent, just to prevent it from blowing away. (If you do build windbreaks, situate your tent very close to them for the most benefit.)

Due to the need for tight lines, staking a tent is an important part of winter camping, and it's done differently than it is in fair weather. Those three-season stakes you have will pop back out of the snow before you have a single wall up. Instead, you have a few choices when anchoring your tent. You can buy commercially made snow or "blizzard" stakes, which are broader and stouter than the thin, candy cane–shaped aluminum ones used in summer. About 9 inches long, they're made of aluminum and have holes for the snow to penetrate. Another option is ToughStakes, which are similar in shape but have a flared bottom, like a canoe paddle. Or you could pick up some snow anchors. Sold by many outfitters, these resemble little upside-down parachutes that you bury deep in the snow. Or you can improvise your own deadman anchors.

Making a deadman is easy. Wrap the guy wire, or the tensioned cable attached to the tent, many times around a tent stake, a short piece of pole, a stick, or some other object. Dig a hole in the snow, about 1 foot to 1.5 feet deep. Place the deadman in

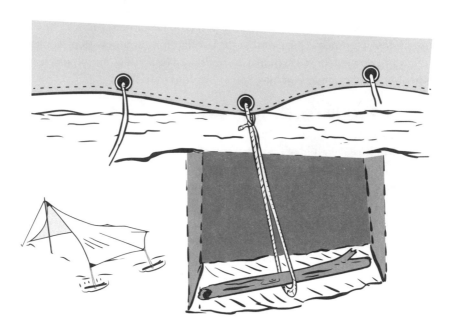

FIGURE 42. Three-season stakes will not properly anchor your tent lines in the snow, but a simple deadman stake will do the job. Wrap each tent cable securely around a stake, a stick, or a similar object then bury this anchor horizontally, about a foot deep in the snow. Pack the snow down firmly. Once it hardens nothing will be able to dislodge it until you're ready to dig it up and go.

the hole horizontally, so that it forms a T pointed away from the tent. Fill the hole, firmly packing down the snow. Once this hardens, you'll have an anchor so solid, you'll have to dig it up when you're ready to leave. In fact, deadman anchors are so effective, they're used by mountaineers in technical rescue situations. (Plastic shopping bags filled with snow can make a good, easily transportable deadman as well.)

With the anchors set at the corners of your tent, insert the poles. Adjust the hitches on your stake wires to make your tent walls taut. Then dig more deadman holes for your guy wires, pulling them nice and tight, too. Repeat the process for your tent fly. After the tent is up, you can trench out a vestibule for your pack and boots, creating a mudroom by the front door.

SNOWCRAFT

Humans have lived in homes of snow for centuries. As we know, snow is one of nature's great insulators. It's malleable and easily worked and makes exceptional building material. You can design and construct a wide variety of shelters using snow, building virtually anything you can imagine, especially if the snow is slightly moist. What follows are descriptions of a few common snow shelters.

Tarp-covered Trench

This is about as basic as building with snow gets. Dig a trench at least wide enough for your sleeping bag. Pile the snow on either side of the trench, making a trough tall enough to stand in. Form the sides into walls with your shovel. Put a tarp over your head, angling it out at either end so any falling snow slides off to the sides and away from the trench. Level the bottom for your sleeping pad. Build stairs up and out, if you want. Carve out areas to store your gear. Some campers like to make bunks on either side of the trench. Also known as a dugout, a tarp-covered snow trench has more natural ventilation than a tent and won't cause as much annoying condensation. Plus, tarps are light, waterproof, and catch more heat than most nylon tents, so the interior of your snow trench will warm quite nicely. But it's obviously not as protective as a tent and should be avoided anytime the forecast calls for warmer weather or rain. (Because the trench is a depression, it's a flood magnet.) In an emergency situation, you can dig a shallower dugout and lay strong boughs flat across the top in lieu of a tarp.

Lean-to

Another simple design. Stretch a line between two trees about 4 feet high and, using a tarp, create a lean-to, pulling the tarp down from the line to the ground. Figure out the direction of the wind and bury the end of the tarp in snow, so the wind is at the back of your lean-to. Place your sleeping pad and bag under the tarp. Shovel snow to create windbreaks at either end, if you want. Build your fire out front, aiming the heat at your sleeping space.

Quinzee

Not to be confused with an igloo, which is a dome-shaped structure built from hardened blocks, the quinzee is a snow mound with a hollowed-out interior. Of Athabaskan origin, quinzees have been used by people around the globe. They take hours to erect but make a very comfortable, warm winter home. The first step in quinzee creation is to build a flat platform using your boots and shovel to harden the snow. (The ideal snow is similar to good snowball snow.) Then shovel snow onto that platform into a pile about 10 feet high and 10 to 12 feet wide, flipping the snow over and using the shovel to pack each layer as you go. This will take some time and effort, so be careful not to overexert yourself and work up a sweat. Use your shovel to shape the pile into a dome

→ **PRO TIP** In winter, you have an ideal medium to sculpt and mold your site any way you like it. Snow allows us to easily build windbreaks, fill in depressions, and make perfectly level platforms for our tents. Be aware that the more you work the snow, though, the harder it will get, due to a freeze-thaw phenomenon called sintering. Think of it like those snowballs that turn to ice with constant cupping.

8

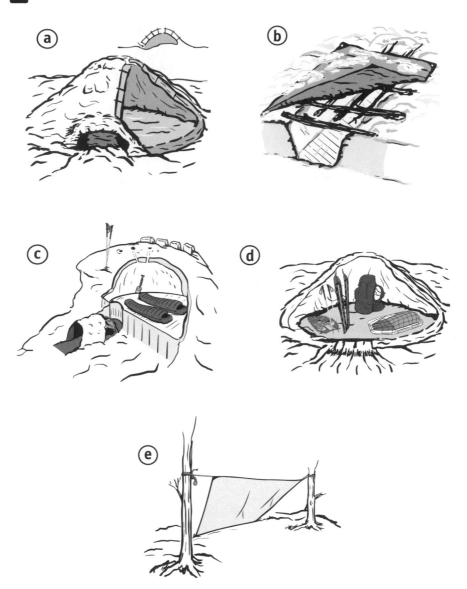

FIGURE 43. Common types of snow structures include: (a) the quinzee, which needs a pile of snow at least 10 feet across and 10 feet tall; and (b) the dugout, a long, wide trench just deep enough to sleep in. The dugout is quick to build and durable in stormy weather, making it a great emergency option. Other choices include (c) the snow cave, which is similar to a quinzee but carved out of existing snow mounds; and (d) the "gearage," a handy, semi-enclosed space made of snow walls, where you can store all of your gear. (e) The lean-to is simplest of all, consisting of little more than a strung line with a tarp hung over the top and buried in the snow at the bottom.

and allow it to harden for about 90 minutes. While it hardens, collect straight sticks about 15 inches long and insert them through the snow, into the roof and walls. These serve as thickness guides during the hollowing-out process. After the snow has firmed up, begin digging a small doorway on the downwind side. Then begin the long, arduous, and wet process of removing mass quantities of snow through the front door, in order to hollow out a cavern inside, making sure the door is the lowest point, which will help funnel out cold air. Keep digging and shoveling snow out until you see the butt ends of the sticks you placed. Make a 3- or 4-inch ventilation hole around one of them at a 45-degree angle to the floor. If the temperature is below freezing, you can pour water over the exterior to make it even stronger, making sure not to cover your ventilation holes. Then do your own interior decorating. Many campers like to carve bunks into the walls and a shelf for a candle lantern.

Because building a quinzee is a time-intensive endeavor, it's best done when you plan to stay in an area for a few days. Plug the doorway with a pack, and you'll be amazed by how warm the interior can get. More than one mountaineer has died of asphyxiation in a quinzee by using a propane lantern or stove, however, so it's best to keep gas appliances out. Quinzees work best when the temperature is 25 degrees Fahrenheit or lower.

Snow Caves

Similar to a quinzee, snow caves can make extremely comfortable and warm shelters, and they're exceptional escapes if caught out in a storm. Snow caves are typically carved out of existing mounds, areas where wind-driven snow has collected in big drifts. This can happen on the sides of small hills or ridges, on stream banks, or beside erratic boulders or fallen trees. When selecting a cave location, make doubly sure you are out of avalanche danger. Use your ski pole to probe potential locations, looking for any interior impediments to digging, such as logs or boulders.

Once satisfied, begin excavating by making a tunnel about 3 feet long, up and into the mound. Then start hollowing out a chamber. The entrance tunnel will serve as a cold air funnel, and you want to make sure your sleeping platform is higher than the ceiling of the tunnel. This allows heat to rise into your bedroom. Hollow out a chamber, leaving the ceiling and walls about 15 inches thick. You can measure using the same kind of guide sticks as in the quinzee process. You'll also need a ventilation hole, which should be at a 45-degree angle from the sleeping platform. Use your pack to cover the door. With only a candle inside for heat, you can raise the temperature to about 40 degrees, regardless of how cold it is outside. Many campers keep a shovel handy inside, in case of collapse, and mark the entrance with a bough or ski pole so they can find it in heavy snow or low visibility.

8

"Gearages"

At home, you keep your tools and transportation in your garage. In camp, you can do the same. Many cold-weather explorers dig a nook at their site (away from their sleeping area) for their sled, extra supplies, skis and poles, and all the other gear that gets us into the winter woods. To create a gearage, stick your skis, snowshoes, poles, and ice ax vertically into the snow. Make piles of food totes and dry bags and organize as you see fit. Build a quick snow wall around the area to keep everything from blowing around. Bring some extra black plastic contractor bags to lay over your pile at night, making it much easier to clean off the snow in the morning. These bags also attract sunlight, keeping whatever's underneath warmer. At the end of the trip, you can use them for hauling out wet gear or trash or a multitude of other uses.

> **→ PRO TIP** Be sure everyone in camp knows what's where. It won't do to have people tearing apart the gearage for the first-aid kit if it's in the kitchen.

SLEEPING WARM

Assuming you've followed the basics of bringing two layers of sleeping pads and a cold-weather sleeping bag rated to the temperature at which you're sleeping, there are a handful of extra tricks for staying warm and snug in your tent. Here are a few.

- **Be dry.** Change out of your sweaty clothes and into the next day's thermals. Going to bed damp is a good way to stay chilled all night. Some people bring a set of sleepwear and leave it in their bag.

- **Fluff your bag.** Give your sleeping bag a shake before you get in at night to evenly distribute the loft or down.

- **Find a friend.** Two bodies equals twice the body heat, whether in the same bag or the same tent.

- **Don't touch the walls of the tent.** We all remember hearing this anytime it rained on a camping trip growing up. The same holds true in winter. When your bag hits the wall, it gets chilled from conduction.

- **Eat and hydrate.** This provides your body with the fuel it needs to generate warmth as you sleep. You can even bring a little snack to bed with you, so if you wake up cold in the middle of the night, you can eat it and warm right up to help you get back to sleep.

- **Wear a hat.** Your head is one of the few parts of the body that is occasionally uncovered while you sleep. A toque helps keep it toasty, in case it escapes the mummy sack.

- **Socks rock.** A fresh, dry pair does wonders.

- **Make a puffer buffer.** Some campers like to wear their puffer jacket or vest to bed and sleep in a lighter bag. Or they tuck these lofty items around themselves so there is less space to heat in the bag itself.

- **Warm your water bottle.** Heat water in your water bottle and place it near your feet for a bit of radiant warmth. This also keeps the next day's water from freezing.

- **Zip your jacket.** If you have an extra jacket or vest, zip it around the base of your bag to keep your feet snug.

- **Go to bed warm.** Sit by the fire to warm up before turning in. Going to sleep cold makes more work for your body. Doing a few sit-ups in your bag can raise your body temperature, as well.

- **Go when nature calls.** No one likes to get out of a warm sleeping bag and step into the cold to urinate at night, but urination is part of how the body manages heat and circulation. Work with the system.

MANAGING CONDENSATION

When we breathe at night, we exhale moisture. The heat from our bodies changes from a vapor to a liquid when it hits cold surfaces. And wet gear heats up and dribbles in our tent. All this wetness causes our bags and the interior of our tent to get soggy. When everything is damp, we get colder. Try these tricks to combat this problem.

- **Take off your jacket.** It's great to be cozy in your sleeping bag at night, but if you feel yourself getting too warm, remove a layer or open your bag a bit. Perspiration feeds the condensation problem.

- **Candlelight helps.** A candle lantern, positioned safely, can raise the temperature enough in your tent to dry off those drippy walls.

- **Throw in the towel.** Put an extra towel in your pack for wiping moisture off the walls of your tent.

- **Keep your chin up.** Resist the temptation to bury your head in your sleeping bag. This causes all your exhalations to clam up the interior of your bag, which can lead to a chill.

- **Ventilate.** So often in winter, we seal up our tents to prevent cold air from seeping in, but this compounds condensation. Utilize your tent's ventilation system. Leave a door or window open a crack to allow air to circulate.

➜ PRO TIP Space blankets are made from a thin plastic coated with a metallic, reflecting material and are waterproof, breathable, and direct as much as 70 percent of your body heat back toward you. Weighing in at less than half a pound, they can make an impromptu clamshell lean-to over you, or you can simply wrap them burrito-style around your sleeping bag. Some winter campers even use these inexpensive, reusable thermal tarps as their only shelter, foregoing a tent altogether.

8

- **Brush off snow.** Before you get into your tent, bang your feet together and whisk the snow off, tracking in the least amount of added moisture you can.

- **Use a vapor barrier** in your bag to keep the moisture from escaping.

- **Bag it.** Put anything wet in a dry bag and keep it shut at night.

OPERATING IN THE COLD AND DARK

Night falls earlier during the winter months, and the temperature falls with it. A lot more of your time in camp will be spent wearing a headlamp than on those summer forays you're used to, and the cold is omnipresent. These conditions turn many people off to winter camping. Their loss. There are plenty of ways to stay warm, happy, and well lit.

- **Warm your boots.** Put a hot water bottle in your boots for a few minutes in the morning before you lace them up.

- **Boot liners.** Put yours down by your feet in your sleeping bag, and they'll be warm and dry in the morning.

- **Hand warmers.** Stuff a few of these in your pocket to keep your digits warm. Put them in your sleeping bag before you turn in and into your boots before you put those on. Warmers are cheap and can brighten your mood quickly.

- **Keep your headlamp handy.** Most winter campers keep a headlamp nearby at all times. Having it right next to your pillow at night makes those cold trips to the bathroom easier.

- **Use lithium when you can.** Make sure the batteries in all of your winter electronics are lithium. Alkaline batteries use water-based electrolytes, which can freeze. Lithium batteries work well in the cold, and they're lighter, to boot. They are slightly higher voltage than alkaline batteries, however, and not all electronics can handle them, so make sure yours can before venturing out.

- **Light bright.** Bring a few more lights than you might in summer—and a lot of extra batteries. Your lights will be on longer than you're used to.

- **Let the healing begin.** If it gets extremely cold, rubbing petroleum jelly on exposed skin helps prevent chapping and frostbite.

- **Extra socks and bags.** Wrap some warm extra socks in a plastic bag; big zipper-closure bags or the plastic grocery sacks will do. If your feet get wet, you can wear the socks and line your boots with the plastic until you get back to camp.

- **Keep the pot on.** Having a ready supply of hot water for hot cocoa, coffee, and tea always perks up the masses. And take a thermos so you can have hot drinks throughout the day.

8

- **Enjoy the stars.** Many winter explorers are tempted to turn in right after dinner due to darkness and exhaustion. Then they wake up at 3 A.M. and have hours to kill. Stay up, sing songs, and take in the star show. The crystalline skies of winter make the constellations really pop.

- **Build a fire.** It's not always possible, because many places these days don't allow or discourage it, but a campfire brightens everyone's day. And know that winter lessens the impact of a campfire.

- **Eat.** You need the calories to stay warm.

- **Bring a book.** Hours of exertion and long nights can lead to turning in early. A good book, preferably one by Andrew Vietze, is always good company.

8

CHAPTER 9

ACTIVITY GEAR AND SKILLS

→ Winter Hiking   162
→ Snowshoeing   165
→ Skiing   170
→ Splitboarding   176
→ Ice Climbing   177
→ Pulks   179
→ Fat Bikes   182

→ WINTER HIKING

Even when it comes to something as basic as putting one foot in front of the other, winter adds layers of complexity to outdoor exploration. You need to be cognizant of the weather forecast, of the time of day, and of snow conditions. And although you should always have safety equipment with you at any time of year, the need magnifies tenfold in winter. You might be able to get away with taking off on a whim in summer, carrying only a water bottle. It's not wise, but you probably can survive it. Just strolling out the door in winter, unprepared, carries infinitely more risk.

The simple act of walking is more difficult in winter. Unless you're prepared for the conditions, you can end up post-holing in no time, making little forward progress. So, yes, winter may be an unforgiving season, but it's also a spectacularly beautiful one, and easy to enjoy with a little planning and effort. And with a few key tools—traction devices, such as Microspikes; crampons; and snowshoes—you will be able to handle whatever conditions nature puts in your path.

HIKING IN TRACTION DEVICES

When hiking in winter in areas that are snowy but not covered with ice, other traction devices, such as Microspikes, are useful additions to your winter gear. They're light, easy to put on, come in a wide variety of styles, and are fairly inexpensive. When you're going for a hike early in winter before the ice fields form, these can be ideal to tuck into your backpack for use at higher elevations. They also feature virtually no learning curve—you can simply strap them on and go.

Models vary. Some traction devices look almost like the bottoms of galoshes: rubber bands that you pull on over the soles of your boots, with little cleats beneath the ball of the foot and at the heel. Others have rows of teeth underneath the front half of your boot. Some that you step into, like baskets, look more like the chains that you put on your car tires, with metal coils crisscrossing beneath your feet. Others feature chains with spikes at the toe and the heel. They all are comfortable to walk in and require little change in your stride, although some work best when you dig in your toe.

HIKING IN CRAMPONS

Big gnarly spikes, crampons make all the difference when climbing up snowy and icy pitches. Walking in crampons is not as simple as walking in more basic traction devices, like Microspikes, however. You can't just strap them onto the soles of your boots and trot up the mountain. You need practice wearing these sharp teeth, and you should seek out a bit of training before you venture off onto the slopes. Usually paired with ice axes, crampons allow you to hike safely on steep inclines, but those steep inclines could lead to a steep fall, so you need to know how to self-arrest—that is, to stop yourself from sliding—before you can safely take to the iced-over hills.

A traditional pair of crampons features twelve points, ten facing down and two facing forward. These tines are extremely sharp and can easily puncture a boot or rip through snow pants, so you need to walk deliberately. These days, manufacturers sell a variety of crampon types, some of which have half the points of traditional pairs. Some are rigid, for mountaineering-type boots, whereas others feature flex bars, which work better with boots that are less stiff. You can also purchase crampons that slide under skis, which provide supreme traction on ascents.

The secret to using these devices is to make sure you have at least two points of contact with the mountain on each step, either an ax and one foot or both feet. As you head uphill, you'll generally use the front points of each crampon, bending your front knee and digging in with that foot, then placing your ax, and only then moving your other foot. Under some conditions, it helps to step sideways, lifting one foot

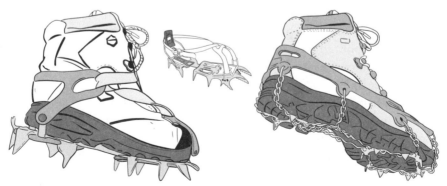

FIGURE 44. Crampons (left) and Microspike-like traction devices (right) are simple to attach and can make hiking on slippery or frozen terrain easier and safer. Which type of device you choose depends on your hiking conditions and level of experience.

over the other to climb. In especially steep terrain, you might even use your ice ax with both hands in front of you, walking pigeon-toed so you don't stab your feet. On the descent, you'll usually walk heel first, especially in loose snow, although there are times when you might step sideways or herringbone your way down.

As with most specialized gear, you should take a lesson or two before setting off on your own. This is especially important for learning how to attach your crampons correctly, something at which many beginners fail. In addition to giving lessons, many outfitters rent crampons, so you can explore whether this type of travel is for you. By getting comfortable on these spikes on your own time, you'll be ready for a safe and fun adventure when you do head out.

When to Wear What: Crampons Versus Snowshoes Versus Other Traction Devices

You're heading out with friends on a winter weekend, and you're not sure whether to wear your crampons or a different sort of traction device. There are a couple factors at play, the primary ones being the angle of incline you're planning to hike and the depth of the snow. If you're wearing metal coil-type traction, such as YakTrax, you want to stay on level ground. If there's a bit of incline and the ground seems too slippery for your hiking boots, pull out your Microspikes. That's exactly what these little cleats were designed for. They'll give you the traction you need below treeline on slick trails or even above treeline, in areas where there's a little snow and ice or the slopes are not steep. When you start going up, however, especially on ice, densely packed snow, or a mixture of rock and ice—or anytime you're concerned your traction devices might slip—switch to your crampons. They'll give you a good firm grip and allow you to dig in your toes when needed. When you feel yourself sinking into the snow, pulling your boots up and out of the flakes, it's time to strap on your snowshoes.

POLES

Trekking poles are a must in winter. Many hikers like them year-round, but they're more useful than ever during the cold-weather months, when the terrain tends to be slippery and full of surprises. Your poles help you check snow depths, test for thin ice, and provide extra stability when you're on snowshoes or slick ground. Although your three-season hiking poles will work fine in winter, they're not ideal. We recommend poles specifically designed for snow, often called snowshoeing poles, which feature bigger baskets. Attached at the base of the pole, these little devices prevent your poles from sinking too deeply, playing the same sort of role that snowshoes do for your feet. The larger the basket the more flotation it provides. (You can also buy winter baskets for existing poles or trekking poles that come with additional baskets, extending the poles' use into other seasons.)

Winter-specific poles generally have latch-locking systems rather than the traditional twist mechanism featured on three-season poles. Twist poles can pose a problem when your hands are cold and wet, slipping every time you turn. They can also let snow or ice collect in the lock itself, causing the mechanism to fail. Winter poles also have longer grips, which can help when going up- or downhill sideways. Always let your poles dry before collapsing them at the end of a trip to prevent moisture from collecting.

→ SNOWSHOEING

In 2016, a cartographer stumbled across an oval of birch and twine while making maps at 10,000 feet in the Dolomite Mountains, on Italy's Austrian border. He gave the curious item to archaeologists who carbon dated it and announced that the laced wooden device was the oldest snowshoe ever discovered, dating back almost 6,000 years. Popularized in North America by the Algonquin tribes of the Northeast, snowshoes have come a long way from their humble, trip-happy beginnings. And they've evolved more in the past 50 years than they did in the previous 6,000.

Today, manufacturers design snowshoes in a wide variety of styles. You can find the traditional bent-ash-and-leather shoes, which many old-school hikers still use. Or you can buy modern plastic and aluminum decks with their own crampons and crank-tightening systems. They all do the job, which is to keep us on the surface of the snow as much as possible. Like the fat paws of a snowshoe hare, snowshoes distribute weight over a wider area than a boot, allowing us to float on the top of a snowfield.

The advent of skinnier, more user-friendly snowshoes over the past few decades has resulted in an explosion in snowshoeing as a winter sport. Modern shoes are simpler to put on, offer better traction, and are easier to maneuver in than ever before. Hikers everywhere began to add the cold-weather months to their calendars.

Most winter campers choose between snowshoes and skis for getting out into the bush. Snowshoes tend to be more straightforward for beginners, and they can go places that skis can't, such as off-trail or up sheer slopes, opening up more territory to exploration. Many travelers bring both on their cold-weather trips, selecting whichever works better for the terrain of the day. For quickly traversing long, level, open distances, skis are hard to beat. For around camp, on steep inclines, or in densely forested areas, snowshoes make more sense.

→ PRO TIP When snow conditions change on the trail from cold and dry to warm and wet, or when you're crossing frozen ponds or small streams, snowshoes tend to accumulate ice under the crampon harness on the shoes' bottoms. This can go unnoticed until lack of solid contact with snow or ice causes the hiker to lose traction, slipping and sliding and possibly being injured. The "ice ball" is extremely difficult to chop away from the snowshoe, taking time and risking unwanted exposure to the elements. This also can happen with traction devices, such as Microspikes. As temperatures change throughout the day, check for ice accumulation with the help of fellow trekkers who can take a quick look without slowing down the whole group.

9

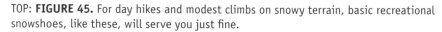

9

TOP: **FIGURE 45.** For day hikes and modest climbs on snowy terrain, basic recreational snowshoes, like these, will serve you just fine.

MIDDLE: **FIGURE 46.** Not for use with a heavy pack or on rugged terrain, fitness snowshoes are designed for running or other exercise on well-maintained, snowy trails.

BOTTOM: **FIGURE 47.** Mountaineering snowshoes tend to be heavier and more expensive than other varieties, but with aggressive traction and the ability to handle loads up to 300 pounds, they are the shoes to get if you're going to be breaking trail in deep snowpack.

TYPES OF SNOWSHOES
Traditional
Up until the 1970s, everyone used traditional ash-frame snowshoes, and a few people still like them for aesthetic or nostalgic reasons. Most have the traditional "racket" shape, but some, like those used by the Cree nation, have pointed tips and long beaver tails. Wood shoes tend to be slightly more flexible than modern models, but they require tying rawhide laces, which can be a pain when wearing gloves or mittens.

Modern
In the 1970s, a manufacturer from Washington introduced a snowshoe constructed of aluminum with neoprene decking. Nicknamed the "Western" snowshoe, these light and easy-to-use frames revolutionized the snowshoeing industry. This style has developed over the years, and these days, snowshoe makers use stainless steel, aluminum, and injection-molded plastics to create their shoes. Most have cleats under the toes for maximum traction, even in icy conditions, and employ clasps or buckled bindings that are much more user-friendly in cold conditions. They're now offered in models designed for recreation, fitness, and mountaineering.

Recreational Snowshoes
These are the most common snowshoes found at outfitters, and they're great all-around decks for beginners. They come in a wide variety of styles and materials. Most use plastic or aluminum for the frame and have a row of crampons under the binding for digging in when needed. Some are rounded, whereas others have pointed tips. Some plastic models have rails of carbon steel teeth; others have cleats at the back for additional traction. Bindings might be buckles, rubber straps, locking clasps, or even cranks. Sizes vary by weight and expected load, with longer decks for bigger individuals and heavier packs. Recreational shoes work best for hikers with light loads on flat, relatively level landscapes. Most will do fine for day hikes and modest climbs.

Fitness Snowshoes
As the name suggests, fitness—also known as racing or aerobic—snowshoes are intended for jogging or otherwise exercising on snowy terrain. They are built narrow, usually of lightweight aluminum, and often feature V-shaped tails and beefy bindings that will hold on to your boots or trail shoes when moving at a clip. Many have specialized suspensions to handle the vigorous pounding of a runner. These are not the snowshoes for expedition use or hiking with a pack; they are more appropriate for groomed trails or crusty snows.

Mountaineering Snowshoes
These rackets are specifically designed for use on trails and peaks while carrying a heavy pack. Stout and rugged, they provide aggressive traction, with crampons

9

under the toe and at the rear, often with teeth on the side rails, too. Made of aluminum or plastic, the decks can handle loads up to 300 pounds or more, and they come in various sizes for different body types. The bindings have extra flex for climbing and hang on even when you're breaking trail in deep snowpack. They tend to be heavier than fitness or recreational models, as well as more expensive.

> ➜ **PRO TIP** Recreational or "hiking" snow-shoes provide the most bang for your buck. You can wear them contentedly into the backcountry, knowing they're made for that purpose, but you can also use them for an afternoon jog, making them a good multipurpose option.

HOW TO CHOOSE SNOWSHOES

Buying a pair of snowshoes is much like purchasing hiking boots: You have to decide where and how you will use them then find a pair that's comfortable and best suits your needs. Some traditionalists like the look and feel of wooden models, but that style is not as effective in backcountry situations where some form of crampon is needed and is rarely used today. Most people go for modern styles, but which should you choose? There are a handful of considerations.

- Perhaps most important is the binding. Are the snowshoes you're considering easy to get on and off? You put on and remove your snowshoes several times on an average winter adventure, usually while wearing gloves or mittens, and you don't want it to be a hassle. Clicking one or two buckles or cranking a knob is much easier than tying laces or attaching a handful of straps.

- Plastic or aluminum frames? This is a personal preference. Both serve you fine under most conditions. Some plastic models have the added ability to attach a tail, which helps when you're carrying a heavy pack. Plus, they can be used as shovels in a pinch. Others have a "televator" that lifts the heel on the ascent, reducing fatigue.

- Check the crampons. If you plan to use your shoes largely for climbing, you want an aggressive bite that can handle ice. Models with heel cleats help when you're descending slopes. If you think you'll be hiking in less mountainous regions, you don't need as many teeth.

- What about your boots? Think about what boots you'll be wearing with these snowshoes. Better yet, bring them with you to the store when you're trying on snowshoes. Some bindings work better with wider, heavier boots than others.

- Rent before you buy. You might want to consider renting and trying different styles from your local outfitter. It's a relatively inexpensive way to sample various styles and narrow down your options based on what works best for you.

9

FIGURE 48. Although your stride needs to be a bit wider than usual to avoid stepping on the insides of your snowshoe frames, walking on level ground in snowshoes (a) is intuitive and not much different than walking normally. If your snowshoes have built-in heavy-duty crampons (b), or while ascending and descending slopes, you will sometimes need to exaggerate your heel lift and dig in your toe in order to make progress.

HOW TO CARE FOR SNOWSHOES

Most snowshoes will provide you with many years of service, although, like anything else, they'll last longer if you take good care of them. Wipe them off or dry them after each use. Store them somewhere out of the sun. While wooden shoes are rare these days, if you nostalgically have a pair, check them for cracks and varnish the frame to prevent rot. Rodents love rawhide lacing, so hang your shoes somewhere critters can't reach. With modern aluminum or plastic shoes, clean off dirt and debris before putting them away. Inspect the straps and buckles. Check the cleats for rust. Look for any broken rivets in the deck and replace them. If there are issues you can't fix yourself, many outfitters repair snowshoes for a fee.

9

HOW TO GET UP WHEN YOU FALL
By Ryan Smith

Think of it as a sign of progress rather than failure: Falling on snowshoes or cross-country skis is part of learning a new skill. Although it's never enjoyable to fall, practice makes perfect. Try righting yourself on varying grades and standing up from both your right and left sides. Working on these skills in a simulated environment will save you time and effort in a real-life scenario. With a little practice and determination, you'll be back on your feet in no time.

1. Remove your backpack if you're wearing one.

2. Roll onto your side. On sloped terrain, position your feet downhill.

3. Still on your side, plant the crampon of your slope-side snowshoe into the ground for better traction.

4. Use your poles as a brace to help you stand up, first on your slope-side leg and then on your outer leg.

➔ SKIING

Although snowshoeing is an excellent option for exploring the backcountry, skis possess their own distinct advantages. Under the right conditions, they allow you to travel farther faster and, for many people, they're simply more fun. Few sensations in the winter woods beat skiing fast down a hill.

There are many varieties of skiing. There's the alpine version done at resorts, with big plastic boots and a lot of fancy clothes. There's cross-country or nordic skiing, with its skinny skis and free heels. And there's the combination of the two, in telemark and backcountry skiing, which allow you not only to climb hills but to descend intense black-diamond slopes. Just remember: Whenever you are skiing, splitboarding, or otherwise recreating in the backcountry, always make sure to wear an avalanche beacon.

TYPES OF SKIING
Nordic/cross-country

Like snowshoeing, cross-country skiing dates back thousands of years—in this case, 5,000, to the Sami people of Scandinavia—and has boomed in popularity during the past 50 or 60. Ancient peoples used skis for the same purpose we do today: to get places faster than trudging through snow. The sport takes a while to master, but once you've done so, you can traverse miles of backcountry in short order.

Nordic skis are much narrower and longer than their traditional downhill cousins, and they feature binding systems that allow the heel to lift off the ski, so that skiers can kick and propel themselves along flat or undulating terrain. Again, like snowshoes, cross-country skis come in an array of different styles, depending upon

9

intended use. Touring skis are built to travel distances, often in the backcountry, and they're generally used by people doing the traditional kick and glide. Racing and skating skis are narrow and shorter and are usually worn on groomed trails, which can be found at resorts and parks. Skiers on skate skis mimic the motion of ice skaters and can hit high speeds.

The beauty of nordic skis is their adaptability to a wide variety of conditions. You might start a day slogging through deep powder only to find yourself ending the afternoon on thin, icy, granular snow at higher elevations. Nordic skis can handle both types of conditions with aplomb. You can thread through a forest, ski across open meadows and wide lakes, and herringbone up one side of a hill only to fly down the other side. Thanks to gliding skis, on a good day, you can traverse at double the speed of someone walking on snowshoes.

Alpine Skiing

Otherwise known as downhill skiing, alpine skiing takes you down steep mountainsides at exhilaratingly high speeds. Most alpine skiing takes place at resorts, where trails are carved down the sides of peaks, and lifts transport skiers upward so they can zip down groomed slopes again and again. Some skiers like to venture to backcountry areas and try their luck off-trail, bombing down crazy pitches and making fresh tracks. The affluent among them hire helicopters to fill the role of the chairlift, carrying them to the summit.

Downhill skiers wear boots of solid plastic that click into large bindings at both the toe and the heel, locking them in place. Although this is crucial for downhill skiing, it greatly complicates moving across flat ground.

Due to the inherent dangers involved in hurtling down the side of a mountain at high speeds, it's recommended you take a few lessons before attempting to ski on your own. Ski resorts everywhere offer lessons.

Backcountry

Sometimes called alpine touring or randonnée, backcountry skiing is a bit of a hybrid between downhill and cross-country skiing. Backcountry skis are wider and shorter than traditional nordic skis and have sharp metal edges, like alpine skis. The accompanying boots are the offspring of a hiking boot and a cross-country ski boot, with rugged Vibram soles, insulation for warmth, and a toe that attaches into the binding. The big difference is that the binding features a locking system at the heel like an alpine ski.

With backcountry skis, you can kick and glide over long, flat distances, but you can also carve your way down incredibly steep slopes with a fixed heel. When you encounter rock instead of snow, you can slip off your skis and use your boots alone. And when you begin to climb serious pitches, you can slide climbing skins over the bottom of your skis to provide them with grip. Typically made of mohair or nylon, climbing skins are long strips that loop over the tip and hook to the back of your skis, allowing you to scale rugged inclines without removing your skis by using tiny hairs that slide in one

9

direction and grab in the other. Backcountry skiing has grown dramatically in popularity in recent years, as downhill ski resorts have become crowded and expensive.

Telemark

Telemarking is similar to alpine touring in that it marries the touring aspect of cross-country skiing with the steep, high-speed descents of downhill skiing. Telemarking just does it differently. Telemark skiers use the free heel of nordic skiing to cover long cross-country stretches and also use skins for climbing. Then, when it comes time to speed downhill, they employ the telemark turn, a technical move in which the skier drops one knee, as if lunging, so that the skis remain parallel but one extends half a ski length in front of the other, with the heels remaining free. Although not a beginner's move, when perfected, this turn gives telemarkers the freedom to zoom downhill at speeds not far removed from those of alpine skiers. Telemark ski bindings are stouter and sturdier than other nordic ski bindings.

SKI BOOTS

Boots vary depending upon the type of skiing and the binding used. Alpine skiing boots are heavy-duty affairs constructed out of hard, molded plastic. Consisting of an interior boot within an exterior shell, they're difficult to walk in, causing the wearer to lean forward slightly, and they have huge, clasping, buckle-closure systems. Some of the more advanced models feature an interior suspension, much like sneaker gels, to provide shock absorption. Alpine "hike and ride" boots look much the same as their traditional alpine siblings, but they boast a pull at the back that releases the cuff of the boot, allowing you to stride normally instead of at the angle of a traditional downhill boot.

Nordic ski boots are much smaller in profile, although they, too, come in a variety of styles. There are brightly colored, thinly insulated, high-top models with zippers and around-the-ankle clasps, as well as clumpy, old-fashioned, lace-up boots with big plastic bars at the toes to accommodate the traditional three-pin ski binding systems. Backcountry ski boots, meanwhile, look for all the world like thick, insulated, winter hiking boots with Vibram soles. Underneath, however, lie grooves designed to fit into ski bindings. Many high-end models feature built-in, zip-up gaiters to keep laces snow free.

As with any boot, it's crucial to get a good, comfortable fit. We certainly recommend clomping around the store to get a sense of how any pair suits you. If boots are too loose, you risk blisters, and you'll have poor control over your skis. If they're too tight or poorly insulated, your feet will get cold, making frostbite a possibility. And unless you want to buy a new set of bindings for your skis, it's imperative you purchase boots that fit your skis' specific binding type.

9

SKI POLES

Salespeople at ski stores often tell you that, for nordic skiing, your poles should fit under your armpits. But pole length is really a matter of personal preference. Many skiers prefer poles as tall as their shoulders, allowing the skier to reach out and grab the snow, really digging in. Others like a shorter pole, preferring to push off closer to the ribs. Most everyone who skate-skis wants a pole on the longer side of things. Like boots and bindings, poles vary depending on the intended use. If you're recreational touring, your pole likely will be light, with a small basket that can plunge deeper into the snow than a larger basket. If you're racing, you want an even lighter pole, with an even smaller basket. Mountaineers usually carry a heavy-duty pole with a bigger basket at the bottom because they typically trek through deep snow. If you're backcountry skiing, you might want a telescoping pole that's adjustable

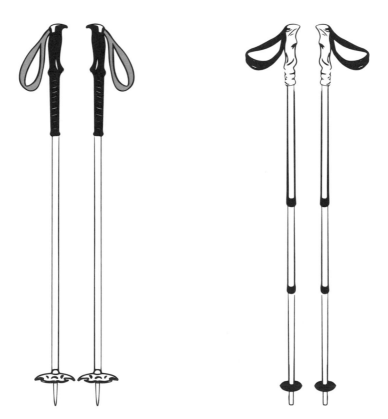

FIGURE 49. Ski poles and winter trekking poles (left) generally have larger baskets than three-season trekking poles (right), a feature that keeps your poles from sinking too far into the snow and helps with stability.

9

in length, extending it longer on the ascent and shorter on the descent, with a larger basket at the bottom. Downhill poles are always considerably shorter than cross-country poles and have bigger baskets to keep fast-moving skiers from being slowed down by deep-plunging poles.

WHERE TO LEARN TO SKI

Learning to ski is a fun but time-consuming process, and you most certainly will spend a good amount of time on your backside. No matter what type of skiing you're interested in pursuing, plan on days of getting comfortable and a lot of time getting yourself back on your feet. For these reasons, the best places to learn are usually at or near ski resorts. Most downhill areas have full-scale teaching facilities, where you learn and practice the basics until you're ready to venture higher up the mountain. Many of the big ski resorts have their own—or partner with—nordic ski centers, where you can pay for lessons and try out your skinny ski skills on groomed trails. Likewise, several big outfitters offer courses in skills including telemarking, backcountry skiing, and basic ski touring.

HOW TO SKIN

In order to enjoy exhilarating runs through virgin powder, you have to first make it to the top of the mountain. That's where skins come in. These are long strips of mohair or nylon fabric that fit on the base of your ski and provide traction. With a good pair of skins, you can climb any slope you want to ski, thus liberating you from expensive, bustling ski areas and their boring slopes. Any peak you scout and climb, you can ski down—assuming you have permission. Many skiers find this freedom quite a rush and enjoy the thrill of finding peaks to ascend and descend. One of the beauties of skins is these simple strips get people out into the beautiful backcountry and away from the crowds.

They couldn't be any easier to use. Slide the loop over the tip of your ski, smooth the skin down the base, allowing the adhesive to bind to the ski, and use the hook at the tail. Let the plush, or those little grippy fibers, do the rest. They work by grabbing the ground in one direction and sliding in the other. The idea is basically the same as cross-country skiing. If you're skinning correctly, you're gliding forward on your skis, rather than picking up your feet and walking. Most climbers who skin ascend sections at a time, making small switchbacks to avoid going directly up steep slopes.

Skinning Tips

- When ascending, switchback your way up the peak.
- Make sure your pack is well balanced.
- Kick your foot forward, sliding; then place most of the weight on your heels.
- Remove your skins from the tails, peel them halfway back, and use a "cheat

9

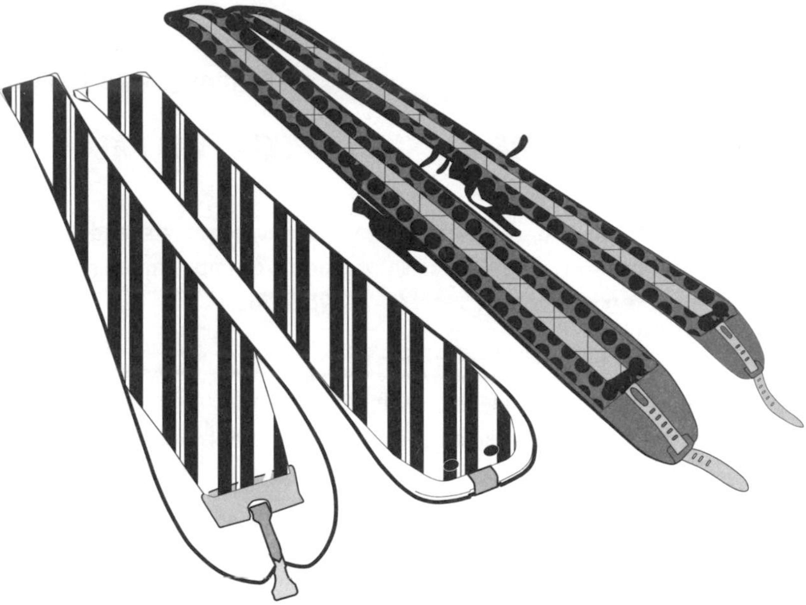

FIGURE 50. Skins are handy when you need to ascend an incline while wearing backcountry skis, and they're easy to attach. Simply slip the skin over the tip of your ski, smooth it along the ski base, and loop the skin back around the ski tail.

sheet" or "skin saver" (a no-stick panel that covers the sticky bottom) to lengthen the life of your skins. Try to cover as much of the glue as possible.

- Apply a bit of paraffin wax over your skins to keep the snow from clumping on the bottom.

- Put your skins in your jacket between climbs to allow them to thaw and dry a bit.

HOW TO CARE FOR YOUR SKIS

Caring for your skis is a bit of an art, regardless of the type of ski you use, but there are many ways to do so. You'll prolong their lives by making sure you remove snow and dirt with a soft cloth each time you put them away. If you strap them together and store them dry, the edges won't rust. That's all easy. The more difficult part of ski maintenance is waxing and sharpening the edges. Waxing the base makes the ski glide better and prevents snow and ice from building up—and this includes the smooth part of popular "waxless" skis. Waxing also fills in any scratches and defects, making for a smoother ride. Many serious skiers wax their skis after every day on the slopes. Others do so every three or four trips. A wax job requires heating the wax with a clothes iron, dripping it down the length of the ski, ironing it smooth, and then scraping off any excess, leaving the ski with an even coating. Because it's so involved, many skiers take their skis to an outfitter to be serviced. When there,

9

skiers can also have the edges sharpened with a file, removing any burrs or sharp spots. Filing is more technical than waxing, and most skiers have it done once a season. Remember to be careful when carrying skis with freshly sharpened edges.

HOW TO GET BACK UP ON SKIS WHEN YOU FALL
By Ryan Smith

Because skis aren't equipped with a crampon underfoot, beginners tend to have a harder time standing up after a spill than snowshoers. It's important to assess the terrain first to figure out where you should point your skis.

1. Remove your hands from the pole straps.

2. Bending your knees and using your arms to push off the ground, shift your upper body over your skis, keeping your feet about hip-width apart. It's sometimes easier to shift your weight onto your downhill ski while your other leg remains bent.

3. Using your poles, push to the uphill side of your body to help you stand up.

4. Dust yourself off, put your hands back in the pole straps, and ski on.

→ SPLITBOARDING

Splitboarding is to snowboarding what alpine touring is to downhill skiing. The sport utilizes a snowboard that can split into two halves, allowing boarders to climb peaks with skins as if they were on skis. Splitboarders "ski tour" their way to the top, similar to how a backcountry skier using skins would, and reassemble their two halves at the summit so they can shred their way down. This clever bifurcation bestows the same freedoms on snowboarders that their ski cousins enjoy, getting them out into the backcountry and away from resorts and crowds.

SPLITBOARD GEAR

The first piece of equipment you'll need to splitboard is the board itself. For all intents and purposes, these resemble snowboards, except with a series of S-hooks or clasps on the deck that fix the two pieces together. A good board is more expensive than a traditional snowboard, setting you back several hundred bucks. Next up are the specialized bindings, which flex to give you the free heel needed for touring then lock back into place for riding. Many splitboarders wear regular snowboard boots. Others buy boots specifically designed for splitboarding. These have additional flex; grippy, crampon-ready outsoles; and adjustable lacing systems that tighten or loosen with the twist of a dial. Backcountry boarders also carry telescoping poles that extend for touring and shrink to fit inside a pack on the descent, as well as specialized, extra-wide skins for traction.

9

WHERE TO SPLITBOARD

Like backcountry skiing, splitboarding has really taken off, with more manufacturers making gear and more outfitters offering instruction. The first step, of course, is to learn how to snowboard, and lessons are available at just about any resort. Then you'll have to master the use of skins, which you can also pick up from many ski areas and outfitters. Then you'll need time practicing splitboard-specific techniques. An alternative is to sign up for a splitboard course through one of the many alpine skills schools that offer them.

HOW TO CARE FOR YOUR SPLITBOARD

Caring for splitboards is much like maintaining a snowboard or a pair of skis. Most experts recommend waxing the base several times a season, ideally after every run. And you should sharpen your edges, which are vital on a splitboard, at least once a year. Check that your latches and bindings are in good condition and free of ice or dirt. Clean your board with a soft towel and put it away dry. Some boarders recommend applying a coat of wax when you retire the board in the spring and scraping it off when breaking it out again in winter.

➜ ICE CLIMBING

Ice climbing is another of those technical mountaineering skills that requires advanced training and can't be covered in enough detail in a book of this type. It's a serious pastime with serious consequences if you get in over your head. That's why many consider it an extreme sport. Ice climbing takes you up sheer walls of ice, and you have to know what you're doing simply to assess whether the ice is stout enough to hold your weight. If you don't know your jumars and your prusiks, your bollards and your front points, best take some lessons.

Many outfitters and mountaineering schools offer ice-climbing classes. Many of the same places that teach rock climbing offer ice-climbing instruction in the winter.

HOW TO CARE FOR CRAMPONS AND ICE AXES

Moisture is the biggest enemy of both crampons and ice axes. Store them wet, and they will rust and eventually weaken. The best thing you can do for them is to wipe them clean with a soft cloth after each use, removing any dirt and grit. Then hang them and allow them to dry. Some users like to oil their crampons before storing them. Any kind of oil will do.

Occasionally, your crampons or other spiked traction devices will need sharpening. You can easily tell when it's time by inspecting the teeth. They should be sharp but not razor-sharp; pressing the point into your hand should hurt but not cut the skin, and a

9

light touch shouldn't hurt at all. You can touch them up yourself with a mill bastard file (don't use a powered wheel) or take them to an outdoor gear shop. When you're giving the tines a once-over, do the same with the buckles and straps, and tighten any loose screws. Once you're happy with the condition of your crampons, store them in a puncture-proof case or cover the points somehow. Over the years, winter hikers have come up with a variety of innovative ideas for this. Favorites include using an old foam mat or a plastic cutting board to cover the points then wrapping them in a piece of webbing or cutting the top off a clean, 2-liter soda bottle and storing your crampons inside. Ice ax heads need to be covered, as well, and you can fashion your own protective cover using a padded leather glove or a section of garden hose sliced down the middle. Many people use a tennis ball to cover the point.

HOW TO USE AN ICE AX
By Matt Mills

The ice ax is an essential mountaineering tool—arguably the essential tool—when climbing large, glaciated peaks or ascending steep routes on any mountain in winter. When exploring Maine's Katahdin or New Hampshire's Mount Washington in winter, using an ice ax—along with crampons—is not only recommended. It's a necessity.

STRUCTURE OF THE ICE AX
Ice axes are made up of two main components: the head and the shaft. The shaft, which is typically constructed of lightweight metal, is the longer part of the ax that often has a triangular spike at the bottom. The head (usually steel) has two main parts: the pick and the adze. The adze is broad and flat, for digging, while the sharp pick on the opposite end is used to pierce snow and ice. Some feature a hammer rather than an adze.

TYPES OF ICE AXES
There are two main types of ice axes: technical climbing axes and general mountaineering axes. Whereas technical axes are shorter, have a curved shaft, and are primarily used on vertical ice-climbing routes, general axes are longer, straighter, and predominantly used as self-arrest devices on mountaineering routes. Self-arrest, or the act of stopping an unexpected fall down a steep slope without the aid of ropes or other climbers, is a skill all mountaineers should be prepared to execute.

HOW TO HOLD AN ICE AX
While ascending or descending, hold the ax with the shaft pointed at the ground, spearing it into the snow with every step. Grip the ax with your palm directly across the head and your thumb under the adze. When hiking in a group and not on terrain where you might be self-arresting, keep the spike pointed forward, so that anyone not paying attention behind you doesn't get poked in the face. If you are carrying your ax on your pack and the spike is pointed up, make sure to cover

it with a tip protector. You can use a leash to secure the ax to either your wrist or your harness. This prevents you from losing your ax if you drop it. With the ax held properly, climbers must follow two main rules:

1. Always carry the ax in the uphill hand and switch hands whenever the terrain changes. During a climb, the uphill side of a route may reverse due to topographical changes. Likewise, the way you position your body while climbing can dictate which hand is uphill at any time.

2. Carry the ax with the adze facing forward and the pick facing backward. This ensures that the ax is already well positioned for a self-arrest maneuver.

HOW TO STOP A FALL

In the event of a fall, secure the shaft with your free hand, pull the ax up and into the shoulder/chest area, and then drive the pick into the ground with full-body-weight force. If the ax is positioned properly—in the uphill hand, pick facing back—when the fall occurs, the climber will be able to quickly insert it into the ground with the force necessary to stop a fall without losing the ax. During self-arrest, it's important to lift your feet slightly off the ground to avoid inadvertently catching your crampons in the ice and breaking your legs or pitching yourself into the air. Though broken legs are preferable to flying off a cliff face, so pick your poison.

A MULTIDIMENSIONAL TOOL

Ice axes are not limited to self-arrests. You can use the adze end to chop steps into snow or ice. You can use it as a stability tool, akin to a single trekking pole. And axes can serve as temporary anchors on steep sections of a route; you can employ simple ice-climbing techniques for short stretches by punching the pick into the ice and using the ax as a hold. The latter use can be especially helpful on steep, icy descents.

SEEK QUALIFIED TRAINING

Having an ice ax in hand won't be enough when that unexpected fall happens; you need to know how to use it properly. Seek qualified training before attempting a route that requires an ice ax. In the same way that reading a trail description doesn't eliminate the need to carry a map, simply studying self-arrest techniques will never substitute for real, hands-on experience.

➜ PULKS

9

Pulks—a fancy name for a pullable sled without runners—provide a big advantage in winter: We can bring more stuff. We can travel farther, explore more, and do so in relative comfort, thanks to the amount of gear we can transport. If you want to get into the backcountry for several days of cold-weather adventure, get yourself a pulk. If you have a child who also needs gear transported, a pulk is for you. If you are ferrying much of the gear for a group, pulk up. And if you want maximum comfort in the middle of winter, it's a pulk every time. People have been dragging their gear behind them for millennia, and sledges (heavy-duty gear transport sleds), in particular, have long Arctic traditions.

You'll have some decisions to make when it comes to your pulk. You can buy a commercial pulk designed for winter adventuring with a professionally crafted harness system or you can buy a less expensive "expedition" sled (a long, deep model with tall sides) from the hardware store and DIY (see Figure 51 on page 181). Regardless, a pulk greatly expands the amount of gear you can bring. Some winter campers even use them to truck in dry firewood (if local regulations allow it) or shrink-wrapped bundles of BioBricks (a firewood alternative made from compressed organic matter).

TIPS FOR USING YOUR PULK

- Pick the right sled. The plastic sleds your kids ride all winter long work fine for the occasional weekend trip, but they're not something you're going to want to use for years on end, due to their relatively thin skins. On the other end, the big black rubber sleds you see towed behind snowmobiles are too bulky for human-powered locomotion. You can find a variety of "expedition sleds" at outfitters and even some big-box or hardware stores.

- Crossing the PVC piping in your tow lines adds great rigidity to your pulk, which is very helpful when descending, reducing the chances it will catch up and clip your heels.

- If you find that your pipes ride up your hips, they're likely too short. Replace them with longer ones. It's worth the extra few bucks it costs to buy another pair and cut them to the right length.

- Put the heaviest items in the center rear of the pulk. Position lighter loads toward the front, making it easier to lift the bow of the pulk over any obstacles.

- Try to even out your load as much as possible to avoid tipping or dragging to one side.

- Don't pile on so much gear that the pulk becomes top-heavy, making it more likely to wipe out when you turn corners.

- Make sure the weight of the belt is positioned at your hips.

- Some people like to use one or two large duffel bags to keep gear compact.

- The bulk of snow will hit the front of the pulk, so put the most weatherproof items there.

- After you've loaded up, tip your pulk to see what's loose or at risk of falling out.

9

FIGURE 51. A pulk lets you transport more gear (and food!) on your winter expeditions than you could carry on your back. To build your own, follow these steps: (a) Begin with a long, deep sled of the sort you can buy at a hardware store. (b) Drill three or four evenly spaced holes on each side, plus a couple more at the rear. (c) Weave 3/16-inch nylon utility rope through the holes from back to front. (d) Thread the rope through two 7-foot lengths of ½-inch PVC pipe, making a loop at both ends of the rope and attaching a carabiner to each loop. (e) Use a piece of Velcro to fasten the pipes in an X. (f) Repurpose an old backpack or weight-lifting belt into a pulk belt that can hook onto the pipes via D-rings and carabiners. (g) Secure webbing or a cargo net over the pulk's load to keep gear in place while you're hiking. (h) You're ready to bring your assembled pulk on your next adventure.

9

DIY PULK

- Drill three or four evenly spaced holes on either side of your sled and a couple more at the rear.

- Starting at the back, weave ³⁄₁₆-inch nylon utility rope through the holes until you reach the front.

- Thread your rope between two lengths of ½-inch PVC pipe, cut to 7 feet long, leaving enough rope at the end to make a loop at both ends of the rope. Attach a carabiner to the two loops.

- Use a piece of Velcro to keep the two pipes in the shape of an X, giving added stiffness to the poles. Some people drill holes and use a bolt for this purpose.

- Make a belt out of an old backpack belt or a weight-lifting belt. Anything that will accept a D-ring to attach your carabiner will work. You can use your own backpack's hip belt, although that makes it more difficult to take off your pack. If you don't want to go to the trouble of making a belt, you may be able to get by using the ice ax loops at the bottom of your pack, provided you have two of them.

- Secure webbing or a cargo net over your gear to keep it in place while you're on the move. Tarps are time-honored for this purpose, too, and we all know how handy they are in the woods.

Many people have their own designs for do-it-yourself tow-behinds. Some like to screw two eyebolts at the front of the sled for mounting the rope. Others use a PVC pipe through these eyebolts and attach the extending pipes using elbows. Still others like to weave webbing through holes drilled in the sled's side for tie-downs. Some reinforce their drilled holes with grommets; some make their own hip belts out of webbing, padding, and buckles; some attach aluminum runners to the base of the sled to keep it traveling in a straight line. There are countless options. Figure out what works for you. You can make a sled with all the hardware, pipe, belt, and rope for less than $50.

HOW TO CARE FOR PULKS

Like anything else, pulks last longer if you take care of them. Clean and dry them when you get home. Fill in cracks with melted wax to make for a smoother ride. Tighten screws and grommets. Because they are so easily built, pulks sometimes get neglected, but it's much easier to maintain an existing pulk than it is to build another.

9

→ FAT BIKES

In the past decade, fat bikes—or those mountain bikes with cartoonishly oversized tires—have begun to appear on winter trails everywhere. In some locales, they're even outpacing cross-country skis in terms of sheer number in the winter woods. It's easy to understand the appeal: They are a heck of a lot of fun when conditions are right;

they're beginner-friendly; and they allow the cycling set to join the rest of us in the backcountry, as fat bikes are designed so that they are easier to ride on soft surfaces, such as snow or sand. Anyone who can pedal a bike can enjoy one. Of course, bikes can have a big impact on trails, and even when those trails are covered by snow, some conservation areas do not allow fat biking. As always, make sure to check in with the appropriate land management agency before toting your bike into the woods.

Many ski resorts have added fat bikes to their offerings, hoping to expand their business away from the slopes, and they're commonly available to rent or buy at bike shops. Like anything else, you might want to rent or borrow one before splurging for one of your own. Fat bikes are not cheap.

FAT BIKE TIPS

- Just as winter hiking is more taxing than summer trekking, fat-tire riding requires more energy than traditional mountain biking. Don't expect to cover as many miles on snow as you would on the road or dirt.

- Use bar mitts (a.k.a. pogies). These big handlebar-mounted mittens keep your hands much warmer than gloves alone.

- Take off your toe clips. Flat pedals are much easier when wearing winter boots.

- Lower your tire pressure. Letting out air, down to 5 or 6 psi, allows your fat tires to become even fatter, thus gripping more trail.

- Don't fight the ruts. Just as when you're skiing, your tires will correct to the groove every time. Go with the flow.

- Sit down. If you stand up and really pump the pedals, your tires are more likely to spin. Steady, consistent pedaling is the way to go on snow.

- Unless you have spiked tires, avoid ice.

- Be prepared to work extra hard in powder, just as you would breaking trail on skis or snowshoes.

- Avoid black-diamond trails. They're killer for beginners.

BASIC FAT BIKE MAINTENANCE

As with non-fat-tire bikes, you can do a lot of maintenance at home, although you should take your bike to a local shop for anything you don't feel comfortable handling. If you're ready to tackle some basic maintenance, follow these tips.

9

- In winter, you want your tire pressure around 5 or 6 psi.

- Inspect your chain, ensuring that all of the links look good and it's not getting rusty. A bit of bike oil goes a long way. Lube liberally, wiping off any excess.

- Check and tighten your grips and mitts. Loose grips make for a frustrating ride.

- Remove your toe clips and leave them at home when winter biking.

- Tighten loose bolts and screws.

- After several rides, take off the wheels and check your hubs to make sure the bearings are in good shape. With the low air pressure of winter, rims can bend more easily.

- Check your brakes before you head out. If you have an air bubble, pump the brakes a few times to remove it. If this fails, turn the bike upside down. If that fails, take it to the shop, unless you know how to bleed your brake line.

- Don't forget to look at your brake pads. They typically need replacing every 2,000 miles.

- A can of compressed air does wonders getting into hard-to-reach areas.

- Wipe down your tires and stanchions with a soft cloth.

- Always remove any accumulated salt, whether with a good rinse or a product like Salt-Away.

- When you return from a winter ride, make sure you dry your bike thoroughly. Bring it inside to allow moisture to evaporate. Set the bike up so that the drain holes are on the bottom and let it drain. Never put your bike away wet.

9

CHAPTER 10
A DISAPPEARING SEASON

➜ **Impact on Future Recreation**   186
➜ **What AMC Is Doing**   187
➜ **Get Involved**   188

The sad truth is, you should get out and explore the winter wonderland around you now, because it is changing. Winter as we know it is slowly but inexorably becoming harder to find. Climate change has reached dangerous levels, and we're currently teetering on a precipice, like a mountaineer swaying on an ice-covered ridgeline. If we don't act soon, it will be too late to save the natural world as we know and love it. It's already sliding out of our grasp.

The planet's average surface temperature has risen almost 2 degrees Fahrenheit during the 20th century. That may not sound like much, if you think about stepping outside on a day that's 29 degrees versus a day that's 31 degrees. But consider this: According to NASA scientists, during the last ice age, when the Earth was covered in sheets of ice as tall as Appalachian peaks, temperatures were only 5 to 9 degrees colder than they are now.

The effects of those two degrees have already proved dramatic. The oceans are slowly rising. The polar ice caps are melting. Wildlife is migrating north. You can see the recession of glaciers from space. The majority of the warming has taken place in the last half-century; the five hottest years in recorded history have occurred since 2010. The temperature graph of the last century looks like a mountain incline, and it's only going to continue rising.

As the season of cold, winter may well be the hardest hit. A 2014 study from the Massachusetts Institute of Technology found that two paradoxical things are likely to occur as the Earth continues to warm. The first is we'll experience more extreme snowfall events. In other words, bigger blizzards and nor'easters that drop larger amounts of snow than we've seen in the past. This is consistent with the number, frequency, and intensity of the wildfires, hurricanes, floods, and droughts occurring in recent years across the globe. Second, areas including the Northeast likely will see their yearly snowfall average slowly decline. In essence, North America will receive more snow in short, violent bursts but less across the season as a whole. The study suggests that, by the end of the 21st century, snowfall totals for the northern hemisphere may decrease by as much as 65 percent. Winters likely will get shorter, as warmer temperatures create longer shoulder seasons. Communities in the northern half of the United States generally are warming faster than points south and can expect to see the most dramatic change. Scientists believe the Northeast to be particularly vulnerable.

All of this sounds rather faraway, right? The end of the 21st century is someone else's problem, say the cynics. But the changes are already affecting today's outdoor adventures.

CLIMATE CHANGE FACTS

- Percentage of climate scientists who agree global warming is very likely due to human activity: **97%**

- Carbon parts per million in the atmosphere from 400,000 BCE to 1950: **below 300**

- Carbon parts per million in the atmosphere, 1950: **310**

- Carbon parts per million in the atmosphere, 2019: **400**

- Warmest global year on record: **2016, as of 2019**

- Percentage of decline in arctic sea ice per decade: **12.8**

- Rate of ice loss in Antarctica: **127 gigatonnes per year**

- Rate of ice loss in Greenland: **286 gigatonnes per year**

- Millimeters of rise in global sea level per year: **3.2**

- Millimeters of rise in global sea level since 1880: **230**

➔ IMPACT ON FUTURE RECREATION

What does all of this mean for outdoor adventures? Virtually every pastime will suffer. Anglers will have to contend with invasive species and the changing runs of their favorite species. Wildlife watchers will see many populations decline, as animals lose habitat to wildfires and other natural disasters. Hikers will be forced to deal with higher temperatures and fewer water sources, closures of favorite areas due to extreme weather events, and more ticks. Surfers will see their favorite breaks dissolve as oceans rise. Divers and snorkelers will witness the death of coral reefs and the demise of many underwater species, due to the warming and acidification of the sea.

Those of us who love winter will be most affected—and it's already happening. Researchers from Oregon State University estimate that North America's snowpack is already down by 30 percent from what it was a century ago. Dangerous

10

and violent storms are becoming more prevalent, and spring is arriving sooner in many places. Warming and fluctuating temperatures are making ice unsafe. Winter-dependent businesses, like ski areas, are struggling to keep their lifts open. According to the National Ski Areas Association, 20 percent of U.S. ski areas have closed in the past 20 years, as snowfall has become less reliable.

AMC has witnessed Earth's rising temperature firsthand. In 1930, the organization's legendary White Mountain hutmaster Joe Dodge began a program of daily weather monitoring on Mount Washington that continues to this day. These numbers form some of the best long-term data sets available for studying the planet's warming. Over the past 80 years, New England's highest mountain has definitively warmed. Temperature records show it, and you can see it with your own eyes. The snowmelt comes an average of two weeks earlier in Pinkham Notch than it did in 1930, and plants at lower elevations in the White Mountains flower weeks earlier than they used to.

→ WHAT AMC IS DOING

AMC has long championed sustainability, honoring the organization's original mission statement, from 1876: "to explore the mountains of New England and adjacent regions, both for scientific and artistic purposes." The organization has designed its huts, lodges, sporting camps, and offices to be as environmentally efficient as possible, not only to lessen the carbon footprint but to provide a model for the guests who visit. AMC is directly involved in advocacy work related to clean energy, land and water conservation, and open spaces.

AMC has also made a commitment to climate research. AMC partners with an array of organizations, from parks to universities, to study how rising temperatures are affecting and changing the mountainous areas of the Northeast. This has resulted in an array of groundbreaking studies on air quality, including alpine acidification, ozone at elevation, and haze and visibility.

Fifteen years ago, AMC began a $70 million initiative in Maine's North Woods to study the effects of climate change while promoting responsible forestry and conserving vast tracts of land. Besides being one of the nation's last wild places, the surrounding 100-Mile Wilderness region is an ideal setting to study the impacts of climate change. It is both a critical watershed and a large carbon sink and has enough untouched acreage to provide the sort of connected habitat required to absorb large-scale environmental changes. In these woods, AMC has been able to study, and even minutely slow, climate change and to educate thousands of visitors and local schoolchildren about conservation.

In 2002 AMC began a new program called Mountain Watch, in which volunteers document their environmental observations—especially flora—while hiking. Flowers are effective forecasters of climate change, and through Mountain Watch, volunteers have added a great deal of data to AMC's database of knowledge on plant life, air quality, and visibility in the White Mountains of New Hampshire.

10

Citizen science is now easier than ever, thanks to the iNaturalist app. AMC has teamed up with the interactive smartphone application, making it even simpler to document the flowering and fruiting plants you see on hiking adventures. Download the app on your iPhone or Android, hit the trail, take pictures of the plants you see, and you become a citizen scientist. The photos you produce are geotagged with the date, time, and location, providing professional climate scientists with hard data. It's a great way to help.

→ GET INVOLVED

Winter isn't dead yet. Although many political factors have led some outdoor lovers to disregard the dire situation we're in, climatologically, there is still time to act. Write your local politician. Work on your carbon footprint. Use less electricity. Buy a more efficient car. Volunteer outdoors. And join and support some of the organizations listed below.

Appalachian Mountain Club
10 City Square
Boston, MA 02129
617-523-0655; outdoors.org

Sierra Club
2101 Webster Street, Suite 1300
Oakland, CA 94612
415-977-5500; sierraclub.org

Protect Our Winters
4676 Broadway Street
Boulder, CO 80304
303-900-4027; protectourwinters.org

National Audubon Society
225 Varick Street
New York, NY 10014
844-428-3826; audubon.org

APPENDIX A

PERSONAL GEAR CHECKLIST

ITEM	NUMBER RECOMMENDED	HAVE	NEED
Personal Equipment			
Backpack	1		
Sleeping Bag (zero degree)	1		
Sleeping Pad	2		
Small Stuff Sacks	as needed		
Garbage Bags	as needed		
Water Bottles	2 or 3		
Water Treatment Method	1		
Water Collecting Pot	1		
Bowl	1		
Cup	1		
Spoon/Spork	1		
Headlamp	1		
Multitool	1		
Compass	1		
Whistle	1		
Lighter/Waterproof Matches	1		
Extra Batteries	as needed		
Sunglasses/Goggles	1		
Emergency Kit (duct tape, space blanket, paracord, glow sticks)	1		
Corrective Eyewear	as needed		
Lip Balm	1		
Sunscreen	1		
Toothbrush	1		
Toothpaste	1		
Moist Towelettes	1		
Toilet Paper	1		
Hand Sanitizer	1		
Prescribed Medications	as needed		
Feminine Hygiene Products	as needed		

Note: Items in italics are part of the recommended Ten Essentials.

ITEM	NUMBER RECOMMENDED	HAVE	NEED
Personal Clothing			
Waterproof Hiking Boots	1 pair		
Camp Booties or Boot Liners	1 pair		
Warm Wool/Fleece Socks	3 pairs		
Liner Socks	3 pairs		
Underwear	2 pairs		
Bras	1 to 2		
Long Pants (waterproof, breathable)	1		
Shell (waterproof, breathable)	1		
Long Underwear Bottoms (medium weight)	2		
Long Underwear Top (lightweight)	2		
Long Underwear Top (expedition weight)	2		
Sweater/Midweight Fleece	2		
Warm Jacket	1		
Puffer Jacket	1		
Puffer Vest	1		
Sun Hat	1		
Warm Hat	1		
Waterproof/Breathable Outer Gloves/ Mittens	1		
Insulating Gloves/Mittens	1		
Liner Gloves	1		
Balaclava/Scarf/Snood	1		
Emergency Device (Spot, InReach, etc.)	1		
Optional Personal Equipment and Clothing			
Waterproof Backpack Cover	1		
Bivy	1		
Hydration Bag	1		
Cell Phone	1		
Hat Liner	1		
Gaiters	1		
Camera	1		
Camp Chair	1		
Small Camping Towel	1		

Note: Items in italics are part of the recommended Ten Essentials.

ITEM	NUMBER RECOMMENDED	HAVE	NEED
Camping Equipment			
Shelter (tent/tarp)	as needed		
Snow Stakes	1 set		
Camping Stove (winter ready)	1		
Stove Platform	1		
Fuel Bottle/Canister	as needed		
Cooking Pot Kit	1		
Cooking Pot Grip	1		
Cooking Frypan	1		
Cooking Spoon	1		
Cooking Spatula	1		
Cooking Ladle or Small Measuring Cup	1		
Gray Water Strainer	1		
Whisk Brush	1		
Liquid or Creamy Food Containers	1		
Food Stuff Sack	as needed		
Kitchen Hand Soap	1		
Water Bladder	1		
Bearproof Rope System	1		
Shovel	1		
Zipper-closure Bags (large)	as needed		
First-Aid Kit	1		
Gear Repair Kit	1		
Map	1		
Optional Camping Equipment			
Binoculars	1		
GPS	1		
Bear Canister	1		
Bearproof Electric Fence	1		
Fire Pan	1		
Camp Lantern	1		
Camping Saw	1		
Water Treatment: Pump	1		
Water Treatment: UV Light Pen	1		
Water Treatment: Gravity Feed	1		

Note: Items in italics are part of the recommended Ten Essentials.

ITEM	NUMBER RECOMMENDED	HAVE	NEED
Winter Expedition Equipment			
Avalanche Beacon	1		
Avalanche Probe	1		
Altimeter	1		
Barometer/Weather Radio	as needed		
Rope	1		
Snowshoes	1 pair		
Crampons/Traction Devices	1 pair		
Skis	1 pair		
Skins	as needed		
Sled/Pulk	1		
Ice Ax	as needed		
Stuff Sacks	as needed		
Extra Tarp	1		

Note: Items in italics are part of the recommended Ten Essentials.

APPENDIX B

PARTICIPANT INFORMATION FORM

PARTICPANTS	
Group Leader	
Group Contact (if different from Group Leader)	
Name	Info (cell phone, email, etc.)
Name	Info (cell phone, email, etc.)
Name	Info (cell phone, email, etc.)
Name	Info (cell phone, email, etc.)
Name	Info (cell phone, email, etc.)
Name	Info (cell phone, email, etc.)
Name	Info (cell phone, email, etc.)
Name	Info (cell phone, email, etc.)

TRIP DATES	
Departure Date	Estimated Departure Time from Trailhead
Return Date	Estimated Return Time to Trailhead
Late Party Emergency Call Time	

ROUTE	
Meeting Spot	
Departure Trailhead	
Return Trailhead	
Route Description (Names of trails from departure to return)	
Campsite 1 Location	Date
Campsite 2 Location	Date
Campsite 3 Location	Date
Campsite 4 Location	Date
Campsite 5 Location	Date
Campsite 6 Location	Date

ROUTE EVACUATION POINT(S)
Evac Point 1
Evac Point 2
Evac Point 3
Evac Point 4

VEHICLE(S) AT TRAILHEAD(S)		
Departure Trailhead		
Vehicle 1 – Type	Color	License plate number
Vehicle 2 – Type	Color	License plate number
Return Trailhead		
Vehicle 1 – Type	Color	License plate number
Vehicle 2 – Type	Color	License plate number

EMERGENCY
911
Search and Rescue phone number:

APPENDIX C

EXPEDITION PREPARATION CHECKLIST

	ROUTE PLANNING
	Select a route.
	Check public or private land regulations for this area.
	If needed, contact public or private agencies to inquire about camping, parking, or other fees.
	If needed, make campsite reservation.
	If needed, get fire permit.
	If needed, plan and organize vehicle shuttle or dropoff and pickup.
	If needed, create waypoints for the route, campsites, trailheads, and evacuation points on your GPS.
	Check most recent weather forecast for your hiking area.
	Gather safety information from each participant (experience, emergency contact, medical information, etc.)
	Leave pertinent information with someone reliable and ready to contact search and rescue authorities if you are not back or have not checked in according to your plan. See Appendix B: Participant Information Form.

	MENU PLANNING
	Prepare a questionnaire/survey to inquire about food allergies, dietary choices, preferences, and caloric needs for members of your group.
	Coordinate meal preparation, if more than one person is involved.
	Create menus, remembering the increased need for calories in winter.
	Inventory your current food supplies and make a shopping list for the missing items.
	Repackage food for ease of transport.
	Plan and prepare dry and wet spice kits.
	Pre-cook any meals, if possible.

	EQUIPMENT AND TRANSPORTATION PLANNING
	Check camping stoves for winter use.
	Calculate stove fuel needs.
	Fill stove fuel bottles.
	Determine shelter needs and check all tents, bivys, etc. for damaged or missing parts.
	Check batteries for each electronic device and headlamp; replace as needed and bring plenty of spares.

	Check conditions of pulks, ropes, axes, and other winter gear.
	Check and refill first-aid kit(s).
	Check repair/utility kit.
	Check to make sure you have the Ten Essentials.
	Establish who will transport what equipment when on the trail.
	Organize meeting location, carpool time, and departure time for the trailhead.
	Plan driving route.
	Check road map or enter GPS coordinates for the trail

APPENDIX D

DRINKING-WATER TREATMENT METHODS

The beautiful, clear streams and remote ponds of the mountains seem as pure as the snows from which they were formed. They look clean and clear and probably taste delicious! But every backcountry traveler should know that drinking this water without treating it brings the risk of ingesting microorganisms that could lead to gastrointestinal discomfort, serious illness, and potential chronic concerns. Protozoan parasites, such as *Giardia lamblia* and *Cryptosporidium*, can cause acute gastrointestinal illness (diarrhea, cramping, vomiting), and these parasites can occur in any untreated water. Water sources with heavy human impact can also contain viruses, such as hepatitis, or bacteria, such as *E. coli*.

For hikers who want to greatly lower the risk to themselves and their fellow travelers, there are several good options for treating water and reducing the likelihood of a protozoan, bacterial, or viral infection. These water treatment options include boiling, filtering, ultraviolet radiation, chlorine-based chemicals, mixed oxidant systems, and iodine. All of these options remove or kill giardia and crypto, as well as any additional protozoa or bacteria in the water. Viruses, which are too small to be captured by filter systems, can be eliminated only with chemical treatment, boiling, or UV light. And this does not only apply to water from streams and ponds: Melted snow and ice must be treated in the same manner as any other water.

Adapted from *AMC's Mountain Skills Manual* (AMC Books, 2017; outdoors.org/books-maps)

EFFICACY OF WATER TREATMENT METHODS		
Treatment Method	**Advantages**	**Disadvantages**
Boiling	▪ Rapidly treats larger quantities ▪ Reliable and inexpensive ▪ Works on all known pathogens	▪ Makes only hot water so requires ample cooling time for some uses ▪ Relies on stove or fire ▪ Requires fuel ▪ Imparts a taste
Pumping	▪ Leaves no taste ▪ Great for clean, clear sources	▪ Bulkier and heavier than other options ▪ Requires maintenance ▪ Requires effort and time ▪ Does not protect against viruses ▪ Interior parts can freeze and crack
Ultraviolet light	▪ Fast ▪ Easy to operate	▪ Battery dependent ▪ Must not be dropped or crushed in pack ▪ Alkaline batteries can freeze; lithium ion batteries have a slow treatment rate when very cold
Chlorine dioxide (chemical)	▪ Cost-effective, especially drops ▪ Easy to use ▪ Requires little trail time ▪ Mostly neutral taste impact	▪ Must have adequate supply for length of trip and size of group ▪ Requires 4 hours for complete confidence against cryptosporidium ▪ Drops can freeze
Mixed-oxidant systems (chemical)	▪ As effective as all chlorine-based treatment options	▪ Battery dependent ▪ Requires rock salt ▪ Some aftertaste ▪ Requires 4 hours for complete confidence against cryptosporidium ▪ Batteries can freeze

EFFICACY OF WATER TREATMENT METHODS (CONTINUED)		
Treatment Method	**Advantages**	**Disadvantages**
Iodine (chemical)	▪ Small and light ▪ Easy to use ▪ Inexpensive	▪ Strong aftertaste ▪ Not safe for certain populations ▪ Not recommended for extended use ▪ Requires 4 hours for complete confidence against cryptosporidium ▪ Takes longer to use in winter
Straws	▪ Small and light	▪ Can take quite a bit of suction to get water through the straw ▪ Inner workings can freeze

DRINKING WATER TREATMENT METHODS FOR BACKCOUNTRY AND TRAVEL USE

Contaminant	Potential health effects from ingestion of water	Sources of contaminant in drinking water	Boiling[1]	Filtration[2]	Disinfection[3]		Combination of filtration and disinfection[4]
					Iodine* or Chlorine	Chlorine Dioxide	
Protozoa Cryptosporidium	Gastrointestinal illness (e.g., diarrhea, vomiting, cramps)	Human and animal fecal waste	very high effectiveness	high effectiveness — Absolute ≤ 1.0 micron filter (NSF Standard 53 or 58 rated "cyst reduction/removal" filter)	not effective	low to moderate effectiveness	very high effectiveness — Absolute ≤ 1.0 micron filter (NSF Standard 53 or 58 rated "cyst reduction/removal" filter)
Protozoa Giardia intestinalis (a.k.a. Giardia lamblia)	Gastrointestinal illness (e.g., diarrhea, vomiting, cramps)	Human and animal fecal waste	very high effectiveness	high effectiveness — Absolute ≤ 1.0 micron filter (NSF Standard 53 or 58 rated "cyst reduction/removal" filter)	low to moderate effectiveness	high effectiveness	very high effectiveness — Absolute ≤ 1.0 micron filter (NSF Standard 53 or 58 rated "cyst reduction/removal" filter)
Bacteria (e.g., Campylobacter, Salmonella, Shigella, E. coli)	Gastrointestinal illness (e.g., diarrhea, vomiting, cramps)	Human and animal fecal waste	very high effectiveness	moderate effectiveness — Absolute ≤ 0.3 micron filter	high effectiveness	high effectiveness	very high effectiveness — Absolute ≤ 0.3 micron filter
Viruses (e.g., enterovirus, hepatitis A, norovirus, rotavirus)	Gastrointestinal illness (e.g., diarrhea, vomiting, cramps)	Human and animal fecal waste	very high effectiveness	not effective	high effectiveness	high effectiveness	very high effectiveness

[1]**Boiling** can be used as a pathogen reduction method that should kill all pathogens. Water should be brought to a rolling boil for 1 minute (at altitudes greater than 6,562 feet [>2,000 m], boil water for 3 minutes).

[2]**Filtration** can be used as a pathogen reduction method against most microorganisms, depending on the pore size of the filter, amount of the contaminant, particle size of the contaminant, and charge of the contaminant particle. Manufacturer's instructions must be followed. More information on selecting an appropriate water filter can be found at cdc.gov/crypto/factsheets/filters.html. Only filters that contain a chemical disinfectant matrix will be effective against some viruses.

[3]**Disinfection** can be used as a pathogen reduction method against microorganisms. However, contact time, disinfectant concentration, water temperature, water turbidity (cloudiness), water pH, and many other factors can impact the effectiveness of chemical disinfection. The length of time and concentration of disinfectant varies by manufacturer, and effectiveness of pathogen reduction depends on the product. Depending on these factors, 100% effectiveness may not be achieved. Manufacturer's instructions must be followed.

[4]If boiling water is not possible, a **combination of filtration and chemical disinfection** is the most effective pathogen-reduction method in drinking water for backcountry or travel use. Manufacturer's instructions must be followed.

***Important:** Water that has been disinfected with iodine is NOT recommended for pregnant women, people with thyroid problems, those with known hypersensitivity to iodine, or continuous use for more than a few weeks at a time.

Other treatment methods can be effective against some of the above pathogens:

Ultraviolet (UV) Light can be used as a pathogen-reduction method against some microorganisms. The technology requires effective prefiltering due to its dependence on low water turbidity (cloudiness), the correct power delivery, and correct contact times to achieve maximum pathogen reduction. UV might be an effective method for pathogen reduction in untreated or poorly treated water; there is a lack of independent testing available on specific systems. Manufacturer's instructions must be followed.

MIOX® systems use a salt solution to create mixed oxidants, primarily chlorine. As a result, refer to the category above for chlorine disinfection. Manufacturer's instructions must be followed.

In addition to using the appropriate drinking water treatment methods listed above, you can also protect yourself and others from waterborne illness by **burying human waste** 8 inches deep and at least 200 feet away from natural waters and **practicing good personal hygiene** (wash hands before handling food, eating, and after using the toilet).

Source: CDC Fact Sheet for Healthy Drinking Water, cdc.gov/healthywater.

APPENDIX E
LIST OF CHARTS, TABLES, AND FIGURES

CHARTS AND TABLES

Efficacy of Stove Types, 62
Windchill, 73
Avalanche Survival Probability, 96
Recommended Daily Water Intake, 129
Personal Gear Checklist, 189 (Appendix A)
Participant Information Form, 193 (Appendix B)
Expedition Preparation Checklist, 195 (Appendix C)
Efficacy of Water Treatment Methods, 198 (Appendix D)
Drinking-Water Treatment Methods, 200 (Appendix D)

FIGURES

1. Warm front, 19
2. Cold front, 21
3. Cloud types, 25
4. The WISE system for layering clothes, 31
5. Hiking boots, 40
6. Pac boots, 41
7. Double boots, 41
8. Mouse boots, 42
9. Nordic ski boots, 42
10. Gaiters, 43
11. How to pack a backpack, 49
12. Bivouac (bivy) sack, 53
13. Tarp shelter, 54
14. Stove types, 60
15. "Burrito wrap" for a hypothermia victim, 72
16. Emergency snow goggles, 75
17. Avalanche types, 78
18. Snow cornice, 80
19. Tree well and vegetation trap, 81
20. Moats, bridges, and undercuts, 85
21. The "find-me cross," 95
22. Searching for an avalanche victim, 97
23. "Rule of thumb" for animal viewing, 99

24. Ticks, 102
25. Example of a summit on a topographic map, 107
26. Example of a saddle on a topographic map, 107
27. Example of a drainage on a topographic map, 107
28. Example of a ridge on a topographic map, 107
29. Example of a slope and cliff on a topographic map, 107
30. The parts of a baseplate compass, 109
31. Earth's magnetic field, 111
32. Orienting a compass to a map, 114
33. Finding Polaris, 121
34. Animal tracks, 124
35. Backcountry water treatment methods, 131
36. Preparing tinder, 144
37. Tipi fire, 147
38. Lean-to fire, 147
39. Log cabin fire, 147
40. Leave No Trace fire, 147
41. Bear hang, 150
42. Deadman stake, 154
43. Types of snow structures, 156
44. Crampons and Microspikes, 163
45. Recreational snowshoes, 166
46. Fitness snowshoes, 166
47. Mountaineering snowshoes, 166
48. How to walk in snowshoes, 169
49. Ski poles vs. trekking poles, 173
50. Skins, 175
51. Make your own pulk, 181

INDEX

➔ A

Acadia National Park, 2–3
alpine/downhill skiing, 171
animal tracks, 124
Appalachian Mountain Club (AMC)
    climate change and, 187–188
avalanche airbag packs, 51
avalanche beacons, 122
avalanches, 76–79
avalanche rescue, 95–98
avalanche survival probability, 96
    beacons/probes, 122
    slope meters, 121
avalung/avalanche airbag pack, 97–98

➔ B

backcountry camping, 152–161
    setting up tents, 153–154
    sleeping warm, 158–159
    snowcraft, 154–157
    tips for coping with darkness, 160–161
backcountry cooking, 148–150
    meal/menu planning, 134–137
    stoves, 59–63
backcountry lodges, 150–151
backcountry skiing, 171–172
backpacking gear, 47–66
    backpacks, 47–51
    cost considerations, 64
    gear care and maintenance, 63–65
    gear malfunctions, 65–66
    kitchen gear, 59–63
    personal gear checklist, 189–192
    shelters, 51–54
    sleep systems, 54–59
backpacks, 47–51
    maintenance of, 65
barometric pressure, 27–28
Baxter State park, 2, 22
bears, 99–100, 124
bicycling. See fat bikes
binoculars, 121
bivouac (bivy) sacks, 52–53

boot dryers, 44
booties, 43–44
boots, 39–43
    maintenance of, 65
    ski boots, 172
bunkhouses, 153

➔ C

cabins, 151
calorie burn, 126–127
campfires, 142–148
    cooking over, 63, 148
    fire building techniques, 145–148
    fire principles, 143–145
    Leave No Trace (LNT) principles, xiv–
        xvi, 148
camping, 141–160
    backcountry camping, 152–161
campfires, 142–148
camp siting, 141–142
    kitchen setup, 149–150
    Leave No Trace (LNT) principles, xiv–xvi
    personal gear checklist, 189
    structures, permanent, 150–152
canister stoves, 60, 62
celestial navigation, 120–121
changing of route/turning back, 92–93
chemical water filtration, 131–132, 197
children, trips with, 6–7
climate change, 15, 185–186
    AMC and, 187–188
    impacts of, 186–187
clothing considerations, 29–46
    boots, 39–43
clothing maintenance, 45–46
    cost considerations, 44–45
    fabric choices, 33–34
    outerwear, 34–36
    personal gear checklist, 189
    protecting extremities, 36–44
    thermodynamics, 32–33
    WISE system, 30–32
clouds, 24–25

cold fronts, 20
compasses, 108–112
    map and compass navigation, 110–112, 114
condensation, 159–160
condition reports, 14
continental weather systems, 19
contingency planning, 10–11
conversion packs, 51
cornices, 79–80
cougars, 101, 124
crampons, 163–164
    care of, 177–178
crevasses, 84

➔ D

day packs, 48
dehydration, 127–129
destination planning, 7–9
dew/frost point, 28
dogs, trips with, 7
double boots, 41–42
down sleeping bags, 56
drinking water, 129–134
    common contaminants, 200
    freezing of water, 133–134
    treatment methods, 198–200
    water sources, 129–130
    water treatment/filtration, 130–133
dry bags, 51

➔ E

emergency situation survival, 88–95
    changing of route/turning back, 92–93
    evacuation, 90
    general principles, 88–89
    getting lost, 93–95
    search and rescue, 90–91
    technological tools, 121–123
environmental challenges, 76–86
    avalanches, 76–79
    cornices, 79–80
    rock/ice fall, 80
    tree wells, 81
    vegetation traps, 81
    water crossings, 82–86
evacuation, 90
expedition preparation checklist, 195–196
external frame packs, 48–49

➔ F

fabrics (winter clothing), 33–34
fall recovery and survival, 83–84
    getting up, 170, 175
"fart sacks," 59
fat bikes, 182–183
    maintenance of, 183–184
    tips for using, 183
find-me cross, 94–95
fire building. See campfires
first aid, 67–76
    common ailments, 69–76
    recommended kit, 67–68
    training courses, 69
fitness, 3
fronts, 19–22
frostbite, 73–74

➔ G

gaiters, 43
gear care and maintenance, 63–65
gear considerations. See backpacking gear
gear lists, recommended, 9–10
    first aid, 67–68
    personal gear checklist, 189–192
getting lost, 93–95
Giesbrecht, Gordon, 29
glacier crossings, 84
gloves, 37–38
goggles, 37
Gore-Tex, 35–36
GPS devices, 115–119
    InReach transmitters, 122
    using GPS devices, 117–119
group size considerations, 5–6
    participant information form, 193–194
guidebooks, 13–14
    internet resources, 14

➔ H

hats/balaclavas, 36–37
health and hygiene, 126–140
    body adaptation, 126–128
    drinking water, 129–134
    hydration, 127–129
    nutrition/meal planning, 134–137
    personal hygiene, 137–139
    toilet considerations, 139–140

hikeSafe checklist, 4–5
hiking, 162–165
hiking boots, 40
Huld, Kaj, 76
hunting, 86–87
huts, 151
hybrid construction sleeping bags, 57
hybrid shelters, 54
hydration, 127–129
hypothermia, 70–73

➜ I

ice axes, 177–179
    care of, 177–178
    preseason training, 3
ice climbing, 177–179
ice conditions, 82–83
immersion (trench) foot, 74–75
Inhofe, James, 15
InReach transmitters, 122
internal frame packs, 49–50

➜ J

Jordan, Kevin, 1–2

➜ K

kitchen gear, 59–63
kitchen kits, 61, 63
Koppen classification system, 17–18
Kosseff, Alex, 5

➜ L

lean-tos, 152
Leave No Trace (LNT) principles, xiii–xvii
liquid fuel (white gas) stoves, 59–60, 62

➜ M

malfunctioning gear, 65–66
maps, 13, 104–108
map and compass navigation, 110–112, 114
map reading, 105–108
maritime weather systems, 18–19
meal/menu planning, 134–137
    expedition preparation checklist, 195
    kitchen setup, 149–150
mental challenges, 87–88
meteorological vs. astronomical winter, 16

Microspikes, 162–163
mids, 52–53
mittens, 37–38
moose, 100–101, 124
Mountain Watch, 187
mouse boots, 42

➜ N

National Audubon Society, 188
navigation, 103–125
    additional navigation tools, 121–123
    animal tracking, 124–125
    celestial navigation, 120–121
    compasses, 108–112
    GPS devices, 115–119
    maps, 104–108
    pace setting, 123–124
    route finding, 112–115
    smartphones, 119–120
    understanding coordinates, 117–119
Nordic/cross-country skiing, 170–171
Nordic ski boots, 42–43
North Star, 120–121
nutrition, 134–137

➜ O

occluded fronts, 21
off-trail route finding, 113, 115
orthographic lifting, 21–22
outerwear, 34–36
overboots, 43

➜ P

pac boots, 40–41
pace setting, 123–124
participant information form, 193–194
personal hygiene, 137–139
personal locater beacons (PLBs), 123
pond/lake crossings, 84
post-trip checklist, 12
precipitation, 23
preseason training, 3
prior experience, 2–3
Protect Our Winters, 188
pulks, 179–182
    care of, 182
    tips for using, 180, 182
pump filters, 130–131, 196

→ Q

quinzees, 155–157

→ R

rain jackets/pants, 35–36
recreation gear and skills, 162–184
    fat bikes, 182–184
    hiking, 162–165
    ice climbing, 177–179
    pulks, 179–182
    skiing, 170–176
    snowshoeing, 165–170
    splitboarding, 176–177
rock/ice fall, 80
route finding, 112–115

→ S

safety considerations, 67–102. *See also*
  health and hygiene
    avalanche rescue, 95–98
    common ailments, 69–76
    dangerous animals, 98–102
    dehydration, 127–129
    emergency situation survival, 88–95
    environmental challenges, 76–86
    first aid, 67–76
    first aid training courses, 69
    human element, 86–87
    mental challenges, 87–88
    recommended first aid kit, 67–68
satellite phones, 123
search and rescue operations, 1–2, 90–91
shelters, 52–54
    snowcraft, 154–157
Sierra Club, 188
ski boots, 172
skiing, 170–176
    boots and poles, 172–173
    caring for skis, 175
    learning to ski, 173–174
    skinning, 174–175
    types of skis, 170–172
skins, 174–175
ski poles, 172–173
sky-watching, 24–25
sleeping bag liners, 58–59

sleeping bags, 55–57
    maintenance of, 65
sleeping pads, 57–58
sleep systems, 54–59
slope meters, 121
smartphones, 119–120, 123
snowblindness, 75–76
snow bridges, 84–86
snow caves, 157
snowcraft, 154–157
snow jackets/pants, 34–35
snow moats, 84–86
snowmobiles, 86–87
snowpack, 27
snowshoeing, 165–170
    caring for snowshoes, 169
    choosing snowshoes, 168
    preseason training, 3
    types of snowshoes, 166–168
socks, 38–39
space blankets, 159
specialized winter backpacks, 51
splitboarding, 176–177
spot devices, 123
stationary fronts, 21
stoves, backcountry, 59–63
    maintenance of, 65
stream/river crossings, 83–84
structures, permanent, 150–152
sunglasses, 37
synthetic sleeping bags, 56

→ T

tarps, 53–54
telemark skiing, 170–172
temperature inversions, 22
temperature preferences, 25–26
temperature ratings (sleeping bags), 56
tent platforms, 152
tents, 52
    maintenance of, 65
    setting up in backcountry, 152–154
thermodynamics, 32–33
ticks, 101–102
toilet considerations, 139–140
tracking, 124–125
traction devices, 162–164

trauma, 70
tree wells, 81
trekking poles, 164–165
trip planning, 4–14
    contingency planning, 10–11
    destination planning, 7–9
    expedition preparation checklist,
       195–196
    gear lists, 9–10
    group composition, 5–6
    hikeSafe checklist, 4–5
    Leave No Trace (LNT) principles, xiv
    meal/menu planning, 134–137
    monetary costs, 11–12
    participant information form, 193–194
    personal gear checklists, 189–192
    post-trip checklist, 12
    travel logistics, 11
    trip planning resources, 12–14
two-way radios, 122

U

ultraviolet (UV) water treatment, 130–132,
    197
undercuts, 84–86
UTM coordinates, 118–119

V

vapor barrier liners (VBLs), 58
vegetation traps, 81–82
Vietze, Andrew, 161

W

warm fronts, 19–20
water crossings, 82–86
water sources, 129–130
water treatment/filtration, 130–133
    treatment methods, 198–200
weather considerations, 15–28
    barometric pressure, 27–28
    dew/frost point, 28
    fronts, 19–22
    Koppen classification system, 17–18
    meteorological vs. astronomical winter,
       16
    observation and evaluation, 22–28
    precipitation, 23
    regional weather types, 18–19
    snowpack, 27
weather vs. climate, 15–16
    wind, 26–27
    windchill, 73
wilderness first aid, 68–69
wildlife
    animal tracking, 124–125
    dangerous animals, 98–102
    Leave No Trace (LNT) principles, xvi
wind, 26–27
windchill, 73
WISE system (for winter dressing), 30–32

Y

yurts, 151

ABOUT THE AUTHOR

Andrew Vietze is a Registered Maine Guide and a ranger at Baxter State Park. He's also the bestselling author of more than a dozen books, including *White Pine* and the award winners *Becoming Teddy Roosevelt* and *Boon Island*. The former managing editor of *Down East: The Magazine of Maine*, Vietze has written extensively about the outdoors for a wide range of publications, including *AMC Outdoors*, the *New York Times' LifeWire*, *Time Out New York*, *Explore!*, *Hooked on the Outdoors*, *Down East*, *TravelBrains*, and *Offshore*. His work has taken him from the wilds of northern Canada to the cold slopes of the White Mountains, and from NASA boardrooms to the Travel Channel. A Wilderness First Responder, he has spent 17 years as a ranger in the "forever wild" vastness of the Katahdin region, embarking on countless adventures. He lives in Appleton, Maine, with his wife and two sons. Find out more at andrewvietze.com.

BE OUTDOORS™

Since 1876, the Appalachian Mountain Club has channeled your enthusiasm for the outdoors into everything we do and everywhere we work to protect. We're inspired by people exploring the natural world and deepening their appreciation of it.

With AMC chapters from Maine to Washington, D.C., including groups in Boston, New York City, and Philadelphia, you can enjoy activities like hiking, paddling, cycling, and skiing, and learn new outdoor skills. We offer advice, guidebooks, maps, and unique eco-lodges and huts to inspire your next outing.

Your visits, purchases, and donations also support conservation advocacy and research, youth programming, and caring for more than 1,800 miles of trails.

Join us!
outdoors.org/join

AMC's Mountain Skills Manual

Christian Bisson and Jamie Hannon

This comprehensive guide tackles the essential skills every outdoor lover should master. Beginners will learn basics on gear, navigation, safety, and stewardship. More experienced readers can hone backpacking skills, including trip planning, efficient packing, and advanced wilderness ethics. All readers will set new goals, perfect their pace, and gain the tools to plan and enjoy their next outdoor adventure.

$21.95 • 978-1-62842-025-8 • ebook available

AMC's Real Trail Meals

Ethan and Sarah Hipple

There's more to outdoor eating than trail mix and freeze-dried meals! This compendium of trail-tested backcountry recipes gives readers a wide buffet of lightweight and nutritious meals made with natural ingredients. Adopting a practical, easy-to-follow approach, *AMC's Real Trail Meals* employs handy icons to note which recipes are vegetarian, vegan, gluten-free, kid-friendly, or require kitchen prep ahead of time. Dig into a diverse range of wholesome fare that will keep you fueled outdoors and that you can feel good about!

$18.95 • 978-1-62842-060-9 • ebook available

Best Backcountry Skiing in the Northeast

David Goodman

Earn your turns with this definitive guide to backcountry skiing in New England and New York, covering the 50 best spots for off-slope adventures, including Tuckerman Ravine, Katahdin, and the historic Thunderbolt Ski Trail, with descriptions, elevations, topo maps, and directions for each trip.

$19.95 • 978-1-934028-14-8 • ebook available

The Unlikely Thru-Hiker

Derick Lugo

Derick Lugo, a young black man from New York City with no hiking experience, had heard of the Appalachian Trail, but he had never seriously considered attempting to hike all 2,192 miles of it. And yet, when he found himself with months of free time, he decided to give it a try. With an extremely overweight pack and a willfully can-do attitude, Lugo tackles the trail with humor, tenacity, and an unshakeable commitment to grooming that sees him from Georgia to Maine.

$19.95 • 978-1-62842-118-7 • ebook available